P9-CNC-488
3 9077 06722 3274

Circs/date/last use

958.1047 G216k
Garcia, Malcolm, 1957-
The Khaarijee   OCT 2 2 2009

CENTRAL LIBRARY OF ROCHESTER
AND MONROE COUNTY
115 SOUTH AVE
ROCHESTER NY 14604-1896

HISTORY & TRAVEL

THE KHAARIJEE

The Khaarijee

A CHRONICLE OF FRIENDSHIP AND WAR IN KABUL

J. Malcolm Garcia

Beacon Press, Boston

Beacon Press
25 Beacon Street
Boston, Massachusetts 02108-2892
www.beacon.org

Beacon Press books
are published under the auspices of
the Unitarian Universalist Association of Congregations.

© 2009 by J. Malcolm Garcia
All rights reserved
Printed in the United States of America

12 11 10 09   8 7 6 5 4 3 2 1

This book is printed on acid-free paper that meets the uncoated paper
ANSI/NISO specifications for permanence as revised in 1992.

Text design by Tag Savage at Wilsted & Taylor Publishing Services

Library of Congress Cataloging-in-Publication Data

Garcia, J. Malcolm.
    The Khaarijee : a chronicle of friendship and war in Kabul / J. Malcolm Garcia.
      p. cm.
    ISBN 978-0-8070-0057-1 (alk. paper)
    1. Garcia, J. Malcolm, 1957– 2. Kabul (Afghanistan)—Description and travel.
3. Kabul (Afghanistan)—Social conditions—21st century. 4. Kabul (Afghanistan)—
Social life and customs—21st century. 5. Afghan War, 2001– I. Title.
    DS375.K2G37 2009
    958.104'7—dc22   2009005298

Portions of this book have appeared in slightly different form in the following
publications: the *Kansas City Star*/Knight Ridder Newspapers, *Virginia Quarterly
Review*, *Ascent*, *Missouri Review*, *West Branch*, *Memoir (and)*, *Fourth River*,
Lake Effect, *Tampa Review*, and *Post Road*.

To Bro, his family, and the boys,
and to the many other Afghan and Pakistani people
who showed me kindness, hospitality,
and tolerance as I traveled their countries.

AUTHOR'S NOTE

Between 2001 and 2007, I made six trips to Afghanistan as a reporter. The trips varied in length from three months on my first trip, six weeks on my second, four months on my third, six weeks on my fourth, two weeks on my fifth, and three weeks on my sixth. I've written these stories as I recall them—from memory, reporter's notes, discussions with colleagues, and personal journals.

Contents

Preface

JUNE 2007
Kansas City, Missouri

Afghanistan.

I miss it.

But why? God knows the place is a wasteland, a battleground not just between Americans and the Taliban, but a battleground for centuries, dating back to Alexander the Great and Genghis Khan.

Afghanistan is a disaster looking for a country. Blazing hot in summer. Bone-freezing cold in winter. An ancient place of mountains and deserts and valleys and thousands of years of violent history. It was an agricultural society, but nearly thirty years of war have blown most farmers off the land. The biggest cash crop now is poppies. In Afghanistan, shell craters pock the roads, and land mines number in the millions. It's a country fractured by poverty, tribalism, greed, hatred, and murder.

It's also an open gun market. Every weapon is available. AK-47 military rifles, mines, rocket-propelled grenade launchers, mortar rounds, you name it.

Afghanistan is slightly smaller than Texas and, like Texas, is an amalgam of tribes, most with their own language. The people's lined faces, sunned into leather, map a history of wars and famines, droughts and death. You can see the country's past and future in the vacant eyes of its children. I got to know six of them.

It is a place of vast beauty and terrible silences.

In the nineteenth century the British in India and czarist Russia tried to dominate Afghanistan and Central Asia. "The Great Game," the Brits called it, until Afghans slaughtered thousands of British troops and chased them out of the country.

Over the centuries, invasions resulted in a complex ethnic, cultural, and religious mix in Afghanistan that made nation-building maddeningly futile.

When I began traveling the country, a newspaperman in search of a story, each military checkpoint I passed was manned by a different tribe. Afghanistan had been ruled by the predominantly Pashtun Taliban since 1996, until the government was toppled by a U.S.–led international military coalition in the wake of the terrorist attacks of September 11, 2001.

Ostracized by the rest of the world for its harsh interpretation of Islam and cut off from international aid, the Taliban did not have the money to provide power, running water, garbage removal, and other basic services. The Taliban outlawed kite flying and listening to music; it even proscribed the singing of birds. Women were forced to cover themselves from head to foot in body-length veils, called burqas, whenever they appeared in public. Men were required to have a beard extending farther than a fist clamped at the base of the chin. On the other hand, they had to cut their hair short and wear a head covering such as a turban. Possession of depictions of living things was forbidden, including photographs of them, stuffed animals, and dolls. These rules were issued by the Ministry for the Promotion of Virtue and Suppression of Vice. Hundreds of religious police beat offenders—typically men who shaved and women who were not wearing their burqas properly—with long sticks. The simplest joys were taboo.

Once the Taliban was gone, Kabul, the capital, became a jigsaw puzzle of competing interests, each trying to control the capital and the country. Of course, I was an American, a former social worker, who, as a reporter, landed in Kabul with limited journalism experience and no knowledge of Dari or Persian or Tajik or Turkish. After arriving, having to make my way through the political, social, and cultural maze, I found an Afghan interpreter named Khalid. The way I mangled the pronunciation of his name drove him crazy, so I nicknamed him "Bro." We didn't know it then, but we would work regularly together nearly every year from 2001 to 2007. Sometimes my trips were a mere two weeks, sometimes months, but every time, I worked with Bro.

We were an odd pair. Blocky Bro, young and tough, driver and translator, and old, skinny, gray-haired, ponytailed me, neophyte foreign correspondent. I met him when he was twenty-four years old. Pashtun tribe. A stocky weight lifter and wrestler. Thick black hair, mustache, barrel chest, mallet-sized hands, fingers sausage thick. Opinionated, rude, tough, fearless, gruff, surly, gentle. A medical student and family man. A philosopher. My Sancho Panza. Together we faced the consequences of war, life without the Taliban, and Afghanistan's uncertain future.

Bro was born in 1977, twenty years after I was and two years before the Soviet invasion of Afghanistan. He was twelve years old when the Russian army withdrew in disgrace in 1989. Between 1990 and 1995, he and his family lost four homes to the civil wars among rival Afghan warlords. As a teenager he was arrested twice by the Taliban, once for trimming his beard and again for listening to music. He had known only war his entire life. All I had to do to break him up was mutter that so-and-so was an "asshole" or "shitbird" or "dickhead." Bro would burst out laughing.

Bro was a Muslim, of course, and he prayed five times a day, but still he had a randy side. Once he showed me a worn copy of *Sports Illustrated* magazine. On the cover was a smiling, come-hither model in a bikini the size of bottle caps. "I would like to go to Miami Beach," he told me with a wicked smile, "but I could never bring my wife." Then he rolled his head back and laughed, big hands on his stomach, his laughter echoing off the sky.

Bro told me he was not responsible for my life, yet he saved it twice, once when I nearly caused a riot distributing food to refugees and again when we were stopped at a military checkpoint.

Bro told me to stay away from dogs because they were rabid. Then he helped me steal a puppy from an organized dogfight. He told me to be wary of street children. Then he helped me care for six homeless, war-orphaned boys.

Then I left them.

Now I have decided to return. For the boys and Bro. For Afghanistan. For me.

I never foresaw how much I would come to love the cleansing beauty of its cloudless sky over the mountains, the brutal frankness of its deserts, its loyalty and generosity, its mysterious history, even its unexpected fits of anger. All made more alluring because, no matter how deeply I immersed myself, I remained an outsider seeking my place in its culture. The boys, I understand now, had provided that place.

Sometimes I fall asleep in my living room and dream about the frigid house in the neighborhood of Wazir Mohammad Akbar Khan. The *pop-pop* of gunfire. The darkness of Kabul without power. The drone of military aircraft invisible overhead. The blank stares of beggars. Then, in my dream, Bro breaks the dark by firing up a cigarette.

"Where do we go now?" he asks.

Prologue

NOVEMBER 2001
Two months after September 11th my editors assign me to Kabul.

I am to work with another reporter I'll meet in D.C. on the way out. I have two days to get ready. My heart pounds as if I am running to catch a bus that never stops, chest aching. I'm unable to define the emotions I feel, leaving for a war zone. Fear, certainly. Giddy with anticipation. Worried whether I've got the chops for the job.

As for Afghanistan, I vaguely remember the Soviet invasion in 1979 and, as a consequence, the U.S. boycott of the 1980 Moscow Olympics. Nearly ten years afterward I saw the cheesy action flick *Rambo III* in which actor Sylvester Stallone allies himself with the mujahideen rebels and defeats the Soviet army. Other than that, I barely know where Afghanistan is or what to expect.

For reassurance I think back to my days as a social worker, a career I left not long ago. I got my start at the St. Vincent de Paul Society's Ozanam Center in San Francisco, a detox program for homeless alcoholics, where I worked shortly after college. At first I didn't know what to expect then either.

I recall starting work at six thirty, just as the lights came on and the curled bodies snoring heavily on the mats snapped awake to the earsplitting blast of static from a radio one of us plugged in and cranked up. Men lurched up off the floor, blinking, their legs and arms jerking from alcohol withdrawal. The air was thick with the sweaty odor of unwashed bodies and clammy clothes. Toothless. Unshaven. Fingernails stained yellow from rolling cigarettes. The crow's-feet etched around the corners of their eyes revealed years of hard living. I knew everyone by their street names: Alabama, Road Warrior, Loco, Rocky.

"What are you doing in my world?" they would ask me.

What would they say to me now if they knew I was about to enter a far different world on the other side of the globe—a world completely unlike anything any of us knew?

I remove a sheet of paper from my computer printer. "My Will," I write at the top. It won't be legal, but it will obviously be in my handwriting. Should something happen to me, my savings will go to my niece Megan, my two border collies to a friend with three acres of fenced property, my books and furniture to the Salvation Army. The landlord will steam clean my carpet and expunge the indentations made by my two futons, kitchen table, desk, and chair. Then someone else will move in.

When I finish writing, I put the will by the kitchen stove and weigh it down with a glass.

What else? Who else?

I don't have the e-mail address of my ex or I would write her. We lived together in San Francisco for six and a half years before we separated. All sorts of reasons for our split. Kids: she wanted them; I didn't. But if I were to settle on the real reason, it would be that we had stopped loving each other the way we needed to if we were to spend the rest of our lives together. The drift apart had happened gradually. When we finally noticed, we were at a loss to stop it. In the space of two years, I had separated from my ex, quit social work, moved out of our house, and accepted a newspaper job in Philadelphia. I'd like to say I never looked back, but I did and often. I wish she were here now, if only to take me to the airport and hug me good-bye.

I open a window. Joggers splash through puddles. I hear the rhythm of their bodies moving toward me and then past me in an echo that rises and falls, rises and falls. Soft jazz music from the Blue Bird Cafe next door sifts toward me. I glance through bare tree branches and ponder the wine-colored sky. I've never felt at home in Kansas City, but for the first time since I moved here in 1998, I have a yearning to stay. Must be nerves.

What's the expression? Be careful what you wish for: you might get it?

Well, I got it.

I start packing my duffel bag.

I am going to Afghanistan.

PART ONE

Shadows of Home

CHAPTER ONE

Points of Entry

NOVEMBER 2001

Bagram Air Base, Afghanistan

I step out of the United Nations plane into the face of armed Northern Alliance soldiers who tell me to stay put.

Great. I waited a week in Islamabad for a seat on the plane that would take me to Afghanistan. Now that I've landed, I can't move. Here only minutes, I'm already looking at a thirty-hour day.

Mingling with the soldiers is a short, zit-faced kid, an American lieutenant, who looks about twelve, in desert camouflage with bars on his collar. He carries an M16 under his right armpit. He says nothing and looks at the commander. American GIs seemed so old when I was a boy watching them fight the Vietcong on the news. Now I'm at least twice the age of the average grunt.

I look around and see nothing but desert unfurling into forever. Despite the bright sun, lightning forks across distant black clouds revealing dry valleys and diminutive mud huts that seem to have appeared whole, rising up from the barren ground, only to disappear seconds later, consumed by the darkness of the storm. Boulder-strewn mountains marbled with snow stand against the horizon.

I remove my backpack, windbreaker, sweatshirt, and wool shirt, stripping down to my long-sleeved undershirt. Not so bad. The weather I mean. I figured Afghanistan in November would be frigid. No. A little cool, that's all. Gray light filters through the jagged mortar holes in shattered barracks and flight towers. Heat lines curtained with dust weave around the tumbled wreckage of Soviet aircraft.

3

Bagram was built by the Soviet army in 1980 and was named for the village outside its gate. It was blasted to ruins by Afghan fighters resisting the Russians. After the Soviets withdrew, feuding warlords pummeled it again. *Warlords* is what they call themselves. I overhear other journos use the word without a thought. Me, I'm stunned. Warlords? What is this, the Middle Ages?

It feels like it when I look at the ruins of Bagram. Since the Taliban government fell earlier this month, western troops and Northern Alliance forces have occupied what remains of the air base. And that's not much.

The commander of the Northern Alliance soldiers can't find a visa stamp. I don't understand. The Taliban has been overthrown—there's no government, therefore no visa, right?

Wrong. He demands our passports. They must be stamped. We can get them later at the Ministry of Foreign Affairs in Kabul although there is no such place because there is no government.

What? Give up my passport? I don't like it, but everyone else hands over their passports without a thought. I'm new at this.

"Give him your passport, mate," a BBC correspondent says to me. "You won't get off the base if you don't."

The commander walks away with my passport, the one lifeline that connects me to the United States and home. We board a bus and drive down a dirt road toward the front gate. As far as I can see, weeds consume acres of rubble. Doors hang uselessly from the hollow frames of burned buildings, and sparrows dart through the empty barracks.

Small groups of expressionless Afghan soldiers watch us pass. Some wear U.S. Army fatigues. Others wear traditional Afghan garb, the *salwar kameez*, and sandals. A *salwar* is a loose and comfortable trouser that is wide at the top and narrow at the bottom, and a *kameez* is a long shirt or tunic. The men wrap prayer shawls around their shoulders, squat beside tiny buckets of coal, and hold their hands out to the flames. Each man carries a different kind of military rifle retrieved from the scrap heaps of forgotten battlefields.

These men survived the Soviet occupation of the 1980s, the civil wars of the early 1990s, and the Taliban's six-year reign. Who, they must wonder, are we? Friend or yet another occupier?

■ ■ ■

American soldiers the size of football players in T-shirts, jeans, berets, and scarves observe our van slow to a stop.

"Special Forces," my colleague Jonathan whispers to me. German shepherds scouring the rocky ground for mines stop and sniff in our direction. The Northern Alliance commander opens the door, and we follow him out. He tells us to wait and runs behind the van to a parked truck filled with Afghan soldiers on another dirt road.

"Where're you from?" one of the American soldiers asks Jonathan.

"I'm out of Washington," Jonathan says. "Flew in from Islamabad today. You?"

"Ohio. How long will you be here?"

"Don't know. I don't know why we stopped. We'd like to get going."

The soldier walks a few feet away, turns to take another look at us, and slips his sunglasses on. "I'd like you to get going," he says.

The Northern Alliance commander returns and grins. He has found the mythical visa stamp, a small square piece of wood. He asks each of us for forty American dollars. We shuffle into a line. I lend a French doctor with Médecins Sans Frontières the money, because she only has francs. The commander smacks our passports with his stamp. A faded green triangle shows up on my page. Forty bucks. Nice racket. I follow Jonathan onto the van, my passport safe in my pocket.

We exit the base into an empty bazaar. A Northern Alliance soldier shuts the gate behind us, a rusted towering patchwork of discarded aluminum siding. We stand subdued in the emerging silence that follows the clatter of its closing, lost in an unrecognizable immensity that threatens to consume and discard us like flotsam. The French doctor calls to me. A van waits for her. She offers Jonathan and me a ride into Kabul.

The roads are the first indication of what years of war have done to Afghanistan. Pitted with craters that could swallow our vehicle whole, they resemble little more than shattered paths. Discarded military hardware litters the roadside in a museum display of late-twentieth-century tanks, jeeps, and rocket-propelled grenade launchers. Our driver speeds past all of it without so much as a glance. He slaloms between the deepest holes, throwing us out of our seats. We bang our heads against the roof as we swerve over the lip of one crater and slam into another.

In response, the driver accelerates even faster. By the time the Taliban assumed power, Afghanistan was broke. Simple things like road repair went unheeded. Dodging potholes and bomb craters is sport, a four-wheel-drive, horn-blaring free-for-all without the inconvenience of traffic cops.

Everywhere is the pockmarked moonscape of modern war: hollow, windowless shells of bombed-out homes and businesses. Stacks of metal doors and window frames and piles of broken bricks. More abandoned tanks list at odd angles among the rocks and dry streambeds. Russian tank treads serve as speed bumps. Rusty armored personnel carriers riddled with bullet holes are used as guard huts at military checkpoints. About fifteen thousand Soviet soldiers died in Afghanistan. This is what the army left behind.

After an hour we enter Kabul and pass long lines of vacant factory buildings, unused for ages. I see none of the streetlights, billboards, or skyscrapers that I naturally associate with cities. Smoke rises from adobe-style huts on the sides of the ten-thousand-foot mountains that ring Kabul. Open markets glut the narrow roads. Impassive-looking burros haul wagonloads of wood and maneuver through the stalled traffic at steady, stoic trots. Merchants push barrows filled with toothy, grinning goat heads—a delicacy, our driver explains.

We're dropped off at the InterContinental Hotel, a sprawling four-story complex on a hill in south Kabul where the United Nations holds nightly press briefings. We are to meet two other colleagues, a photographer and another reporter, who arrived in Kabul a week ago.

Inside the dank, spacious hotel lobby, the world's war correspondents huddle in groups, blow on their hands for warmth, and wait for someone to tell them when the Northern Alliance will call its next press conference. Many of these journos followed the Northern Alliance into Kabul as American bombers pounded the Taliban from the sky. The bags beneath their eyes carry the weight of sleepless days and nights. They wear hats and bandanas covering greasy hair. They look at me, the newbie, relatively well rested, showered, and in clean clothes. Wait, their looks tell me, just you wait.

The InterContinental looks like it was swank at one time but not now. Generators hum but no lights come on. Above my head, the ceiling is riddled with holes where tiles have fallen. Cold clings so closely to the worn red couches and chairs that none of us sit in them except Northern Alliance soldiers whose breath rises with ours toward the ruined ceiling.

A handwritten list taped to the glass doors of the briefing room names reporters killed in Afghanistan. Three near Jalalabad in the southeast, one farther north toward Mazar-e Sharif. Humanitarian-aid workers have also been recently shot at. Another list of hand-scrawled advisories warns of mined roads and areas outside Kabul where bandits routinely hijack passing vehicles.

A young man comes up behind us and asks if we need a car.

"Peter Bosch send you?" Jonathan says, referring to the photographer already here.

"Yes, Peter, yes, come."

"You'll take us to Peter?"

"Yes, yes."

"To Peter's house?"

"Please. Yes. Come."

Jonathan looks at me and smiles, but something tells me this isn't our guy. Then again, Jonathan has years of overseas experience and knows what he's doing. Central Asia, the Balkans, Southeast Asia. He's a wiry guy with thick black hair and enough nervous energy to orbit the earth. He constantly looks around like some fidgeting meth head. But he knows this turf; I don't. This is only my second overseas reporting gig and the biggest story of my lifetime. I'm tired, jumpy. That's all.

I've been a reporter for only three years, a career I chose when I left social work. The call of working with the homeless, the finger-snapping "hey man, I'm living on the edge dealing with the element" rap had lost its allure over time. I had outgrown a young man's belief in the romance of poverty. The daily numbing of my heart as I dealt with the same people over and over again drained me. My clients worked hard at destroying themselves, and more often than not they succeeded.

So after fourteen years I found myself suddenly unemployed, a former English major in need of a job. As a social worker I had published a monthly newsletter. I decided to give the reporting business a try and look at life from the outside in, instead of being "in the middle of the mix," as my former clients would say.

After a brief internship at the *Philadelphia Inquirer,* the *Kansas City*

Star hired me as a police beat reporter. Car wrecks and house fires, freaks who made false 911 calls for fun, and drive-by homicides filled my nocturnal shifts between 4:00 p.m. and midnight. But when I was sent to cover crime stories in expanding suburbs, I felt lost in pristine subdivisions among designer-dressed kids and cookie-cutter homes. The neighborhood watch signs I read applied to me as much as anyone. In my off hours, I roamed desolate inner-city streets, sat in the foul doorways of boarded-up storefronts with homeless men and women, and spoke of my work in San Francisco seeking balance in my life.

Then I got a break when I went to Sierra Leone for the *Star* with a group of local doctors who had missionary zeal. What I saw and experienced there—the violence, the poverty, the famine, and helplessness—changed my life. I became an overseas junkie. I loved the chess game of making my way through a place where no one spoke English, the streets were a maze, and the guy around the next corner could be friend or foe.

When terrorists attacked New York City and Washington, D.C., on September 11th, I pushed past my shock and saw an opportunity. I told my editor I wanted to go to Afghanistan. He smiled and said nothing. Right. Give to the newbie the biggest story of the new century. Reporters with greater experience than mine wanted the same gig and had earned it. At least I asked. Neither of us mentioned Afghanistan again. Then in mid-November he called me into his office. An American-led international military coalition had entered Kabul.

"You still want to go to war?" my editor asked.

I was a forty-four-year-old man who had just finished writing a Thanksgiving Day feature about a woman who liked to dress as a pilgrim and entertain schoolchildren. "Yes," I said, "I do."

I caught an assignment working for the Washington bureau of Knight Ridder. The *Kansas City Star* was part of the vast Knight Ridder corporate chain, one of the largest newspaper publishers in the world. They didn't know anything about me or my level of experience. To them I was a warm body. No one thought I was the second coming of Hemingway, and neither did I. They needed reporters. And I needed out.

We leave the InterContinental in the man's yellow car, so battered and dented he keeps the doors shut with wire. A mob collects around our car, pleading with Jonathan and me to hire them. The interior turns dark from the press of bodies against the windows. Our driver blasts his horn, curses, inches forward through hands and faces that part slowly until we emerge onto a road in the pale light of sunset.

We drive through tortuous side streets and stop at countless houses only to be told at each one that we have the wrong address.

"How come you don't know where the house is?" Jonathan asks finally.

"Yes," the driver says smiling.

"You work for Peter?"

"Yes, Peter, yes."

Jonathan pulls out his wallet and looks at a scrap of paper.

"We want house number three on Fifth Street," he says.

"Yes."

"Yes what?"

"Yes."

"He doesn't know where the house is," Jonathan says. "He doesn't work for Peter. He barely speaks English."

I settle into the backseat and relax a little, congratulating myself somewhat smugly that after all those years of working with dope fiends, brother, I can spot a bullshitter. I may be green, but I know ghetto.

"We'll go back to the hotel and see if Peter is there," Jonathan says.

The car wobbles and lists. The driver parks across the street from a Northern Alliance military barracks and gets out. Flat tire. Jonathan and I remove our laptop computers, satellite telephones, and backpacks to the sidewalk so the driver can get the spare tire out of the trunk. Then I put my equipment back inside the car. Jonathan stands by his on the sidewalk. We notice children flying kites from rooftops in mock aerial dogfights. The contrails of an American B-52 fade above them.

In short order Northern Alliance soldiers encircle us. They touch our clothes and pat our pockets. Jonathan worked in India years ago and speaks to them in Urdu, a language akin to Dari, the dialect of northern Afghanistan.

"Where you from?" a soldier asks.

"United States," Jonathan says.

"America good, Taliban very bad."

Our driver throws the flattened tire in the trunk, wipes his hands on his clothes, and tells us to get back in. The soldiers shake our hands and saunter back to their barracks talking loudly. I move my gear from the backseat to the trunk. Jonathan grabs my arm.

"Where's my laptop and phone?"

"I don't know."

"Where is it?"

Maybe the driver put it in the car. I check the backseat. Nothing.

"Where!"

"I don't know!"

"They took it," Jonathan screams. "They took it!"

The soldiers look back at him. He and the driver confront them, and they all talk at once, shouting accusations until the rising volume of their voices becomes meaningless noise. Jonathan storms back to the car, watched by the soldiers. They stand together, the looks on their faces not my idea of a welcoming committee but of fighting men who consider us nothing more than hors d'oeuvres.

"They say they didn't take it! You lied to us!" Jonathan shouts at the driver. "You don't work for Peter!"

"Yes, Peter, yes."

"They took it!"

Jonathan gets in the car and tells the driver to take us back to the InterContinental. Maybe, maybe, he left it there. We both know he didn't, but it's a way to put off the inevitable admission that we lost three thousand dollars worth of equipment.

"This could cost me my job!" Jonathan screams.

I keep quiet. He was hustled plain and simple. You'll never make it, my first supervisor told me when I started as a social worker signing homeless drunks and drug addicts into detox. You've never been on the street. You're not an alcoholic. These guys'll eat you alive.

Well they didn't. No they didn't. And they won't here.

Jonathan stares at me. I look back at him and say nothing. I feel abashed by my sense of satisfaction. I knew he'd been hustled, but I say nothing. I begin to feel oddly more at ease than I had in Kansas City, where I felt lost in the soccer mom miasma of Midwestern family values. I repress a smile and relax a little. Pressing his hands against his face, Jonathan weeps.

Jonathan calls Peter from the hotel on my sat phone, screaming into the receiver about how he's been robbed. Peter sends his driver, who takes us back through the bazaar to a neighborhood near where we had our flat. Turning down a narrow, rubble-strewn street, he stops at a two-story cinder block house.

Next door and across the street, Afghan soldiers stand outside houses where their commanders live. Blankets serve as doors. The white houses are riddled with mortar holes, the paint chipping off in curls. Sheep and goats graze in mountainous trash heaps lining the street.

"Had some trouble?" Peter asks, meeting us at the door, a mocking tone in his voice.

"Trouble? You could say that," Jonathan says bitterly.

Peter grips my hand. He towers above me. His straw-colored, shoulder-length hair and heavy beard remind me of mountain men depicted in frontier paintings for Easterners too timid to tread west of Ohio. Like Jonathan, he has the years of overseas experience I sorely lack. Twenty years working in the Caribbean, South America, Africa, and the Middle East.

"Put your bags up and let's get going," he says.

"Where?"

"You got a UN briefing to cover tonight at the InterCon, cowboy."

"We just came from there."

"Then you'll know your way around."

"I just got here."

"It's twenty-four–seven from here on in. We'll get something to eat first at the Herat, a restaurant near here. Great kabob."

Never having eaten kabob, I'll take his word for it. I throw my backpack in a corner and go outside and stretch my arms above my head feeling whipped. An ashen sky presses down on me, and I turn up my collar against the hard weight of it.

"You ready?" Peter says, tugging on a pair of jeans and a red plaid shirt. He puts on a beret and an army jacket. He ties a checkered prayer shawl around his neck and lights a cigarette.

I dig into my pocket for my apartment keys. Front door, mailbox, back door. The air was damp and bitter the morning I left for Afghanistan. Across the street my neighbor Charlie waved out his window. His wife piled empty beer boxes on the street for the garbage man. An elderly woman collected her shopping bags at the bus stop, wiped dew off the bench with a handkerchief before sitting down.

Holding my keys provides the ballast I need, although my memories of home already seem far, as if I dreamed them, as if I'm slowly coming awake and they're drifting out of focus, sinking to the bottom of everything I've known and experienced, consumed by the vast sky, cool wind, endless desert, and desperate ruin.

"Let's go," Peter says.

I look down the street, watch women in body-length veils, their faces concealed behind stitched masks, scour gutters for usable trash. Some of them notice me and approach, moving through wisps of fog settling over the street.

"Look like a bunch of Darth Vaders," Peter says.

"Money, mister," they shout holding out their hands.

I dig into my pocket for a dollar bill. It's all I have.

"You're doomed, dude, if you start giving them money," Peter says.

I approach the Vaders, their filthy palms outstretched. They grip my fingers, and I shake my hand to free myself.

"Careful, cowboy. They'll suck you dry."

The women call to me. I feel a familiar tension in my neck stretching down into my back, a stiffness that always started when the homeless shelter I managed was full and I had to turn people away. This too familiar sensation makes me sorry yet relieved because I understand it. I've been here before.

"I'm okay," I tell Peter.

CHAPTER TWO

Encountering Afghanistan

DECEMBER 2001
Kabul

Morning.

I am curled up in my sleeping bag, procrastinating. My breath hangs in the air like the outline of a ghost; ice rims the windowsill. Two out of four coils on my space heater glow an orange that rises and fades, rises and fades, like a faltering heartbeat before it sputters and dies out completely.

Damn, it's cold.

Shivering, I reach for a pamphlet lying on the floor from HALO Trust, an international charitable organization that specializes in cleaning up the debris of war, especially land mines. One of their staff spoke at the UN briefing last night at the InterContinental. "Too many farmers were returning to their land before mines had been cleared," the man said. He didn't know how many had died or been injured as they crossed their booby-trapped fields. I decide to check it out but will keep the story to myself. Last night Jonathan warned me that reporters would steal my ideas if I was stupid enough to share them.

I'll need a shooter. I'll see what Peter has going today and talk to him and no one else.

I hear the bathroom door open, put aside the pamphlet, and kick out of my bag and grab a towel. Peter sprints past me in the frigid hall, a towel around his waist, hair rising and falling, a trail of wet footprints and steam fading behind him.

The hot bathroom warms me, and I close the door to maintain the heat lingering from Peter's shower. I strip out of my long underwear and turn on the water and soap my hair. Suddenly the bathroom light shuts off. No power. In seconds the water turns glacial. I jump out of the shower and clasp my arms across my chest. I wait for the power to come back, for the water to warm again.

Nothing doing.

With my hair still soapy I hold my breath and duck my head under the frigid water and scream.

After I dress, Peter shows me the countless pockets in his vest that he fills with digital disks for his camera. In some pockets he keeps blank disks; others hold disks already filled with photographs. If he were to be killed, Peter tells me, I am to make sure I recover the completed disks from his body so his work won't be lost.

"What would you want me to save of yours?" he asks.

I hold out some notepads scrawled with my rushed handwriting. Peter glances through them.

"This is all you have? Nobody could read this."

I take my notepads from Peter. I'll call my folks on my satellite phone tonight. No particular reason. After this reassuring conversation, I'm thinking maybe I should.

I step out the front door into pools of blinding sunlight. Our housekeeper, the landlord's brother-in-law, wobbles up on a bicycle that looks older than the country. His damp hands grip mine in greeting and then he coughs. Peter gives him some antibiotics he brought from the States. Whatever the housekeeper has, neither of us wants it.

Squinting at far-off mountains tipped with sunlight, I think of the points of a prism. I remember an early morning drive I took in the desert outside Santa Fe years ago. The flat land was splayed with different shades of red light, and the mountains were gradually stripped of shadows. For a moment I forget I'm in Afghanistan.

By midmorning Peter and I are waiting at the Ministry of Foreign Affairs for our press credentials. Afghanistan is in shambles; there's no such thing as regular hot water and electricity; there's no government, only a bunch of Northern Alliance soldiers occupying government buildings; but we need credentials.

We give passport-size photographs of ourselves to a secretary. He hands us forms to complete.

We move onto a balcony that overlooks an enclosed courtyard. Dead plants and trees stripped of leaves lay exposed to the sun. Stones square off dirt plots where gardens once blossomed.

"He pointed a gun at me," a freaked-out British journo is telling anyone who will listen. He cleans his glasses, talks fast. "He's a doctor and he pointed a gun at me. I'd been following him for a week. Perfectly cool about it until this morning."

"What hospital?"

"Indira Gandhi Hospital. The place is bloody awful. No power. Filthy. The odor about killed me. He's been fine all week. Then today, he's working on a boy with pneumonia. The boy's dying."

Freak Out lights a cigarette, inhales, and lets smoke stream out his mouth.

"He's dying, about six years old, I'd say, and I'm getting it all down. Sad, mind you, but great stuff. Then the doctor looks at me. He bloody looks at me and pulls a pistol out of his pocket. I'm thinking, 'Hold on.' And he waves it around. Gets right in my face with it. Tells me I need press papers to be in the hospital. I've been following him all week with only my passport! He doesn't care. He's flipped, man. Starts shouting at me. Gun in my face and the kid dying between us. Hell, I'm not going back. The man's blooey. All this just this morning. Fuck all, eh? He was fine all week. Great stuff. I don't understand it."

The secretary calls for Peter and me. He hands us our credentials, two slips of creased paper with our photos stapled to a corner of each one. We head to the door. Freak Out grabs me by the elbow.

"Fuck all, mate. His gun right in my face. Bloody, bloody fuck all country, do you hear me? Bloody fuck all country."

Peter and I take a taxi to the HALO Trust office, a square building riddled with cracks and rising at a slant above rubble on a side street that is little better than a gutted alley. An armed guard shows us through the gate to a dust-covered room where a weary-looking man, sunk deeply in a torn leather chair, gestures for us to sit beside a broken space heater. He introduces himself, Farid Homayoun, the director of the Kabul office of HALO Trust, then pauses while a barefoot boy enters with a tray of tea, dust puffing up around his feet.

"How can I help you?" he asks in English.

I explain that we are reporters and want to follow one of his demining teams.

"It is very dangerous," he says.

He hands me a flyer with a map of Afghanistan. Dozens of areas suspected of being mined dot the map around Kabul. Who knows which army is responsible for strewing the mines that are killing people, that leave amputees begging on the street clutching at my clothes? Some of the mines were dropped by the Soviets, others by opposing Afghan armies during the civil wars. The United States dropped its share of mines pursuing the Taliban. No one agrees on the numbers. The United Nations estimates that between 640,000 and a million mines have been laid in Afghanistan since the late 1970s; the Northern Alliance claimed five million; the U.S. State Department suggested ten to thirty million. That would mean two mines for every Afghan survivor of the Soviet occupation.

Clearing the land of mines is slow work, Homayoun tells us, with fourteen HALO Trust teams of twenty-nine men moving inches at a time with metal detectors and trowels, poking into the dirt hoping to find something that could blow their faces off. This month, since the teams began clearing the Shomali Plain fifteen miles north of Kabul, they have found as many as ten mines a day. I passed through the Shomali when Jonathan and I drove in from Bagram.

After years of warfare and drought, the Shomali had spread before us broken and defeated, over eighty miles of wasted hills, scrub brush, shriveled streambeds, rusted army tanks, trucks, and shell casings. Once known for its vineyards, now it's a junkyard of abandoned Soviet military hardware.

"Where the teams are now, we have been there two weeks and cleared only five kilometers," Homayoun says. "This morning we have already evacuated one casualty. We are dealing with Soviet mines, mujahideen mines, Taliban mines, Northern Alliance mines, and unexploded U.S. cluster bombs. People actually think they can avoid mines like one would walk on stones across a stream so as not to get wet. This is not so."

"We still want to go."

"The teams have left for the day. You'd have to meet them where they are working. Just a minute."

He shouts into the hall, and a sullen, bulky young man fills the doorway.

"This is Khalid, my nephew," Homayoun says. "He speaks English. He'll take you."

"Khalid," I say extending a hand. "I'll pay you thirty dollars."

"I have to piss," he says.

Okay. He's different.

Khalid whispers in Homayoun's ear.

"He won't work for less than fifty dollars a day," Homayoun tells me. "That's what his friends make working for foreign journalists. He says the *khaarijee* robs him."

"He says what?"

"*Khaarijee.* It means a man who comes from outside. You are khaarijee."

"Remind him, would you, that he's the one outside pissing. Thirty."

Homayoun lets out a deep breath and slumps in his chair. His sun-worn face carries the weight and stoic expression of an old sculpture that has confronted centuries of harsh winds and over time has been stripped to a minimized profile; sharp nose, hollow cheeks, lines eroded deep into his forehead.

No doubt some of his men have been among the casualties. He doesn't need me giving him a hard time, but goddamn. I offer his nephew a job, and he pisses right in front of me. I'm tired, confused, and more than a little anxious; I'm in no mood for nonsense. I want a story on land mines. Period. I need to see one of Homayoun's de-mining teams. Today.

Khalid finishes pissing and comes back to Homayoun, who tells him I won't budge on my offer.

"The khaarijee rob me!"

Peter wraps an arm around his shoulders, encircling his throat.

"Listen, Bro, we don't have time, *capisce?* Thirty. Most of the day is gone, understand? Now what's the problem?"

Khalid squirms, rolling his head. Peter turns, winks at me.

We both know Khalid is right. Most journalists hire drivers and translators for fifty to sixty dollars a day. Television crews pay as much as a hundred dollars a day. I want to keep Khalid down to thirty to stretch my budget. I've already forked over fifteen hundred dollars in rent for a frigid house. After years of destitution, Afghans are making up for lost time. If I have to, I'll go fifty. I'll still be getting a driver and a translator for the price of one.

After a moment Peter releases Khalid. Furious, Khalid steps away and adjusts his clothes. Muttering to himself, he leads us to a dented gray van and gets in. He drums his fingers on the steering wheel, fuming. Peter sits next to him on the red passenger seat. Khalid doesn't move.

"You going to start the engine, Bro?" Peter asks.

"My name is Khalid."

"Khalid?"

"No. Khalid. *Khaaalid.*"

"I can't pronounce that."

"Why? What is so hard?"

"Chill out, capisce?"

"What is this *capisce?*"

"Different languages," I say, getting between the two of them. "Say my name. Malcolm."

Bro struggles and finally settles on "Markum."

"No," I tell him. I pronounce my name again. He shakes his head. "You see the problem? But let's forget it, Bro. Okay?"

"Yes, why not, khaarijee."

"Why not," I say.

Bro drives without caution, increasing his speed whenever he narrowly misses a crater or oncoming bus. Red-painted rocks line the roadside, a warning that the area has not been cleared of mines. Bro leans on the steering wheel so hard that he raises the left wheels off the ground to avoid a truckload of refugees returning to Kabul.

"This is not a good day to die, Bro!" Peter shouts.

"In Afghanistan every day is a good day to die!" Bro shouts back. He glances at me and smiles. Payback, I think, and despite myself I laugh with him.

Bro stops when he sees a group of men wearing blue flak jackets and plastic face masks. They probe the ground with thin metal rods, metal detectors, and trowels. Farmers prod mules across the hard ground, past the de-miners, oblivious of the danger beneath their feet.

We get out of the van and approach a man Bro knows. Peter takes out his camera and screws on a lens cap. I pull my notepad from the back pocket of my jeans. The man yells at us to stay on the road. He jabs a finger at the ground, and we hear his metal detector squawk. He removes a small brush from his pocket and gently dusts off the edge of a green Soviet antitank mine partially buried in the dirt. As he works, he tells us he discovered the mine after combing a four-foot-square section of ground for three hours.

Bro asks him to repeat himself several times before he translates. Sometimes they talk for minutes at a time. Jesus. I tap my pen against my pad. I've never worked with a translator before, but it doesn't seem that it should take all day.

"What was your question again?" Bro asks me.

"My question is, how many mines has he found today?"

"What does it matter?" Bro says. "There are too many mines in Afghanistan. What is your next question?"

"I need him to answer that question."

Bro asks it again. I can't believe it. My first day on the job and I must persuade my translator to translate. Makes no sense. I'll hire another one tomorrow. Might have to pay the typical rate, but at least I'll get a cooperative one.

"Just this one mine."

"I can't make a story out of just one. How about the others? How many have they found?"

"He says this morning he evacuated an injured man. He was returning to his village and lost a leg."

"So we can assume he found at least one other mine? The one that got the farmer?"

"He is only one man and there are too many mines for him to find. What is your next question?"

Jesus.

The de-miner studies the mine and ignores us. His team walks to a cluster of mud huts surrounded by broken antiaircraft guns about two hundred yards away. He places a packet of nitroglycerin by the mine and attaches a fuse. I am distracted by a growing line of buses. Families get off to watch the explosion. After so much fighting, I would think this would be old hat.

"Khaarijee, we should go," Bro says and tugs my arm.

The fuse snaps and shrivels inching toward the mine.

We run to the huts. Through a broken wall we watch a narrow

line of blue smoke rise above the weeds. Wind whistles through cracks above us. A mouse scrambles over my boot. Sheep amble past the hut, a farmer tapping them with a stick to urge them on.

Before I see the explosion, I feel the air shift. The roof shivers, and the ground heaves. A geyser of dirt spews into the air from the road, and we bolt out of the hut before it collapses.

Bro, Peter, and I follow the de-miners back to the road. The half-time entertainment is over, and traffic starts moving again. Peter puts the lens cap back on his camera, and I shove my notebook into my hip pocket.

"May I have one of your cigarettes?" Bro asks Peter.

Peter shakes one loose from his pack. They smoke, relax, exhaling in long sighs. I leaf through my notes. Suddenly my fingers begin to tingle. I look at Bro and Peter, and they look back at me as the three of us feel an invisible shift in the weight of the air.

A second explosion throws us to the ground. My heart races. I want to scream with exhilaration and fear. I raise my head and look over my shoulder. Around us de-miners push themselves off the ground cursing. Sheep run toward the road.

"What the—?" Peter says, glaring at me as if the explosion was my fault.

"There! Crazy man!" Bro shouts, pointing at the farmer we had seen earlier.

His sheep had found an unexploded bomblet on the path behind the hut. They lingered around the yellow object. Sniffed it. Rolled it with their noses. The farmer wanted to keep them moving. Sheep, he explains, are very slow. He picked up the bomblet and threw it aside, and it exploded.

"I didn't know what it was," the farmer explains.

He turns, looks at the de-miners smirking at him.

"Then you understand," the farmer continues. "This is my home. The Talib took my land. They are gone. I want to go home."

Bro waits for me to say something, but I don't have any more questions. We watch the farmer leave.

"That is sad. Where is he to go? This is his land. But it will kill him. You have three mines, khaarijee."

I turn away from his sarcastic look. He glances at his watch and then squints at the fading afternoon light.

"We should return to Kabul," he says. "Bandits drive the roads at night."

"We have nothing to eat at the house," Peter says. "Where can I buy some meat?"

"There is a village not far from here."

We follow the empty road, pink in the late afternoon light, until we see the village. It reminds me of etchings in antique Bibles; the mud brick compound, the towering wood doors fitted with thick metal knockers, the clay pots and ovens, the chickens, cows, and goats roaming free amid heaps of hay. Barefoot men wear turbans and plain flowing gowns, their thick long beards stained brown around their mouths.

A butcher's open-air stall stands at the side of the road. Knives hang from the walls and the heavy skinned carcasses of sheep droop off rusted hooks. Flies buzz around piles of bloody hides on the dirt floor. Behind the stall, brown sheep tied to stakes move their fat mouths over the dry ground beneath the remains of a Soviet antiaircraft gun.

The butcher cuts a slab of meat and throws it on a wood table. Boys gather around the hut and watch. A curled HALO Trust poster with a large X drawn through illustrations of mines and bombs peals off the wall. One gaunt boy wears a prayer shawl over his head. He tugs it to cover his swollen left eye. Peter squeezes the meat and blood rises over his finger. The butcher nods and wraps it in newspaper. Peter takes the package and bumps into the boy. The boy winces and raises his shirt. A long pink scar extends from his chest down to his waist. Other pink welts lace his stomach and shoulders. He holds out his hand.

"No money," Peter says.

"Last month, he picked up a bomblet behind the butcher's stall," Bro says. "He didn't know what it was. Like the farmer. Here is another mine for you. Four."

"Enough."

"You asked."

"Now I'm not."

The boy points to a dry patch of land his family farms. I don't see any crops. Bro chases younger children away who sneak up on the boy's blind side, pelting him with stones. He helps the boy adjust his scarf over his eye. Taking my hand, he shows me how to tie the scarf so that it falls behind the boy's neck.

"My brother picked up a mine."

"When?"

"This was in Russian time," Bro says. "He lost three fingers."

"I'm sorry."

"It was not your fault."

Something snaps under my foot. I freeze. Bro's eyes widen, and he doesn't move. Land mine. I close my eyes and try to control my shaking. My guts shrivel, heart hammers in my throat. I go limp, about to fall, and I struggle for balance. My hands sweat. I can't raise my arms to wipe them against my shirt. I face the ground, slowly open my eyes. I'm going to get sick.

A broken piece of aluminum from a Pepsi can sticks out from beneath my boot. I look at it for a long time and then spit. My heart slows, and the pressure in my neck and shoulders eases. I pick up the can to throw it, but my hand refuses to steady itself, and I drop it at my feet. I hear it fall, roll against stones. I hear myself breathing. I feel the wind play with my shirt. Then the boy starts laughing, his high-pitched giggles almost too eager, and I look at Peter and Bro, and we start laughing too.

"Oh, this hurts," Peter says, holding his stomach. "Cowboy, the look on your face!"

"You should take a picture," Bro shouts.

Peter tosses Bro the meat, speckling the ground with blood. Bro drops it in the backseat, and we get in the van. He starts the engine, and the boy steps back and waves. We pick up speed, and dust soon obscures him.

"Not a good day to die, Bro!" Peter yells.

"Never mind him, Bro, drive faster," I say.

Peter gives me the finger, and Bro laughs and accelerates. I laugh with him, and something collapses within me, and I can't stop laughing. I keep laughing until I break into sobs.

"Khaarijee?"

"You okay, cowboy?"

I nod. The meat bounces, sliding against the rear door. I reach back to hold it, my eyes brimming with tears. Bloody bits of paper stick to my fingers.

■ ■ ■

We reach our house before dark and pause to admire the moon, which had started out a dusty orange as we drove into Kabul but grew whiter and whiter as daylight receded with the undertow of nightfall. Sheep grazing in garbage heaps pause in their chewing to contemplate the sky before they bolt away from children shooing them forward with sticks.

I hand Peter the meat.

"Work something out with him, cowboy," he says, raising his chin at Bro.

I hear the *pop, pop, pop* of gunfire and sink in my seat.

"AK," Bro says. "Not far."

I nod, pretending to share his opinion although I've never heard an assault rifle before. I understand enough, however, to appreciate the implication. Militias loyal to rival warlords make up the Northern Alliance. The gunfire we hear may be militias fighting for control of Kabul, or it may be some solitary jackass shooting off his weapon.

"We'll worry if it gets closer," Peter says. He gets out of the van and hefts the meat over his shoulder. A pack of feral dogs at the end of the street raise their noses.

I give Bro thirty dollars.

"You'll come back tomorrow morning?"

"Why not?"

He examines the ten-dollar bills, holding each one against the windshield.

"They're real."

"I will need more money. Not for me. The car. Gas is very expensive."

"Of course not for you. Forty?"

"Fifty."

"And you'll drive and translate?"

"Yes."

"And you'll translate maybe a little faster and just answer my questions?"

"Why not?"

I decide to give him another shot at the job. Why not?

"See you in the morning. Eight o'clock?"

"Why not? *Inshallah.*"

"What's that mean?"

"God willing."

Bro stuffs the money in his pocket.

"My wife waits for me."

"Kids?"

"A daughter."

"I have a niece."

"No children?"

"Not married."

"What is the problem?"

"I'm single. No wife, no kids. No problem."

"Capisce."

"Yeah, capisce."

Bro reaches for my hand.

"Have a good night, khaarijee."

"See you tomorrow, Bro."

He rummages through the glove compartment for a battered note-pad and writes down "Bro" and then asks me to spell my name. He will use the pad for English words he doesn't know or has difficulty pronouncing, he says almost proudly, student to teacher. For now, my name leads his list.

"How do I spell your name?" I ask him.

He tells me and I write it down in my pad, determined to keep my own list and somehow master words and phrases of Dari.

"Call me Bro," he says. "It's better for you, I think." He laughs. "Inshallah, khaarijee. Watch where you walk."

I watch him go as another solitary burst of machine-gun fire pierces the night. Moonlight provides the only illumination. I walk up the drive and open the front door to the pitch-black hall. No power. I rub my face. I'm tried and stiff, feet sore. I wish I had some Dr. Scholl's inserts to put in my boots and then understand how little I have of anything I usually take for granted.

I smell the meat in the kitchen, see Peter moving through the shadows. I blow on my hands and zip my jacket and step into the dark house. It will be cold inside.

CHAPTER THREE

Lay of the Land

DECEMBER 2001
Kabul, Afghanistan
8:00 A.M.

From my bed I hear Bro and two other translators working for Jonathan laughing downstairs.

I slip on my clothes without bathing. We have so little power in the morning that the water warms for only a few minutes at most. I have decided to hold out against the frigid shower for days if necessary, until I can no longer stand myself. I jog down the stairs and heat water for coffee on the kitchen hotplate.

Peter and I pour cups of instant coffee and wander into the living room to see what all the laughing is about. Bro sits gaping at a porn station on the satellite TV. Television was banned under the Taliban, and the landlord had hidden the TV and the dish in the fireplace. He brought them out and hooked up the satellite on the roof when we rented the house.

On the TV, some guy's pale white ass jiggles with each thrust of his hips as he bangs a chick from behind. She coos in French.

A European phone number flashes on the TV screen, offering a subscription. Bro is beside himself, bug-eyed, kneading his crotch. The bouncing tits and writhing ass before him must offer one hell of a cultural release after living for years under the Taliban.

Since the Taliban fell, burqas are no longer required, but local warlords still enforce wearing them. In the current unsettled conditions, women who might not otherwise wear the burqa must do so as a matter of personal safety.

"Jesus," Peter says. "I need more coffee."

"Good morning, khaarijee," Bro says. He stands bent over to adjust his blue jeans. In less than twenty-four hours, he has discarded his *salwar kameez* and sandals and gone Western on me. This, however, may be a temporary change, with little conviction. After all, when the Taliban took over, men stopped trimming their beards to conform to the new rule of law and prevent further persecution, while their women were brutalized.

These days Westerners are flooding Kabul, and change again sweeps through the city, beginning with the sudden emergence of blue jeans and television and porn.

I'm in a land of chameleons.

"We need to make a rule," Peter says, peering over my shoulder. "No porn in the morning."

"What is porn?" Bro asks.

"This," Peter says, pointing at the television.

Bro asks for my pen and takes out his notepad. I tell him how to spell *pornography*.

"TV sex," he writes beside it.

Peter changes the channel to the BBC. In Germany progress was reported in talks to create a post-Taliban government, as the Northern Alliance indicated it was prepared to transfer power to—and proposed its candidates for—an interim administration. At the head of the pack is Pashtun leader Hamid Karzai, a compromise candidate. He grew up in Kandahar and Kabul, where his father was speaker of the parliament. He holds a moderate view of Islam and favors rights for women.

Tribal affiliation means everything here. The Taliban emerged out of the predominantly Pashtun-dominated south. The Northern Alliance, a coalition of mostly Tajik people and other northern tribes, controls the government. The majority Pashtuns resent the rise of the minority Tajiks. The selection of Karzai is an attempt to appease the Pashtuns, but the Tajiks despise them for supporting the Taliban and as a result distrust Karzai.

The newscast then cuts to images of coalition soldiers in southern Afghanistan. American-led anticoalition forces launched a ground offensive against the final Taliban bastion of Kandahar and met only modest resistance. It is feared that Osama bin Laden has escaped into Pakistan.

I walk outside.

"Where do we go?" Bro asks, hitching up his pants.

"I'm not sure, but I have an idea."

I tell him I want to profile life in a liberated Kabul, a story that captures the feel of the place after the Taliban. Bro likes the idea. He extols the virtues of my Afghan neighborhood, the Wazir Mohammad Akbar Khan. As he starts the car, he tells me these rubble-strewn streets make up Kabul's poshest district.

At the UN briefing last night, officials complained that some real estate agents, cashing in on the influx of reporters and relief organizations, were charging as much as ten thousand dollars a month in the Wazir. Our landlord has already advised us that he will boost our rent to three thousand dollars soon.

When Soviet-backed President Mohammad Najibullah ruled Afghanistan from 1986 to 1992, many top Communist officials lived in the Wazir. The mujahideen took up residence here after they drove out the Soviets. Then the Taliban overran the country and with it the Wazir. Now it's the Northern Alliance's turn.

We pause at an intersection and watch an old beggar move along the street on hands and knees. The beggar's face is covered with a rag. I can see only darting eyes. I can't tell if they belong to a man or a woman. Scraps of rubber from blown car tires are strapped to the beggar's hands and knees.

The beggar stops by a group of Northern Alliance soldiers, slips off the rubber pads, and holds out both hands. A soldier kicks the hands, and the beggar moves to the second soldier, who pushes the wretch into a third soldier, who kicks and stomps on the hands, and the beggar wails, rolling against the foot of the first soldier. I think I should do something, but what? I look at Bro.

"Stupid soldiers," Bro says. "Stupid soldiers with guns."

The soldiers laugh, form a circle around the beggar, and start kicking him. The beggar makes ghastly cries. A man wrapped in a prayer shawl and holding a rifle runs out of the house shouting, and the soldiers abandon the weeping beggar and hurry down the street. The beggar crawls to our van and holds out a bruised hand. I try to ignore him by focusing my attention on the man in the prayer shawl as he shakes water off the butt of his rifle. Perhaps he feels me watching him. Turning toward us, he gestures for Bro and me to come inside his house. I wave, thinking that might satisfy him. It doesn't. He jerks his chin toward the door.

"He wants us to have tea," Bro says.

"How do you know?"

"You are a stranger. It is the Afghan way."

I get out of the van and pause by the beggar. Bro takes my arm.

"Not your problem," he says and urges me forward.

We push through a line of dirty clothes, stepping carefully around water-filled pots and pans cluttering the patio. The house has a large kitchen with a stove, refrigerator, and deep cupboards. The bathrooms too are big, with sunken tubs equipped with showers and hot and cold running water. I tell the man I would kill for a hot shower. He takes my hands in his and bows, introducing himself as Abdul Jabar, a Northern Alliance commander. He expects to have a job in the new Ministry of Defense. He encourages me to drop by any time for a bath. I ask if the soldiers assaulting the beggar were his men, but he waves a hand, dismissing the subject as unworthy of his time.

"This is not bad," he says of his house. He holds his arms out with the confidence of a giant embracing his domain. A Taliban official had lived in the house. His job was to measure men's beards, inspect the size of their turbans, and enforce a dress code. Jabar opens a closet with four machine guns to show how hastily the Talib had departed.

"Never did I think I would have the opportunity to live in the Wazir," he tells me.

Looping a gun over my shoulder, he stands next to me, holding his machine gun, and asks Bro to snap a picture. I promise to get him a copy.

A boy carries in a tray of tea. Bits of white plaster from the cracked ceiling fall in our cups, and Commander Jabar dips a finger into my tea, removing the plaster. He considers the tip of his finger and then shakes his hand, flinging the bit of plaster to the floor. Commander Jabar raises his chin at me—an order, I assume, to drink my tea. A fresh dollop of lead poisoning drops from the ceiling into my cup. Around us Northern Alliance soldiers hurry from one room to the next, clearing the house for its new occupant. I take a sip, straining the tea through my teeth to catch any grit that may have fallen in. Bro follows suit. After a few obligatory sips, we thank Commander Jabar for his hospitality and excuse ourselves to explore Kabul further.

I ask Bro to drive me someplace where he would take his family since the Taliban left. He suggests we visit the zoo so that I can see Marjan the lion, a popular attraction, he assures me.

Men and women hunch within the thin spaces between flattened rooftops and the ground in block after block of crumbling buildings. They watch our van with mouths open, eyes wide, evidencing the bewilderment of survivors trapped within the meagerness of what little remains from all they have lost. Farmers coax wheat from the dirt amid the cinder-block ruins of libraries, hotels, and movie houses.

"Are they refugees?" I ask Bro.

"Maybe, yes. Refugees of war and drought. Some are poor and have always been poor. You ask questions as if there are specific answers, but Afghanistan is not so simple."

We pass through the broken gates of the Kabul Zoo, park by a monkey cage filled with cigarette butts, and follow an old man and some Northern Alliance soldiers down a stone path. The old man carries a bucket of raw meat. Most of the exhibits we pass stand empty, bars wrenched apart by explosives. Leaves scrape across the bare floors, and dead trees cast anorexic shadows over the twisted bars. Homeless war widows in filthy burqas, with no place else to seek shelter, sit in some of the cages, their masked faces following our progress down the path, their upturned palms outstretched.

When he was a boy, Bro says, more than a hundred people a day would watch the old man and his staff feed lions, tigers, cheetahs, panthers, bears, and every kind of tropical bird imaginable. At least one hundred animals lived in the Kabul Zoo. In those days it was very crowded. Too many people. Look. Only nineteen animals. Nineteen. He shakes his head.

A miniature Taj Mahal stands cracked like an egg, the only structure remaining in the elephant compound. Two Indian elephants were killed in 1995, when the zoo was the front line between feuding Afghan factions in a civil war that nearly destroyed Kabul. Later that year eighteen African water buffalo were killed. Then the zebras. Mortar fire ripped through a building for parrots. Some of the birds died. Others flew away, filling the black, smoky skies with bright colors.

"What was in that?" a soldier asks, pointing at three trash-filled cages near the ruins of the administration building.

"Monkeys," the old man says.

"And that one?"

"Mountain goats."

"And that one?"

"Brown bears."

"What happened?"

"Killed. The cages are fit only for war widows."

A soldier watches a black bear pace in its cage.

"The bear's snout is raw and swollen—from children beating it with sticks," the old man exclaims, noticing his gaze.

"At first he tried to bite them through the bars," the old man says. "Then he became like an Afghan and accepted his fate."

We stop at a walled enclosure. The old man lowers a ladder over the wall and clambers down it. He stops near a deep hole in a wall. The scarred face of an emaciated lion peers out at him. It is missing an eye and part of its mouth. The old man holds out the leg bone of a water buffalo. The Northern Alliance soldiers shout encouragement. The lion stumbles from its cave, oblivious to the jeers of the soldiers. They throw stones and cigarettes. The lion moves, veering slantwise, its head down. The old man smacks its flank, forcing it to run around the compound like a circus animal. After a few minutes of this, the lion stops on shaking legs and feebly roars its outrage. The old man too seems out of breath. He sits and feeds the lion, and together they contemplate each other, while Bro and the soldiers cheer and the war widows in the cages behind us wail inconsolably.

"During Rabbani time," Bro says, referring to Burhanuddin Rabbani, who was president of Afghanistan during a time of civil war before he was ousted by the Taliban in 1996, "the people had headaches all the time. There was too much fighting. Eight thousand, nine thousand rockets were fired every day. The mujahideen shoot one thousand bombs. Big sound. All the people's minds stop working. After twenty-three years of war, you know the people of Afghanistan have negative minds. Some Afghans come back from the West. They are fresh. But most Afghan people are not fresh."

■ ■ ■

From the zoo Bro takes us farther south to Bagrami Clinic to get vitamins for his wife, who he says is suffering from a cold. We turn off the road and drive over the rubble of a broken wall, past mud brick buildings with gaping holes that stand open to the sky near barren fields where the wall of a compound emerges like a mirage. "The clinic," Bro says, pointing. We drive through an open gate and stop beside a tree hung with sheets drying in the sun. A man emerges from one of the buildings and hesitates when he sees us get out of the van.

"I always think first it is Taliban," he says and then introduces himself as Mir Faziullah, a pediatrician who runs the clinic.

He brushes aside a blanket and leads us into a waiting room and offers us chairs. Bro mentions his wife's illness and Faziullah nods. I look up at the low ceiling made of straw and log beams. Thin curtains cover an open window. Faziullah faces a cabinet and rummages through the shelves until he finds a brown bottle. He pours some pills into an envelope and offers it to Bro.

"This will help," he says.

Bro nods without asking questions.

"What did he give you?" I ask him.

Bro shrugs. "I am not a doctor. How would I know?"

Faziullah smiles as Bro hands him some money. "When the Taliban ruled, I risked my life every day and let our nurses work without covering their faces when they treated men. I could have been executed for that."

I knew that within twenty-four hours of taking Kabul, the Taliban banned women from working except in the medical sector, since male medical personnel were not allowed to examine women. Female medical professionals were forbidden to talk to their male colleagues or patients.

"Why did you take the chance?" I ask Faziullah.

"We agreed among ourselves that the Taliban treated women as property," Faziullah says. "The Taliban cut my hair because it was not the right length. That was just hair. For women it was worse. I was very sympathetic to women. Wearing a burqa is too difficult for the patient. You can't hear the mouth or eye. You can't see what she is saying. What were we to do if a man was sick? A nurse should be allowed to see him. It only makes sense."

"And you were never caught?"

"Almost. Mullahs came by three, four times a month. We took turns watching for them. Sometimes when we were watching the front, a mullah would come through the back, and the nurses would have to hide."

I look outside. Hiding places would have been few in the empty compound. A nurse walks across the grounds and glances in my direction. She stops and stares at me staring at her. Then she approaches. She wears a burqa, the mask rolled above her forehead. Bro explains to her what Faziullah was telling us.

"Where would you hide?" Bro asks her.

"When the Taliban came, I'd close the curtains and cover my face," the nurse says. "Then they would leave and we'd go out without burqas, and all the men could see our faces and didn't care."

"Why do you think she still wears a burqa?" I ask Bro. "The Taliban is gone."

"My wife still wears the burqa," Bro says.

"Really?"

"Only two months ago, she would have been beaten for showing her face. It is not so easy to forget."

The nurse watches us talk. She says good-bye to Bro, smiles at me, and leaves. I watch her walk toward the other building, the burqa billowing behind her like a blue wave rising, open in the dry wind but still clinging to her.

I ask Bro to take me to the InterContinental Hotel to check in with other reporters. Many rent rooms there, since it has become a meeting place for Northern Alliance officials. Nothing, however, is assured.

There is a better-than-even chance that a news conference could convene any minute, called by some obscure official in the transitional government, and I wouldn't know it. Without phones it's impossible for the Northern Alliance to release information to journos in an efficient manner, even if they were so inclined, and there is scant coordination among ministry personnel. InterCon staff post notices, but often after journos have left for the day.

None of the reporters I speak with seem to know of anything, or if they do they aren't saying. The female reporters wrap scarves around their heads, a nod to Muslim dress codes. I overhear two Reuters reporters say that Karzai was officially selected to head a six-month interim

Afghan government. He received word of his appointment over a satellite phone from his elder brother, who was at the talks, while Karzai was north of Kandahar, accepting the surrender of a Taliban commander. I feel a sudden urgency. My editors will want local reaction to feed into the story.

"Hamid Karzai will take the country out of ruin," Bro tells me and slaps me on the back. "He will get all Afghan people jobs. He will build very big houses for Afghan people. He will make Afghanistan very democratic."

I am more than a little skeptical about Karzai's omnipotence. Then again, I'm not the one who lived under the Taliban all these years. Who am I to deny anyone hope?

We get back in the car and leave for downtown to check in at the key ministries: Interior, Foreign Affairs, and Defense.

Two lines of Northern Alliance soldiers facing off in the middle of a main thoroughfare in downtown Kabul stop us. Feral dogs roam the broken sidewalks, urban jackals trot through mazes of rubble. A man looks at the soldiers through the broken gates of the International Red Cross, where medical teams fit prosthetic limbs on mine victims. Burros maneuver through the stalled traffic like biblical creatures burdened by the imperfections of their masters. The soldiers raise their fists and shout angrily at one another, arguing over who is in charge of military checkpoints in this part of Kabul. All of the soldiers carry Russian-made military rifles, in different sizes, scuffed from use. A few have grenade launchers strapped to their backs. Some have on green uniforms and black boots; others wear cloth caps and loose-fitting smocks.

"I was home with my wife and daughter on September eleventh," Bro says above the honking. "We heard what happened on the BBC. We were very sad. It was hard to believe. But then, and I hope you understand, we were happy. We knew this would bring the Americans. We knew the Taliban would be gone. The bombs never fell in Kabul, but on the hills outside of Kabul. The entire sky turned orange and shook with great anger, and we heard the explosions. Then it faded into yellow and black. Everyone ran out to see. We were gratified."

He lights a cigarette and exhales slowly. Smoke clouds the windshield. The winter air burns my lungs, tastes metallic. I switch on the heat.

"We asked what happened and listened to the radio. Today planes crashed into the World Trade Center. Big building fell down. That day the Talib did not say anything about music or check the length of our beards. They were nowhere to be seen. All the people were confused.

"When the B-52 plane bombed, we thought, The king of Afghanistan has come again to save the people. On the radio the Talib called for jihad like in Russian time. All the people say, Fuck off. We like American people."

He turns and grins at me and slaps me on the shoulder, and I realize that throughout Kabul the same smiles flashed and the same shoulder slaps were exchanged when Afghans knew the Americans would be coming.

"At nine at night, very close to our house, two jets come and drop bombs. A truck was completely burning. We were very afraid and hid in the basement. In the morning the first car of the Northern Alliance came to Kabul. Big truck. I run out and buy a shaving machine. 'The Taliban is gone,' I told my mother. 'No, no,' she said. She could not believe it. 'Yes,' I said, 'it's over.' After one hour my brothers shaved. All of Kabul was shaving that day."

We both laugh but are jolted back to the present when a soldier runs forward from the group nearest us, hurls a rock, and sprints back to his line. The rock strikes the head of another soldier, who stumbles, howling and clutching his scalp. Blood spurts between his fingers. He sinks to his knees. Both groups surge forward, and in seconds the street dissolves into a stew of arms and legs, thwarted punches and kicks. Distorted faces snarl with rage. Their hot breath fractures the cold air. Prayer shawls fall on the pavement. Sunlight glints off rifle butts. Agitated dogs circle the fight, snapping at legs. Other dogs chase after children begging on the street. The children run, dodging between the cars. Bro reaches over my lap to roll up my window. "Rabies," he says. A boy jumps on the hood of our car, followed by a lunging dog.

Our car rolls forward, and I watch the boy run to the sidewalk, the dog lost somewhere between the cars. Bro casts an almost bored eye at the commotion around him, and I am reminded how I walked without a thought through the chaos of homeless people gathered in parks. I have yet to grow accustomed to this environment as I had my previous life.

Leaning over the steering wheel, Bro maneuvers past the soldiers to a side street, where he accelerates past rubble-strewn lots until we reach the Ministry of Foreign Affairs.

A reed-thin guard taps on my window. I roll it down, and he pokes his head inside.

"Hello, mister!" he shouts in my face. "Hello, my American friend!"

We follow him inside a barren concrete office, rubbing our hands against the cold. He sits behind a desk. A faded green carpet lies bubbled and uneven beneath his feet. Shadows fill the dark corners where space heaters offer thin orange glows of warmth. The guard holds a tattered copy of an English grammar book, which he scrutinizes upside down. I ask to see it and turn it right side up and give it back to him. He taps a notebook. I sign my name, profession, and country of origin.

"How are you?" he asks, exaggerating each word with over-the-top enunciation.

"Good."

"You are welcome."

"Thank you. What do you know about Hamid Karzai?"

"Michael Jordan, basketball, yes?" he says and raises a hand.

I high-five him. "Yes, Michael Jordan."

"Who is Michael Jordan?" Bro asks.

We split after a few more high-fives and failed efforts at getting anything out of him about Karzai. Richard, a freelance reporter I met at the InterCon, waves to us from across the street. Before 9/11 he lived in Bangkok, banging out copy on computers at a bank where his companion worked.

"Have you heard about Karzai?" I ask him.

Richard shakes his head as if it is absurd for me even to ask.

"Mad! We're all mad!" he shouts and points.

Glancing over my shoulder, I see a photographer trying to snap a picture of a woman begging. A gawking crowd of men gathers around him. Their shadows spike the ground in long lines, ruining his shots. Annoyed, he passes his hat, demanding payment for the privilege to stare at him. The men oblige, stuffing money into his hat. The photographer can't believe it.

"I'm not a monkey!" he screams.

The men press closer and begin laughing, and the photographer rants.

"Mad!" Richard cackles, "mad, mad, mad!"

A block from the Foreign Ministry, the medieval world of downtown Kabul unfurls in a sprawling display of vendor stalls and draws me toward it to wander like a lost time traveler in its raucous bazaars.

Everything is for sale: donkey-drawn carts loaded with firewood, tea, water buffalo hoofs, heaps of blue jeans and Gap T-shirts that were donated to aid agencies but have somehow ended up on the street. Lumbering, wide-eyed water buffalo moving with the deliberate determination of storm clouds, chickens, sheep. Jagged chunks of soap. Sacks of wheat and flour and dates. Peanuts heaped on blankets where beggars sleep, each with one upturned palm thrust into the scuffling traffic of so many sandaled feet. Wood furniture. Shoes, wrinkled as if someone still stood in them curling their toes. A powerful odor of diesel, sweat, and raw meat fogs my senses.

Afghan soldiers of all ages patrol the streets, their heads turning along with Bro's at an unfamiliar sight: women, unaccompanied by men, strolling down the street in burqas pressed and clean, paying heed to no one. Everywhere around us. It is shocking to the soldiers, who for the first time in years may gaze at them without the threat of vice police sweeping through their midst, wielding chains.

Bro tells me these women were likely doctors and lawyers before the Taliban and consequently have the confidence to silence the ignorant, gawking soldiers around them with their poise, almost daring them to voice a challenge.

"I myself have a biology degree," Bro says. "Stupid soldiers."

The women move on without looking either left or right, one foot after the other, but despite their outward confidence, I sense hesitancy in their steps, as if the ground might break beneath their feet at any moment.

Bro drives slowly and asks the women their names, where they are headed, do they need a ride? They pay him no mind.

Watching Bro flirt with the women, something he never would have done under the Taliban, I think of his wife and her fears and ask him how much longer he thinks she will wear a burqa.

"I tell her to take it off, but she wants it. She wants to see if Talib come back. I tell her no more Talib, but she is not so sure," he says.

We park near a man selling knives. Posters of skimpily clad Indian actresses decorate his stall, a soft-porn depiction of desire that feels almost explicit for the lust it creates in the soldiers pausing to examine it with their fingertips. They touch the breasts and crotches, jerking their hands back lest they get burned. Cassette tapes with similar photographs sell for one dollar. Distorted music blares from old boom boxes that must have been hidden for years and that the knife seller now uses to weigh down a blanket displaying his knives, all of them cut from discarded mortar shells.

We cross the Kabul River. Under the bridge the river lies barren, shriveled from drought, except for a few puddles staining the cracked clay bed. Goats drink from the puddles beside women washing clothes and others who scoop water for drinking into plastic containers. Children play in the mud, competing with dogs for dead fish.

"Please, in the name of God, help me," a woman cries. She rocks against the rail of the bridge, cradling her infant son. I glimpse her eyes, darting back and forth behind the tattered stitches of her burqa.

"I'm very poor. Help me. My husband died in Taliban time, help me."

I search my pockets for money, but a man shoves me out of his way, and I stumble back against the rail. Bro grabs my arm.

"This is no place to talk," the man snaps at Bro.

"Yes, I know this," Bro says. Turning to me, he repeats the admonition. "She is no one to talk to. She could have married again if she wanted."

He takes me by the arm, pushes us forward through the crowd.

"Mister," the woman shouts after me, "please, in the name of God, help me."

I look back at her, but Bro keeps pushing me down a small, damp alley. Merchants fill the narrow, rutted street, unpacking their goods: pots, pans and knives, sandals and jackets, spices, fruits and vegetables. Boys drag the carcasses of freshly butchered lambs and cows off carts and wrap them in newspaper. Near us, a young man thrusts open the wavy metal doors of his shop and steps inside the gloom. He rubs his hands against the cold and swats cobwebs off ghostly blue, green, yellow, and white burqas suspended from the ceiling. Seeing us watch him, he offers us tea and complains about the passing of the Taliban.

"In Talib time, each day I sold at least thirty burqas. Maybe I sell two, three a day today."

When sales were brisk, brides bought white burqas for their weddings. Wealthy women bought burqas manufactured in Korea; most of the rest settled for Pakistani-made burqas. Villagers on the outskirts of Kabul favored green and yellow burqas over the sky blue design fashionable in the capital.

"I still sell burqas in the outer provinces, but only God knows how long that will last," he says. "What will I do now? Who knows?"

He experienced days when women ran into his store bleeding, flogged by the vice police for not covering their faces. He hid one woman in a back room until the Taliban stopped looking for her.

"They had beaten her with cables in the face. I let her wash her face and then she left. I don't know if I ever saw her again. If I did, her face would have been covered, and I wouldn't have known."

I ask about Karzai, but he has never heard of him. We watch the commotion churning past his shop. Men pushing wheelbarrows stuffed with produce jostle among dense pockets of shoppers. Small boys whip donkeys hauling wagons weighted with sacks of flour. Money changers, waving fistfuls of Afghan bills, shout the latest exchange rates, jumping out of the way of Northern Alliance soldiers, who slash at the crowds with their belts to break up the congestion.

Bursts of truck exhaust explode black clouds of diesel into the air. Slow-moving cars rattle through crowds with incessant beeping, barely missing bicycle riders weaving through the narrowest openings. Small boys stand on buckets and wave socks, candy, and perfume, shouting in high-pitched voices, "Buy, buy, buy!"

A woman in a tattered blue burqa stops by his stall. The burqa salesman shoos her away. She looks at me. I'm mindful of what happened on the bridge. "*Boro!*" the burqa salesman tells the woman. "Go!"

A blind man led by a boy shuffles behind her with an upturned hand. I wave him off too, but the burqa salesman digs into a dented coffee can for five hundred Afghanis, about fifty cents, and hands the money to me.

"Give to him," he says.

I do, wondering, Why this guy and not the woman? But I know the answer without asking. The Taliban may be gone, but the punitive attitude toward women remains. It is not something the Taliban created but rather something they took further than any other government. I should take the money and follow after the woman until I find her. Here, I'll say, this is for you. But I don't. I see no reason to anger the men around me. I have enough on my plate. I am not a social worker here. There it is. I don't feel good about it, but there it is. I too am a chameleon.

But I can't get the woman off my mind. The image of her nags at me. I tell Bro I want out of here. He drives us to the nearby Herat Restaurant for lunch. Grease spits off hot coals, and orange flames flare around the lamb roasting on grills. War widows in blue burqas squat in shadows on the sidewalk. They see us park and swarm the van.

"My husband died," a woman says.

"I am twenty-five," another woman declares. "No man wants me. I am old."

Bro translates, but I cut him off. I've heard enough. We walk into the restaurant, and the women start tapping a window near where we sit at a warped wooden table. Waiters huddled around a wood-burning stove watch us. Bro closes a pair of faded pink curtains, cutting the women off. They continue tapping. A waiter stops by our table.

"Beef kabob. It is good," Bro says.

"Okay."

The waiter leaves. Bro slaps the window to stop the women's tapping.

"My daughter is ten months old today," he says. "My wife is pregnant. I hope for a boy. Under Karzai he will go to good school."

"Another kid already? Bro, you need to give it a rest."

He laughs, then shouts to the waiter for two Cokes.

"My marriage was arranged. I visited her for seven months, once a week, after our parents agreed to the marriage. Then we married. Under Taliban, I could not go out alone with my wife. They would ask me, 'Who is she?' 'My wife.' 'You lie,' and they would cable me. I had a relative who wore a necktie to his wedding. The Taliban stopped him on the road and said he was only to wear a turban and white gown. They arrested him, and he missed his wedding."

The waiter carries two plates heaped with rice mixed with beef, raisins, and shredded carrots. Bro complains that the meat is fatty, and the waiter digs into the rice with his fingers, removing the meat. He returns seconds later with another chunk of meat steaming in his palms and plops it on Bro's plate.

"Under Islamic law, I could marry four women, but I won't. You are old not to have wife."

"I was with a woman for six and a half years, and then it ended," I explain.

"Were there no more women?"

"So far, no."

"What happened to her?"

"Moved to Southern California, got a job. Met someone else."

"Who?"

"I never met him. I was told by a mutual friend that they dated, broke up, and then he came back to her and said he could not live without her. I felt that way too, but I didn't go back to her."

We scoop the meat into our mouths with pieces of bread. The waiter brings us a box of Kleenex for napkins.

"Why didn't you go back to her?" Bro asks.

"It was done between us. As much as I missed her, I knew that. And she did too. I still miss her, but I have learned to accommodate her absence."

"Accommodate?"

"To make room for."

I spell it for him, and he jots it down in his pad.

"You see, I love my wife very much," Bro says when he stops writing. "Now with Karzai I will have a very big family."

"She is fortunate you were not killed in the fighting."

"Fortunate?"

"She has had good luck."

"Not like your wife?"

"No, it's not the same thing. She was not my wife legally like your wife, although for a long time I loved her like a wife. She left me because she was not happy with me. I am the one who did not have good luck."

Bro looks at the curtains where the shadowy outlines of the begging women stretch and shrink against the thin fabric. He takes out his notepad.

"Fortunate," he says and writes it down.

CHAPTER FOUR

Relief

DECEMBER 2001

This morning Bro and I cruise downtown, taking the day off. Last night I filed my story about life in Kabul, and now I'm indulging myself with a mission of mercy.

I tell Bro to buy a pound of rice and a half gallon of cooking oil on Flower Street, a commercial district in downtown Kabul, for an impoverished family we'd seen days before. This is my shot at international giving. It's December after all, the holidays only weeks away. In San Francisco we gave frozen turkeys to poor families days ahead of Christmas. Rice and beans are a poor imitation, but here it's the best I can do.

In fact, this will be the first Christmas season openly acknowledged in Afghanistan in five years.

"Jingle Bells" crackles out of a merchant's staticky cassette player for the amusement of Westerners who have converged on Kabul. Small, spare evergreen trees, cut down in nearby mountains, line sidewalks crowded with European and American journalists, troops, and embassy personnel. Afghan and Westerner alike are festive, not only because of the holiday but because of the impending arrival of Hamid Karzai to lead an interim government until elections are held, which tells us Afghanistan is moving on from the Taliban.

Problems, however, remain. No one will say when Karzai will come to Kabul for security reasons. He will enter office with a twenty-nine-member council selected in Germany by various competing Afghan factions and not of his choosing. He will need the support of ambitious

Northern Alliance officials holding some of the most powerful positions in the government.

As Kabul awaits the arrival of Karzai, the United Nations has appealed for twenty-four million dollars from the international community to establish a start-up fund for the new interim government. Some estimates call for $6.5 billion over five years to rebuild. Government employees haven't been paid in five months. More than twenty-eight thousand war widows live in Kabul alone, and at least thirty thousand children survive on Kabul's streets. One physician is available for every fifty thousand people.

I recall the dozens of homeless people I turned away every day as a social worker because I had no room in the shelter. Their numbers don't begin to compare to what I see here.

"People's expectations are high, but where will they be three months from now?" a merchant asks me.

I can't answer.

"It's Christmas," I tell him.

He laughs and shows me a tin box stuffed with U.S. dollars.

"Yes, I know."

Bro and I pass more merchants who promise me great deals on sweaters, sandals, and carpets. A Northern Alliance soldier bargains with a vendor over a box of chocolate, settling on a final price of twenty-five cents. "It's all the same," the merchant says. "No matter the government, everyone wants the best price."

No Taliban, Christmas, Yes, a sign reads.

Happy Chersmess, 2001, a baker writes carefully, lettering a cake with icing.

"Sales of Christmas trees has been very good," another merchant says.

"I am trying to make a doll of the old man with the white beard who rides a wagon in the sky," another man tells me.

Northern Alliance soldiers stationed at intersections use metal cables and leather whips to chase beggars away from Westerners flashing money in a country where the average income is about fifty dollars a month. Every day, desperate men, women, and children swarm me when I step out of my car. Their calloused hands clutch my pockets, fingers scrambling over my clothes, reminding me how as a social worker I would park blocks away from work so I would have five or ten minutes of peace before homeless people saw me and swarmed around me demanding help before we had even opened. I would shove past them without comment, no different than I do here as I push by grasping fingers and remind myself that I can't help everyone, and, unlike in San Francisco, it's not my job in Kabul to do so.

"*Boro!*" Northern Alliance soldiers shout in Dari, thrashing the beggars. "Go!"

"It's all right, it's all right," I'll yell at them. I try to protect the beggars and get away from them at the same time, swinging my arms to free myself from their grasp. Merchants tug at my coat, urging me into their shops. I swat at their outstretched hands swarming around me.

I put the rice and oil in a rented car and tell Bro to drive me into the ruins of south Kabul where some of the fiercest factional fighting between feuding warlords took place after the Soviet withdrawal.

"What?" he shouts.

I wait until the noise passes. Every day we struggle to make ourselves heard above the drone of B-52 bombers and Apache helicopters roaring overhead.

Bro and I leave the pandemonium of Flower Street and jostle down bomb-blasted roads under gray skies seething with storm clouds. Long stretches of rubble reach to the horizon. Men, women, and children linger around tents donated by the United Nations as temporary shelters for refugees. The tents tilt oddly on the uneven ground. Some are arranged on rooftops, beneath which nothing remains but the hollow shells of windswept apartment buildings.

Barefoot children chase us shouting, "Please, mister, help us! Please, mister!" until Bro outdistances them and they fall behind us. We've not driven far when we're stopped at a military checkpoint.

"He is an American journalist," Bro explains to the Northern Alliance commander in charge of the checkpoint. "For him, this time is Christmas, a holy time. He wants to give food to poor families. That is his custom this time of year."

I show the commander the rice and oil.

"We are hungry too," the commander says. Broken shards of concrete crunch beneath the boots of soldiers walking behind him. Other soldiers sit off the road by small fires. They look at a B-52 streaking above us.

"Americans," one says.

The other soldiers nod and stand up. They approach our car hunched against the cold, hands out.

"*Bakhsish*, mister," one says, using the Dari word for *tip*. His breath steams in the cold. Bro offers the soldiers cigarettes. They take the smokes, and Bro lights a match for them. I look around at what appears to have been a residential area.

Gaunt families wander through bomb-shattered apartment buildings. Sheets of plastic provide makeshift walls. The plastic balloons monstrously from the wind, then abruptly snaps inward, drawn by invisible currents. Shadows cast from the orange glow of cooking fires bob and weave.

The commander sucks on his cigarette and contemplates me. He squints an eye as smoke curls above his cheek. Bro gives him three more cigarettes.

"Bakhsish," the commander says.

Bro turns to me, and I hand him two Afghani, the equivalent of twenty-five cents. The commander takes the money, lowers a rope drawn across the road, and waves us through.

We stop at a destroyed office building about a mile past the checkpoint. Trash clings to the broken walls, stained with human feces. A spiral staircase rises out of the rubble to the second floor, where an old man with a long white beard stands on a broken balcony. He looks out over the road.

A dog tied to the rail of the staircase barks at us, slathering saliva in the air. Brown chickens scramble over the parched ground, and donkeys chew on dry grass growing between torn chunks of concrete. I hear the hesitant start-up sounds of a bus wheezing and coughing. The engine finally catches and explodes. The old man winces. Bro and I climb the stairs, giving wide berth to the dog. The old man presses a hand over his heart and bows in traditional greeting. Bro and I do the same. The old man speaks and Bro translates.

"Please, mister," the old man says. "We have nothing to cook with."

"I understand," I say. "That's why I have come."

I had seen him before when I passed this way earlier in the week. He was alone at the top of the stairs, surrounded by about a dozen children. I saw their torn clothes, dirty, lean faces. The old man's white beard was lined with soot. He was rail thin. His tan kurta billowed around him.

The sky was black and an electrical storm snapped coils of lightning into clouds. He had turned slowly, following our car, eyes buried deep in his head.

I know the old man and the children are only a few of the many desperate people I see daily. I can't help everyone, but I can help them.

"I've brought you this," I say, offering the bag of rice. Bro sets the cooking oil on the ground. The old man holds the rice and bows again. A slow smile creases his face. Women emerge from the hall behind him. They gather around the old man and start fighting one another to squeeze the bag of rice. They tear the bag. Their shrill cries make me cringe. Grains of rice fall on the floor.

"We should go," Bro says.

A stooped woman with stringy gray hair shoves the other women aside. The old man lets her take the rice. She raises it to her face, sniffs. She looks at me without expression and then moves away down the hall. Her burqa inflates around her as she turns down another passageway, absorbed into a gloom made darker by the black soot caked on the walls from cooking fires.

"You are very kind," the old man says to me. "I am a farmer. I once grew rice in the Shomali Plain. We come to Kabul City because of drought."

I ask how long he has lived here.

"Six years we live like this. I send my children out to beg in the morning. They go to the bazaar. Early, when goats and lambs are butchered. They bring back scraps of meat. They fight dogs to bring us food."

"That must be very hard. I am sorry."

"We have not seen you for a long time. Why have you taken so long?"

"What do you mean?"

"He thinks you are NGO," Bro explains, referring to the dozens of international "nongovernmental organizations" that provided humanitarian aid in Kabul.

"No, no," I say. "I'm not an aid worker. I'm a reporter. I'm just trying to help."

The old man moves close enough to me that our noses almost touch, the lines in his face deep and hard. He tightens a turban around his head without taking his eyes off me. Men appear behind him, followed by more women and children.

The men crowd around us, smelling of sweat and mildew. They reach toward me and touch my clothes with hesitant fingers, speak in guttural tones. Bro translates. He grips my arm, motions toward the stairs.

"We should go," he whispers.

"Wait. What are they saying?"

We need food.

I have not had anything to eat in three days.

Please mister.

Please mister.

Please mister.

"Let's go," Bro says.

"I want to make sure they don't think I'm an NGO."

"Let's go."

Girls hold scarves across their faces and giggle looking at me. The women slap them. Sharp, hot words echo in the hall, high-voltage shrieks clawing at the walls. A rooster crows. The dog snaps. One man pushes toward me holding a baby.

"My son is sick," he says, holding the naked infant out to me.

"Malcolm," Bro says, moving toward the stairs, "we have stayed too long."

"Bro, what are they saying?"

"Everyone is sick," he says, translating for the old man. "We look for work, but there is nothing."

The old woman who took the rice emerges from the hall, touches the old man on the shoulder.

"He did not bring us enough rice," she tells him.

"We are twelve families," the old man says to me.

"How many people is that?"

The old man frowns.

"Sixty," he says after a moment. "We need more than one bag of rice."

"I'm sorry. I've done what I can."

A rooster crows again. Bro yanks my coat, but I shrug him off.

"When will you come back?" the old man asks.

"I don't know. I'm not with an NGO. This is not a regular thing I do."

"No one ever comes this way. We have no food. It has been a long time since you were last here. And now you did not bring us enough food. After all this time."

"This was something I could do today. Something I wanted to do today."

"Why didn't you bring more food?"

"I'm not an aid worker."

The old man says something, but his voice is drowned out by the din of the women screaming, "Please, mister, money, mister!"

Everywhere I look, outraged faces snarl words I don't understand. Bitter eyes glare. I don't move.

The man holding the baby grabs my hand and pulls me through the throng down the hall. Bro lunges after me. I'm pulled into a long narrow corridor. The man walks ahead of me holding my coat with one hand, his other hand pressed against his stomach. Dry cow manure used for fuel fills barren rooms and stuffs my lungs with its stench. Chickens squawk, scurry ahead of us.

We stop at a room concealed by a heavy blanket. I hear a donkey snorting below us. The man parts the blanket, and a foul rotting odor swamps me. A startled woman looks up, raising a scarf to cover her face. She sits on the floor, back against a wall. Her swollen legs and blackened feet seem detached from her body.

"Both of my wife's legs are broken," the man says, shifting the baby in his arms. "We cannot get her to a doctor. This is my son. He is sick. His mother hasn't any milk."

He holds the blanket, squeezing it until his hand curls into a tight fist and fabric bulges between his fingers. He drops the blanket and pulls up his kameez. A blood-soaked bandage sticks to his stomach.

"We need medicine. Food. How will you help us? Why have you taken so long to come?"

"I'm not an aid worker," I try to explain. "How many times must I tell you?"

"This is from land mine," the man says, tugging off the bandage and exposing a deep red hole surrounded by mottled flesh.

"Don't!" I shout, turning away. "I don't need to see it. There's nothing I can do. I'm not a doctor."

"Where is our medicine? Why do you come if you have no medicine?"

"Because I'm not a goddamn aid worker!"

"What are you going to do for my son?"

"I brought rice. Let's go, Bro."

Bro gives me a hard look. "We should already have gone," he snaps. "Now it will be difficult."

We step around the man and retrace our steps toward the balcony.

"Where are you going?" he shouts after me. I hear the rapid slapping of his sandals on the floor as he runs behind me and grabs my shoulders. I shove him off, keep walking.

"Where are you going?" he demands.

The old man has not moved. He stands on the balcony staring toward the blood-thin line of the horizon. Wind whips his kameez into a tumult of writhing fabric.

"Before drought, the Shomali was beautiful," he says, his back to me. "Every day we beg. Eat a little and then we beg. You are kind, but the rice is not enough."

Men and women follow Stomach Wound and encircle us. Someone punches my back. When I regain my balance, I look for the old man, but he has disappeared. A woman shouts at me, throws the empty rice bag at my feet. Someone kicks me. Another grabs my left arm. I turn ready to land a punch. It's Bro. He holds onto my arm, covers his face with his other arm, and pushes his way out, dragging me with him.

We run down the stairs, leap past the dog lunging at our legs. Stomach Wound follows close behind, shouting at us as the baby bounces in his arms. I slip on the stony ground, fall on my knees, and scramble back up. We reach the car and I turn around. A group of men and women at the top of the balcony scream, "Money, mister!"

Stomach Wound reaches the bottom of the steps, shifts the baby to his other arm, and runs toward us.

"Hurry!" Bro yells at me.

I open my door, and he fumbles with the keys. Stomach Wound scrambles up behind the car and leans on the trunk, rocking us up and down. He kicks the fender. Suddenly he stops and bends over. He stands back up without the baby, arms outstretched above his head.

"Where's the baby?" I say.

"The baby is not our concern."

"Where is it?"

Bro glances in the rearview mirror, leans out his window. I look out my window and see the baby's legs.

"He put him behind the right rear wheel," I shout. "Jesus! Don't back up."

"I can't go forward!"

We are parked about two feet in front of a sheared concrete pillar.

"You can't back up. We'll have to get out."

"No."

The man keeps rocking the car.

"Bastard!" Bro says.

He shifts into neutral and lets the car roll forward, turning the wheels hard to the right. The metal screeches as the car scrapes against the pillar. Stomach Wound follows us, punching the trunk with his fists. When Bro can see the baby in the rearview mirror, he starts the engine and spins onto the road.

I look back. Stomach Wound holds his bandage above his head and shouts after us, the hole in his belly raw and exposed. The ragged bandage snakes out of his hand, whirling into the black sky, while below it the baby sits shapeless in the dirt.

"Crazy man," Bro mutters. "You should not have stayed."

"They thought I was an aid worker."

"People have lost everything," Bro says. "You came with food. You are a good man. But you are not in United States."

"Did you lose your home in the fighting?"

"We lost the home where I was born and had to move in with an uncle. What have you lost?"

Nothing. My mother lost an uncle in the Spanish Civil War. My father was in the navy but never saw combat in World War II. I was too young to fight in Vietnam. Years later my mother said she would have sent me to my aunt in Mexico had I been old enough for the draft.

"You've been lucky not to have been hurt with so much war," I say.

"No, *you* have been lucky. Inshallah, you will stay lucky."

We drive silently into downtown Kabul, park near Flower Street, and get out of the car. Bro feels the crumpled metal where his door had scraped against the pillar. We lean against the hood and cross our arms, keeping our thoughts to ourselves. I stare at the barren mountains, hulking ink blots against the sky.

A boy approaches us with a smoking can of incense. He waves the smoke over the car, a blessing, Bro explains, a spiritual cleansing. Bro brushes smoke against his face, inhaling deeply.

"Bakhsish," the boy says.

Bro gives him two Afghani. The boy shakes his can around me. "Boro," Bro says.

I watch the boy wander off and glance at my watch. It's a little after five o'clock. I've been so busy thinking about Christmas that I've forgotten December is the month of Ramadan, when Muslims fast from sunrise to sunset. They eat only in the evening. Bro must be starving. I point at a man cooking kabob on an open grill.

"You hungry? You haven't eaten."

Bro shrugs, stares at Flower Street where the sidewalks remain crowded with Westerners badgering merchants for good deals on Afghan rugs to take home while the tired tape of "Jingle Bells" continues to play. Afghans crowd into restaurants. Beggars collect on the sidewalks, waiting for traffic to stall. A few move toward us. Bro watches them, tells me to get in the car.

"You will not help any more poor people today," he says. "I will eat later. Let's go."

I watch Bro get back in the car. What was I thinking? I should have known better. But what should I have known? That people suffer and even in the smallest way I can do nothing? At least in San Francisco I could hand out bus tokens, refer someone to shelter, offer a sympathetic ear. None of that matters in Kabul. Here I feel powerless to help.

Bro won't talk to me. He remains furious that we did not leave when he said we should. Because I did not listen to him, we could have been hurt. Killed. He did not survive thirty years of war to die with me. I apologize over and over until I'm as pissed off at him as he is at me. Finally we settle into a sullen silence, and he drops me off at the house.

A Northern Alliance commander next door walks into the house behind me and asks to borrow my sat phone to call his family in Pakistan. He uses my room. One of his men sits outside the closed door, Kalashnikov rifle resting against his knees. He looks at me and smiles. No shoes. Young kid. I offer him socks, but he declines. Tea? He smiles, shakes his head.

I go into Peter's room and watch him edit photos of women who had secretly taught girls in their homes while the Taliban ruled. He wears a battery-operated headlamp strapped to his forehead to see until the power comes back on. He has attached his laptop to a car battery.

Peter motions me to a chair and pours himself a drink. He found a merchant willing to sell booze to Westerners. When the Taliban ruled, he hid dozens of pint bottles in the rafters of his ceiling and buried his remaining stash behind his house. He sells the bottles now for eighty dollars apiece.

Peter thinks it's rum. He strains the gold liquid through his water purifier. The color lightens considerably as all sorts of grit settles at the bottom of the purifier. He pours some in a glass, strikes a match and lights it. A blue flame rises, weaving inside the glass. Peter hands me the drink and a small carton of mango juice to cut it.

"Good stuff, cowboy."

I consider the glass, feel the warmth creeping into my fingers, and blow out the flame. Below me I hear commotion at the front door. I step into the hall, the commander's guard standing tensely beside me. Bro bounds up the stairs, and the guard raises his gun. I jump between them.

"He's with me, he's with me!" I yell.

"Hamid Karzai," Bro shouts, "He's here! He's here! The inauguration is next week."

The guard doesn't move. Bro eases me out of the way and shakes his hand. They kiss each other on both cheeks. Bro says something in Dari, and the guard relaxes. Then Bro embraces me, all hard feeling gone in the wake of the magic soon to be cast by the arrival of Karzai.

"Karzai will find jobs for all of Afghanistan," he says. "He will build schools. We will have new roads. He will..."

As hardened and wise to Afghanistan as Bro is, he seems naive about what a politician can do. Maybe I'm just cynical, I don't know. Maybe his desire for peace runs so deep it allows Karzai supernatural powers. For all I know Karzai may be Afghanistan's Abraham Lincoln-in-waiting. Inshallah, why not? That's not for me to decide. Right now I need more immediate information.

"How do I get into the inauguration?"

Bro pauses, confused at first by the intrusion of my question. I wait until he returns to earth.

"That will be very difficult," he says finally. "You will need a pass."

"Can I get one?"

"Yes, why not? Inshallah, we will try."

■ ■ ■

I soon learn that inshallah is the escape clause for agreements made by Afghan people. Inshallah, God willing, we can do anything. Why not? If it does not happen, it was not God's will. Inshallah, we try another day.

We spend a week trying to get an inaugural pass, but my needs are not those of God. Officials at the presidential palace tell us to go to the offices of the United Nations. The UN guard says I should stop at the Ministry of Foreign Affairs. Mr. High Five greets us at the gate.

"Hello, my friend!" Slap palms. "Michael Jordan!"

"I need a pass for the inauguration."

"Go to the palace, my friend," Mr. High Five says.

"I was just there. They told me to come here."

"I am sorry, my friend. Please sign in."

"I just did."

We return to the palace. The guards tell us to wait. After four hours, I return to the ministry.

"Hello my friend!" Slap palms. "Sign in, please."

"I still need a pass."

Mr. High Five waves us away from his desk. He calls to a security guard to pat me down. He tells me to wait and sends another guard into the ministry.

"What is the problem?"

"No problem, my friend," Mr. High Five says. "Extra security for Karzai."

"Will I get a pass?"

"If you go to the palace."

Round and round we go, day after day. Where it will end, nobody knows. Finally I give up on ever getting a pass. I will sneak into the inauguration. How? I'll worry about that later.

This evening I stop at the InterCon for the nightly UN briefing. There is little news of Karzai. He has avoided reporters and stayed behind the closed gates of the presidential palace, building political support among allies and opponents, many of whom are liable to pounce should he stumble after being sworn in as prime minister. He has already met with U.S. Defense Secretary Donald Rumsfeld at Bagram Air Base. Then he flew to Italy and hunkered down with Afghanistan's exiled former monarch Zahir Shah.

Earlier in the day Ayatollah Mohammad Asef Muhsini, leader of the Harakat-i Islami of Afghanistan, a fundamentalist political faction not represented in the new government, told reporters that Karzai was owned by the West. "But it doesn't matter who supports him from the outside," he continued. "It's important we have democracy and peace. We'll see what his policies are."

Asked about potential strife within the new government before it has even assumed power, the UN spokesman has no comment. Instead he complains that international aid promised by the United States and Europe lags. "The life expectancy of Afghans is forty-six," he says, "and infant mortality is the highest in the world. The country cannot afford these delays."

As I take notes, a *Wall Street Journal* reporter whispers to me that he had been promised an interview with Karzai all week, inshallah, but so far nothing.

I tell him about my futile efforts to obtain a pass and how Bro and I entertained one another joking about the idiotic bureaucracy.

"You think this is funny?" the reporter snaps. "You're telling me you and your Afghan driver tell jokes? I'm running around like an idiot and you're laughing?"

A chunk of ceiling tile suddenly falls and strikes him on the head. He doesn't move. His head droops. The UN spokesman stops talking. Someone laughs. Then we all break into laughter.

"Karzai," the reporter mutters as if his very name is a curse.

Inauguration day arrives under overcast skies. Military checkpoints block nearly every intersection to the Ministry of the Interior, where the swearing-in will take place. The roads empty of traffic except for officials and reporters negotiating our way through roadblocks. Northern Alliance soldiers ask for my pass. I give them five, ten, twenty dollars, depending on the checkpoint and the greed of the guard, and we drive through.

Outside the Interior Ministry, a looming gray building landscaped with broken fountains and empty flower beds, Bro recognizes a driver for one of the generals. They embrace, exchange greetings. Bro whispers in his ear. The driver hesitates, opens the passenger door and waves me over. I get in the backseat. Bro tells me to give him forty dollars. Within seconds I am through the ministry gates.

The driver lets me out near a row of satellite dishes set up by various international television networks broadcasting the inauguration. I join Afghans and other reporters who mob the two doors of the auditorium. Armed soldiers shove us back. A steady drizzle intensifies the fetid funk of our unwashed bodies, sweaty with our desperation to get inside.

The soldiers treat us as if we are Taliban fighters trying to retake Kabul. They raise their rifle butts, wield metal cables, and punch anyone within arm's reach. A few reporters wave yellow passes, but the soldiers have no regard for mere paperwork no matter its color. I surge back and forth with the currents of the crowd, unable to resist its undertow. Without reason or order, the soldiers open the heavy wood doors a crack and permit a few people inside. Then the doors slam shut with a clamorous shudder, and I am crushed within the mob shoving against the guards, an enraged, writhing bundle of Eddie Bauer jackets and turbans demanding entry only to be thrust back once more.

"Keep your arms crossed and out in front of you, so your chest doesn't get crushed," a reporter advises me.

I do as he says. I'm not the biggest guy in the world nor the youngest, and I can't afford a cracked rib. Someone behind me presses his hand on my head, pushing me down as if he is shoving a turtle back inside its shell. He leaps up, squashing me, and tries to scramble over the heads of the mob to the door. Another hand reaches from behind me, grabs my chin, and pulls me back as the man tries to claw his way in. I shove him away and he falls, clutching my ankle as I feel the small space he held suddenly go vacant. A cool dampness washes over my neck for an instant before the space fills with another pressing body, followed by still another surge that thrusts me forward again.

"Tell them I'm with you," a reporter yells to another reporter near the door.

"You're not with me," the second reporter shouts back before she ducks under a guard's arm and dashes inside the auditorium, the doors shutting behind her once more.

"Keep as much space around you as you can so you don't suffocate," a photographer tells me. "If it gets real bad, get down. There's more space around the legs. Like this."

He squats, arms folded across his chest, his face inches behind someone's ass. Suddenly the crowd stumbles backward and knocks him down.

"Hey!" he yells.

I try to grab his arm but am thrown forward onto my knees. The doors open once more, and I scramble inside. An Afghan soldier grabs my collar, hefts me to my feet, and thrusts his gun into my stomach. He pushes me down an aisle past packed rows of seats toward a rear room.

"Afghans have decided to no longer heed the voice of the gun," I hear new Interior Minister Younis Qanooni declare from the stage. "I feel our wrecked ship is finally sailing slowly towards peace."

The guards hold me against a wall and demand my passport. I offer it to one of them, who snatches it from me and examines it upside down. They talk among themselves, agitated, pacing. For all they know, a lot of people who'd like to assassinate Karzai have gotten in almost at random.

They return my passport and hustle me back into the auditorium. I look for a seat but see none. I stand against a wall and watch a short, slim man in a lambskin hat and green and purple Uzbek robe assume the podium. Hamid Karzai.

"We should put our hands together to be brothers and friends," he declares in a high voice cut with static. "Forget the painful past."

He promises freedom and opportunity for women and for members of all religious faiths; to educate Afghans, weed out corruption, rebuild the economy, and create a national army to enforce law and order; to fight terrorism and promote democracy, a nod to the U.S. support that helped him achieve power.

"Dear Afghanistan is ours, and we are the valuable sons and daughters of this land. Everything can happen if we are united."

I am not convinced. He seems to be talking to people outside this auditorium, certainly not to the guard who had dragged me off and is now punching an Afghan man in the face before brushing past me and shoving him into a back room, blood spurting from the man's nose onto my jacket.

Karzai continues talking. He insists Afghanistan can come together and put aside the factionalism of the civil wars. People around me clap in a thunderous roar, shouting agreement, and the hope in the room is palpable, and despite my doubts I applaud too. But do we really believe? I want to think so, but then I see the bleeding face of the Afghan man emerge from the back room bloodier than before and livid with outrage. Whatever he feels I suspect Karzai can't heal.

CHAPTER FIVE

Curfew

JANUARY 2002
Kabul

I slam down the receiver.

I run out of the house, shout for Bro. He stands by his car, still parked on the street. Arms folded, he turns to me.

The night sky unfurls without stars and curtains everything in darkness except for a small patch of light coming from inside Bro's car. Streetlights hover above us with no purpose. After nearly thirty years of war, nothing works here.

Bro looks at me. The jagged flashes of an electrical storm reveal beggars stooped in piles of trash, sifting through foul gutters. Square concrete houses appear ghostly white and then disappear into darkness. A frigid wind inflates my jacket and the hair on the back of my neck rises from the chill.

"Where do we go?" Bro says.

"Bagram. We need to go to Bagram."

"Now?" Bro looks at his watch. "It's 7:00 p.m."

We have been working since eight this morning, interviewing staff of aid organizations. Banditry and fighting across the country continue to hinder relief efforts to freezing and starving Afghans, they told me. One aid worker was killed, caught in the crossfire between feuding Afghan clans.

Bro and I didn't stop for lunch, haven't had dinner. He dropped me off only minutes before. We had tea, relaxed from the long day, said good night. I heard my satellite phone ring as I shook hands with him at the door.

Bro understands my impulsiveness, the sudden demands on his time, but what I'm asking of him tonight involves risks beyond the usual hasty, breaking news story. Far worse than my hapless efforts to help the refugees. He makes a face, kicks at the pavement nervously.

"Curfew," he says, finally looking again at his watch.

I nod. I'm not happy about it either. I'm supposed to file my aid story tonight. It's at least an hour's drive north to Bagram Air Base. But a BBC correspondent has called to tell me that a delegation of United States senators is arriving at nine o'clock tonight. I have no choice but to cover it. I need to get to Bagram.

"Curfew's nine thirty, I know," I say looking at my watch. "If we leave now, we can get to Bagram by eight. If they let us in we'll spend the night on base. If they don't, we'll turn around and get back just in time."

"It's very late," Bro says.

"And getting later. We have to leave. I'll pay you extra."

"It's not the money. I am Afghan. If we are stopped, it will be big problem for me."

"For both of us."

"For me more. I am Pashtun. Do you understand?"

I do. The Northern Alliance patrols the roads after dark. If we're stopped, it won't matter that Bro and his family opposed the Taliban. He's still Pashtun.

"I'll pay you extra," I say again.

Bro has been seduced by his fifty-dollar-a-day salary. When he learned that television crews were paying translators one hundred dollars a day, he asked me for the same amount. I bluffed, told him to apply for another job. There were plenty of translators I could hire for fifty dollars a day, I said, and walked away.

"If you need, I'll write you a letter of reference," I continued, not even looking over my shoulder. "This isn't September 2001 anymore but January 2002. A new year, Bro. Most reporters are leaving Afghanistan. The Taliban is gone. Stories are fewer. I hope you're sure about this."

That scared him. He pleaded with me to keep him. He supports a wife and child. He buys food for his parents and clothes for his six brothers and two sisters. They all live in one house. Each night, Bro counts his earnings out on the kitchen table, lit by a gas lamp. The wavering light dances in the wide eyes of his family bunched around him spellbound as he counts out his money, two American twenty-dollar bills and a ten. Yesterday he bought a new black leather jacket. Money is our bond.

"I am your driver. This is my job. I'll do what you say, but this is dangerous," Bro says.

"I'll pay you an additional fifty bucks. That's a hundred dollars for today."

"You don't understand. What good will money do if I am dead, and where will the money come from then?"

"Nobody's dying."

"This is silly."

I smile and he smirks, chuckling. *Silly* is a word he latched onto after he heard me say it one afternoon when I described a disgruntled bureaucrat who wouldn't let us make an appointment with a government minister. Since then every bumbling guard and official we encounter he dismisses as silly.

"You'll give the money to my family if I die?"

"We'll be in and out of Bagram and back here in no time."

"I need to tell my wife and father."

"Your house on the way?"

"Yes."

I look at my watch, thinking, Stop at his house, five, ten minutes tops.

"Okay," I say, "don't get too overly fucking sentimental. We're coming back."

7:15 P.M., BRO'S HOUSE

"This is silly," he says again, getting out of the car. This time he doesn't laugh.

I watch him go. I look at my watch and wait, listen to chickens rustle in a wire pen inside the gate to Bro's house, a low, flat, concrete building draped in shadows. I hear voices, can't tell if they're coming from his house or another. Then silence. A man bicycles past me, weaving around potholes. Cats yowl, run through patches of murky light thrown by a pocked moon veiled in thin clouds. Women in burqas drift toward me in fog and knock on my window for change. I ignore them. I remember how creeped-out I was when I first saw the Vaders, as Peter calls them. They are part of my world now, and I have the comfort of knowing that tonight will end no differently than other nights when poor women approach me with little expectation of spare change despite their pleas. Just another night, I tell myself. Then I glance at my watch once more. When the women move on, I thumb through my wallet to make sure I have an extra fifty to give Bro.

7:20 P.M.

Bro runs back to the car, a sleeping bag jammed under one arm.

"What did you tell your family?"

"I told them I have to work late and may need to sleep in your house. I did not tell them we go to Bagram."

"I'll get you back in time."

"Inshallah," Bro says, shifting the car into gear.

We rattle down a road potted with bomb craters, heading out of Kabul. I look at my watch. 7:25. We're going barely thirty miles an hour.

Yeah, at least an hour.

8:30 P.M.

The metal gates of Bagram Air Base tower above us. Gaslight from wooden vendors' stalls casts a yellow glaze on the gritty air. Afghan men approach my side of the car talking at once.

"Mister, help a poor man."

"Please, mister."

"My family, they are all sick."

"Boro," Bro snaps. "Go."

The men step back. They peer into the car, rocking it, and again Bro shouts, "Boro!" They scuffle away, shift to another side of the car, and press their faces against the windows.

"I'm going to see if I can get us in."

"I'll wait here," Bro says. "Boro!"

A Northern Alliance soldier stops me, pats me down. He says to wait and talks rapidly into a radio. Another Afghan soldier asks where I am from.

"United States."

"What do you do in Afghanistan?"

"I'm a journalist."

"You have a satellite phone? I see many journalists. All of them have satellite phone."

"What does it matter?"

"May I use to call my family in Pakistan?"

"Only if you get me in."

"I have not seen them for a long time."

"Get me in, and you can talk to them."

"I'll get you in," he says, slipping behind the gate.

I glance back at Bro, can't see him through the crowd of people gathered around the car. I blow on my cold hands. Narrow dirt paths lead from the road to collapsed mud huts, lit from within by wood fires. I twist my watch against my wrist, look at it, pace back and forth. A merchant offers to sell me a prayer shawl. Another guy urges me to buy some nuts. The night stretches low and immeasurably far over the desert, a dark fathomless void beyond the firelight.

After fifteen minutes, an American army officer walks around the gate toward me. I cup my hands around my nose and blow to warm my face. My toes feel numb.

"May I help you, sir?"

"I'm a reporter. I want to get in for the press conference with the senate delegation."

"Sir, I'm sorry you came out this way at this time of night, but I can't let you inside."

"You can't?"

"No, sir."

"Is there a reason?"

"We have a list of reporters, sir. From that list, a pool of reporters was selected. You should be able to get what you need from them."

"No way I can get in?"

"No, sir. I'm sorry."

"Can my driver and I park inside the gate and sleep in the car?"

"No, sir. I'm sorry."

"We won't make it back before curfew."

"I'm sorry, sir."

"We could get killed going back."

"You need to leave, sir."

"How about if we stay on this side of the gate?"

"I wouldn't do that, sir. These people—I don't know, but we can't protect you."

"Well, I had to try."

"Sir?"

"Yes."

"Abdul here wants to know if he can use your sat phone."

"No. I told him he could use it if he got me inside."

"I'm sorry, Abdul," the soldier says.

I walk back to the car, push through the throng to the passenger door. Bro sits inside behind the wheel, looking tense.

"Let's go back."

He looks at his watch, turns the key. Nothing. Turns it again. Nothing. Turns it again. Again. Again.

"What's the matter?"

"I'm your driver, not your mechanic," Bro barks back.

Bro opens the hood. We stare at the engine as if somehow staring will solve the problem. A glut of vendors cranes over our shoulders, shoving us against the car, their stink filling my lungs like cotton. We're given advice, steamy breath layering hot mist over the exposed engine amid the shrill clacking of tongues, excited gestures.

We decide to push the car down an embankment to see if Bro can pop the clutch to start it. He steers the car off the road between rows of red-painted rocks that warn of mines in the area. The car gathers speed, lurches when Bro lets out the clutch. The engine coughs and sputters. I wait, watching, take my watch off and shove it in my pocket. Tired of looking at it. A cloud of exhaust belches out the back, and I hear the engine growl to life.

"Whatever you do, don't turn it off," I shout.

Bro leans out his window, wags an upraised thumb, and laughs. He backs up. I get in, give him a high-five slap to the hand.

We drive away. I take my watch out of my pocket, twist it around my fingers. Bagram has almost disappeared behind us when I feel the car slowing to a stop. I look at Bro. He won't look at me. He gets out, kneels by the right front tire.

"What's the matter?" I ask, knowing without being told.

"Flat."

"Let's get the spare."

"Spare?"

"Extra tire. You have an extra tire?"

"No."

I tug at my beard a few times, biting my lower lip. I put my watch back in my pocket.

"What do we do?"

"Go back," Bro says, getting in the car.

He drives in reverse. The car lists heavily. Small flickers of firelight dance out of vendor stalls, grow brighter. We're immediately surrounded again. Bro explains the problem to the curious crowd. Several men point at a narrow path between several stalls and urge us to follow them to a gated compound I can't see at first in the dark. We drive in first gear, the flat tire thumping. A man leans against the heavy wooden door and slowly pushes it open. Inside, smashed cars rise in uneven stacks. Two grease-stained men emerge from a shack as if rising up out of the ground and chase the onlookers away. They close the gate and examine our tire. Shaggy hair. Patchy beards. Trolls, I think. I breathe deeply, wait and watch.

Without talking, the trolls jack the car up, remove the tire and roll it in a trough of water, waiting until bubbles rise from the puncture. Troll number one taps the ground with his fingers until he finds a small splinter of wood. He pushes the wood into the hole, marking it.

The trolls rummage through toolboxes until one of them finds a small rubber patch and smears it with glue. It sticks to his fingers, and he shakes his hand until the patch falls on the ground. He picks it up, brushes dirt off, rubs more glue on. He removes the splinter from the tire and presses the patch over the hole. He reaches for a hand pump and attaches it to the tire, slowly pushing air into the tube.

He pumps for a long time, then passes the pump to the other troll, who finishes filling the tire. Together they put it back on the battered wheel, remount it on the axel, and screw on the lug nuts. The fat tire shines where it is still wet. The trolls look at us and smile. No teeth. We shake hands. I pay them five dollars and they bow, right hands over their hearts.

"Where do you go?" one of the trolls asks Bro.

"Kabul."

"Now?"

"Think we'll make it?" I ask.

He shrugs.

"Before curfew?"

"Inshallah," he says. "Why not?"

The cratered road leading back to Kabul is lit only by our headlights. Blackness extends beyond our feeble illumination. Fog breaks over the hood of the car. Bro drives fast, swings right, then left around the deepest holes. Our lights graze red rocks on the side of the road, and I close my eyes, exhausted, wondering how all the mines will ever be removed from this country.

The car leaps and my head bangs the roof. I see Bro's hands scramble over the steering wheel as he fights to regain control.

We skid off the road, smashing through a line of red rocks into sagebrush. My head smacks the passenger window. Wheels spin in place as Bro downshifts and we leap back onto the road, slamming into another hole. We're thrown from our seats. My left leg hits the stick shift. Bro grips the wheel, steadying it to a stop. I rub my leg. The car lists to the left. This time I hear the hiss of the flattening tire. We look at each other, get out.

"A different tire," Bro says from the left rear of the car. "That is good."

"Why? Why is that good?" I ask, limping behind him.

"Those men did a good job. It is not their tire that is flat. At least they did not steal from us."

I look around and can't see anything beyond our car. A nether place where we're lost in someone else's stormy dream.

"We're going to have to spend the night here."

"No," Bro says.

"We can't drive. I'll call people in the morning on the sat phone when curfew is lifted."

We turn at the sudden sound of a vehicle approaching. Headlights rise behind us, slowly illuminating the road. Gradually the light fills the night until we're blinded. A truck passes without stopping, rocks our car in its slipstream.

"We can park behind one of these tanks," I say above the noise of the passing truck.

"No."

"Bro."

"I am your driver," he says. "But I am also Afghan. For twenty-four years, as old as I am now, there has been war here. What do you know about that? I know. We can't stay here. Why do you think this road is empty at night? Bandits. We will be killed if we stay here."

I am convinced we won't make it to Kabul driving on a flat. We'll ruin the car, have to get it towed, increasing our problems in the morning.

"Look, I know you're nervous. I'll pay you extra to stay out here. Behind these tanks. No one will see us."

"Why you always talk of money? What does money do for dead man? I told you we should not do this. I told you! You have not seen killing. You have lost nothing. I have!"

His anger stuns me to silence. Bro gets back inside the car, shifts into first gear, and we hobble forward rocked by the repetitive thump of the flat tire. We don't talk, don't look at each other.

Any bandit who sees a car moving this slowly will be drawn to it like a shark to blood, I think. But I don't say anything. I drop a tape of Iranian music into the cassette player. Something to kill the time. Kill the silence between us. Keep my mind off the *thump, thump, thump* of the flat tire and the painfully slow journey ahead.

9:30 P.M.

Each time headlights appear behind us, Bro pulls off the road, and we get out and scramble behind an abandoned Soviet tank and wait for them to pass. Thank God for war debris. I can't see if there are red rocks or not.

"If they stop," Bro says, "don't move, don't breathe. Hide. Hide as best you can."

No one stops. The noise from their engines trails off in the fog. We resume driving. The flat tire slaps noisily against the gloom. I glance at Bro's worried face.

This is not my fault, I try to convince myself. Not my fault.

I look at my watch.

Curfew.

11:30 P.M.

We limp into the outskirts of Kabul and stop at a military checkpoint, the tire an unraveling mound of shredded rubber.

"Where are you going at this time of night?" a Northern Alliance commander asks Bro. Shivering, the commander tugs at a blanket around his shoulders, shifts from one sandaled foot to the other. The new government of Hamid Karzai has no money to provide its soldiers with uniforms, boots, and other basic necessities to keep them warm.

"He is an American journalist," Bro says. "I am taking him to his house. We are returning from a news conference at Bagram."

The commander looks at the back of the car, jams a cigarette in his mouth. "How long have you driven on this tire?"

Bro looks at me and I look at my watch. "Two hours," I say.

"Two hours," Bro says.

"You can't drive farther on this tire."

"His house is not far."

"You are a guest in our country," the commander says, looking at me. "But I have no tea to offer you, or I would ask you to stay. Go. But you will be stopped again."

We push on toward downtown. Padlocked vendors' stalls covered with burlap line the road. The empty streets resemble little more than paths. Dogs howl unseen. We continue driving. Bro talks us through three more checkpoints. My status rises with each stop. He says I'm an FBI agent working for Karzai, a UN official, an aid worker. Anything to keep us moving.

When we reach downtown, a man materializes out of the fog, rears back on his right leg, then lunges forward, extending a rifle. He aims it at the windshield.

"Jesus!" I scream.

Bro slams on the brake, and we drop down in our seats, wiggling as much as we can under the dashboard.

"Aiee!" the man shouts, firing a shot above the car.

12:00 A.M.

Four Afghan soldiers surround us, pointing their rifles at the car. We are at an intersection near a roundabout. Their commander asks Bro again and again why we are out after curfew. Bro explains about the two flat tires. The commander shakes his head. He has a beard that sticks out all over the place like an overused Brillo pad.

"Bad luck," he says.

"Yes," Bro says.

"Where are you from?"

"Kabul City."

"But you are Pashtun?"

"I am from Kabul City."

"I am from the Panjshir," Brillo Pad says, referring to a Northern Alliance stronghold near Kabul. He studies Bro a moment, then looks at me.

"You can't leave until five o'clock when curfew ends. But I will take the American to his house," Brillo Pad says, looking at me.

"Don't leave me here with them," Bro says after he translates, his voice shaking. "Tell them you can't go without me."

Bro, I think, you got nothing to worry about, partner. I've heard too many stories about kidnappings. I'm not going anywhere alone.

"No, no," I say. "I can't leave without my translator. We'll stay here."

"Thank you," Bro whispers.

"I'm sorry, mister," Brillo Pad says to me. "You are a guest in our country, but I am a soldier and must do my job. If you will not leave without your translator, then you will stay. Cigarette?"

I give him one.

"Don't be afraid, mister," he says. "When one fights against someone if you are not the enemy you must not be afraid. I'm not against you. Our goal as soldiers is to resist our enemy and conquer. You are our guest."

"Thank you," I say.

Behind him, soldiers gather around small fires to warm their hands. Many are barefoot. Farther away orange firelight stains the interior of a hut where more soldiers stand. Indian music squawks out of a cassette player. Beggars dart among vendor stalls, picking at scraps on the ground. The soldiers ignore them.

Bro turns in his seat, reaches for the sleeping bag. He unrolls it and pulls it up under his chin. He pushes some of the bag over to me. I scoot toward him, pressing against the stick shift, and cover myself. Bro leaves the car running and turns the heat high. We lower the backs of our seats. Brillo Pad stares at us, walks away. Three other soldiers stay by the car.

"Well, at least you told your family you might be out all night."

"It's okay."

"I'm sorry."

"This is my job. I'm your driver."

We laugh.

"I think you went above the call of duty. Next time I'll listen to you."

"Next time you'll do the same thing," Bro says. "You are a journalist, I am your driver."

"Where do we go?" I say, imitating him.

"Where do we go?" He laughs. "Once they came to my house and asked for my father, but he was not there. Then they asked for my brother, but he was not there. They took everything—our rugs, tables, beds, photographs. There was no joy. Now there is joy.

"My wife wants to go to America. She tells me, 'Get visa at embassy.' I tell her it is too expensive. I want to go to America, but not with her. I think if she saw all the beautiful things in America she would not want to come back. In America women see too many men other than their husbands."

"We call that promiscuous."

"Promiscuous?"

I spell it for him, and he writes it down in his notebook.

"It means seeing someone other than the person you're married to."

"Oh. We have that in Afghanistan too."

"Maybe you could come to the States by yourself first and see how you feel and then send for her."

"I think maybe I would like to go to America alone. Tell me about Miami Beach."

"Miami Beach would rock your world, Bro. You wouldn't want to come back."

He laughs. I take a Bob Dylan CD out of my coat pocket and drop it into the radio's disc player. Bro makes a face at Dylan's nasal tones. He takes it out and replaces it with an Iranian CD. The high-pitched wailing of the singers drills into my temples. I punch it out and we agree to no music.

"I want to go to school in the U.S."

"You can go to school here."

"There are no jobs for Afghans. I studied biology, for medical school in Talib time, but there's no work for doctors."

"Reporters are starting to leave here. You should go back to school."

"I cannot tell you how good it is to make money. What it is like to say I am a driver for journalists. I have told all my professors I drive for a journalist. They have not been paid for months. They see I am doing well. I can imagine nothing else but to drive for journalists."

"You should think of something else. The news will move on. I'll move on."

He doesn't understand my restlessness. He was born into the adrenaline rush of war and wants only peace.

"Inshallah, you will stay in Afghanistan. I could take you to many places. Herat, Jalalabad. Good stories for you."

"Inshallah, we'll get home tonight. Why not?"

"Inshallah."

12:20 A.M.

A soldier taps the window and asks for a cigarette. He wants to know what we are talking about.

"Nothing," Bro says. "It is between us."

"Mister, in Talib time sometimes at home very secretly I watched TV and videocassettes," he says to me. "Many times Taliban would come by our street and put their ear against the houses to see if we were listening to music."

Another soldier leans his gun against the car and shares the first soldier's cigarette.

"One day a woman came to my shop," the second soldier says. "The Taliban said don't talk to woman. But why? They kicked the woman. I could do nothing. Children could not play outside. It was forbidden for them to fly even kites."

The soldiers pause long enough for Bro to translate. Soon he becomes so involved in their conversation, he forgets me.

"What are they saying?" I ask.

"It is nothing," Bro says. "It's between us."

One of the soldiers apologizes.

"I am sorry, mister. You are a guest in our country, mister. But we are soldiers doing our job. We are talking. About life. About how it is to be Afghan. We have known only war all our lives."

Bro says something to him, and their conversation resumes without me.

■ ■ ■

I hear a shout, wake up beneath the sleeping bag, my nose pressed against the fabric. A soldier runs to a spot where the light beams of a vehicle thrust through the fog.

"Aiee!" the soldier shouts, firing a warning shot.

The vehicle appears to be some sort of military Land Rover. The soldier eases out of his crouch and approaches it.

"I need to piss," I say to Bro.

He nods, rolls down his window, and says something to our guards. They wave for me to leave the car. I walk a few feet away and relieve myself.

"Aiee!" a soldier shouts behind me at the same time I feel a blast of air over my head, followed by a sharp crack.

I close my eyes, drop to my knees and hunch my shoulders, the sharp odor of urine filling my head. I slowly open my eyes. The soldier who stopped the Land Rover runs toward me, rifle extended. I raise my hands. Soldiers around the car yell at him, move toward me. I hear Bro shouting.

"Bro, what's going on? Goddamn it, Bro!"

I am surrounded. Three soldiers on my right side scream at the other soldier on my left. My heart seems to fill my throat, wants to burst through my chest. More soldiers come running from the hut, rifles raised. They shove one another, reaching around me. I smell their tobacco breath. Bro's voice rises above the rest.

"He says he thought you were running away," Bro says of the shooter, turning one way and then the other trying to listen to each side. "These guys say he fired at them and could have killed one of them."

He grabs my arm and pulls me off the ground and toward the car.

"You are a silly man!" Bro shouts at the shooter. "Silly!"

The soldier lunges toward Bro, and Bro lets go of me, turns, and raises his fists. I grab him and pull him back. Another soldier shouts at the shooter. Firelight glints off rifle butts. Distorted faces snarl insults, fend off punches and kicks, a stew of legs and arms, dancing shadows in the night.

Finally the commander approaches, swinging a metal cable, striking the backs of the entangled soldiers.

"Boro! Boro!" he shouts.

Bro opens my door. I stand transfixed by the fight, the thrashing cable, the screams. He shoves me into my seat. I notice my crotch. The fly of my pants is wide open.

4:00 A.M.

The commander introduces us to the Northern Alliance soldier who is driving the Land Rover. He will escort us out, the commander explains, adding that curfew doesn't end until five and he could keep us here the additional hour if he wanted. Bro nudges me and I give the commander five dollars. He bows. Bro tells me we should direct our escort to his house because it's closer than mine and near a tire shop.

"I am sorry, mister," the commander tells me for the final time. Bro offers a final round of cigarettes to the soldiers. The one who shot at me reaches inside the car and takes my hand. A fresh gash runs down his right cheek.

We follow the Land Rover down narrow streets between white stucco buildings and piles of trash where boys let goats graze. The sound of our thumping tire will be ignored until we reach Bro's house. The silence that follows when we stop awakens me.

Bro takes me to his bedroom. He says he will sit outside his parents' room, where his wife and daughter are asleep. His wife does not like sleeping alone when he is gone, he explains. He does not want to wake them.

Bright red carpets and pillows cover the floor of his room. An oil-burning stove takes up one corner near a wide bed covered with a red comforter. A copy of the Quran lies on a table beside the bed near a photograph of Bro, his wife, and baby girl. Bro takes the photo, wipes the frame with his sleeve.

"You are too old not to have a wife, Malcolm."

"It happens that way sometimes."

"You are alone. If bandits had killed us you would have died alone."

"And you would have left a widow and orphans."

"But I would have left something of myself."

I take fifty dollars out of my wallet plus an additional one hundred.

"Here," I say, extending my hand. "This is something of myself. One hundred fifty dollars. A day's pay and extra for what I put you and your family through."

He takes the money, counts it.

"They don't know anything about tonight."

"Still."

"I will fix the tire early." He starts to laugh.

"What?"

"When they shot at you, you got in the car with your pants open."

"Fuck you, Bro. At least my pecker wasn't still hanging out."

He laughs harder, and I start laughing too.

"Get me up when you get up."

"The tire shop opens at seven," he says.

"Good. Tomorrow will be a busy day."

"You mean today. We can be promiscuous."

We both bust up laughing. Christ, we're tired.

"I'll have to write some kind of follow-up to the press conference we missed at Bagram tonight. Last night. Whatever night."

We laugh again until it hurts. Bro pockets sixty dollars, gives the rest back to me, a smile still on his face, but he is no longer laughing.

"I am your driver," he says and shakes my hand. "This is my job. Good night."

He closes the door and walks downstairs.

I hold the money for some time before I shove it back in my pocket. We are colleagues, he and I. Maybe after tonight, even friends. I look at the closed bedroom door, imagine Bro throwing a blanket down outside his parents' room. I pull back the bedcovers and slip beneath a comforter and listen to the barking of dogs outside as I drift into sleep.

What seems only minutes later Bro knocks on the door. I look at him bleary eyed. He raises his chin toward a crack in the curtains where sunlight streams through. I hear chattering families beneath my window as they step off sidewalks and merge onto the street. The shouts of vendors mix with the blasts of car horns. Wailing chants from a nearby mosque pierce the morning with prayer.

"The tire is fixed," Bro says. "Where do we go?"

I rub my face and look at him. He smiles and I shake my head. In a minute, Bro, in a minute. I'll think of something.

CHAPTER SIX

A Good Life, Cowboy

JANUARY–MARCH 2002

Bro takes me home. I try the shower, but as usual we have no hot water. I heat a pot of water on the gas stove and, when it warms, wipe myself down with a stained washcloth, jumping from one bare foot to the other on the frigid floor. Peter asks to use some of the water for coffee. He gives me a hard time going out so close to curfew. I'm too tired to get into it with him.

Stirring his coffee, he tells me he wants to attend a cockfight. He has been frustrated with his photos lately. Too many meetings, too many group shots, too many things that don't interest him. He wants something with color, action. Cockfighting had been outlawed under the Taliban. Now it's back.

"That's a story," he insists. "You can write it. What do you say, cowboy?"

"I need to follow up on last night's press conference."

"You missed it," Peter says and throws me a shirt. "Let's go. Bro can drive."

A scrim of dust hovers above the alley and drains the light until there is no light, turning the afternoon into dusk long before sunset. Peter, Bro, and I walk to a rotted wood door that leads into a corridor of mud and clay.

Moving slowly, we crouch beneath a brick walk that spans the narrow passageway, past old men, foul-smelling and ragged, squatting amid caged birds, cramped and confined. Their desperate high-pitched songs

72

follow us deeper inside, past dirt-smeared faces of boys, mere shadows against the walls leering at us, and we keep walking toward a blanket behind which rise the shouts of men.

Peter sweeps the blanket aside. A courtyard littered with broken bits of metal and coal, firewood and dried pieces of bread opens before us. Two-story apartment buildings rise above us, slanting drunkenly into shadows. Blood-spattered roosters circle each other, jabbing their beaks, their multihued feathers damp from exertion. Men squat on their haunches and toss money into the pit.

I listen to them shout as one of the birds leaps, claws extended, poised in one frozen second before striking the air in a sudden fury, tearing down through the floating pall of dust, eyes wide but blank, drawn down by gravity into the chest of the opposing cock, spewing blood. The owner of one of the cocks separates them. He grabs his bird and shoves a wet bandana down its throat, clearing it of blood.

A heavyset man urges the crowd on. He rages at the sky, appealing to an unseen deity for more bloodlust among the apostles of this cockfight. He clenches a drooping bouquet of money in his pumping fist. He shouts louder, ever louder, and I feel sucked in, some part of me primal and lustful, and I search for my own money until I hear something whimper. I turn around but see nothing.

Peter removes the lens cap of his camera.

"Ever been to anything like this before, cowboy?" he asks.

I shake my head. Large slathering black dogs bark and growl and lunge at us, rising up through the cracked ground against the heavy chains that contain them at the edge of a pit. I hear the whimper again and follow the sound to a trash can. Inside, a white puppy cries, scratching at the rusted metal.

Its eyes look as if they have been open a day or two. An old man pours himself a cup of green tea and sits by the trash can. Annoyed by the puppy, he jerks it out of the trash can and shakes it in front of the chained dogs. The dogs snap at it. The puppy whimpers. The old man tosses it toward another dog, which tries to bite it, ravaging the air with its outrage. Restrained by its chain, taut against the ground from where it arose. The puppy freezes in place, legs shaking. The old man tosses it back in the barrel. He strokes his chin, a philosopher of bestial sports.

"Keeps the dogs interested," he says of the puppy. "Makes them want to fight."

"When do the dogs fight?" I ask.

A shout rises from the onlookers. Blood shoots from the chest of one of the cocks.

"After," the old man says, nodding at the cocks. "Then the dogs."

The puppy whines, scraping the sides of the trash can.

"What's going on?" Peter says behind me.

"Dogfight after this."

He looks into the barrel. "Meat?"

"Bait."

"Meat."

I peer into the trash barrel and pick up the puppy. It snuggles against my coat, sneezes. I put it back in the barrel but don't let go of it completely. It scratches at the barrel again, whimpers. The old man looks at me. He holds two crumpled ten-thousand-Afghani notes—about two dollars. He says nothing, but I read the question in his eyes. I hand him some money. He nods and leaves to place a bet. The cocks strut slick and pink with blood. I listen to the noise of the crowd, to the dogs straining against their chains, to the crunch of gravel beneath the old man's sandals as he walks to place his bet.

"Get in front of me," I tell Bro.

I grab the puppy by the scruff of its neck and shove it into my pocket.

"What are you doing?" Peter says.

Fleas and ticks and other bugs that look like black needles thrust into its fur have turned the puppy into a pincushion of vermin. My skin crawls at the thought of these things digging into my skin, and I close my windbreaker around my chest to keep the puppy from touching me. Ears flopping, eyes wide, it stares out the car window as Bro drives.

Peter and I decide it's part Labrador retriever and part everything else and about four weeks old. We name it Maggot. In the evening I bathe Maggot with shampoo mixed with gasoline to kill the bugs. Peter slouches against the bathroom door holding a lit cigarette behind his back.

"Why do you want to break your heart?" he says.

I slather Maggot in suds. The gasoline burns my chapped hands.

"What are you going to do with it when we leave?"

"I haven't thought that far ahead."

"No, you haven't."

We mash lamb, rice, beans, and carrots for dog food. Maggot won't eat and won't drink water. He has diarrhea. His fur stands in dry humps, his eyes filled with mucus. Peter has all sorts of antibiotics. Green pills, blue pills, white pills. What does this one do? How about that one? We don't know, but we mash them up and give them to Maggot anyway. Bro offers me tetracycline tablets, which he uses for his chickens when they have diarrhea. We give him those too.

I keep Maggot in my bedroom. For days I squeeze water and food down his throat with my fingers, but he grows thinner. I bring him with me during the day and feed him between interviews. He sits on my lap and stares listlessly out the window at the remains of bombed buildings and the lines of beggars sprawled on the sidewalk wailing for help. I carry Maggot into interviews with government ministers, who consider the dog with the resigned disgust of people accustomed to Western extravagance.

Peter watches Maggot when I can't.

"I took him out ten minutes ago, cowboy. Still not eating," he says when I return from an assignment.

I continue force-feeding Maggot. He spits up most of the food. I pat him until he sleeps. At night, he curls so close to a battery-operated space heater that he burns his fur. I pull him away, and he burrows into my sleeping bag. I feel his warmth against my ankles, the steadiness of his breathing inside the bag. He shakes sometimes from whatever bad thoughts dogs have when they dream.

Throughout the night, Maggot awakens me at two-hour intervals to piss. I carry him downstairs and open the door. Frigid air blows against my face. I step out into the front yard, feel his ribs expand and contract against his thin skin. The door slams behind me. I wipe mucus from his eyes. When I was a boy, we had a cat that came down with distemper. I would clean its eyes every morning and it would look better, and because it looked better I convinced myself it would get better.

Maggot sniffs the ground. Dogs howl, trot down the street invisible in the fog. The heavy breathing of packs half crazed with hunger. The air tastes bitter, the sky smooth as slate punched with stars. Moonlight casts jagged shadows through the trees. Military helicopters and planes rumble overhead beyond my sight. Occasional gunshots pierce the night and then the steady movement of the dogs resumes amid the howls of mating pairs. Maggot squats, keeps his head turned from me, ears pricked.

"Get on with it," I tell him.

About two weeks after I found him, Maggot awakens me at six o'clock in the morning. Roosters crow amid high-pitched chants rising from mosques. Sunlight begins its ritual melting of the ice on my windowsill. I hear the crunch of wheels against stone, car horns, children playing by the public water well, vendors pushing their carts.

Maggot sits on the floor and stares at me, wagging his tail. He crouches and leaps—the first time he has played. His food bowl is empty for the first time. The water dish too stands empty. His stomach is filled to bursting. Watching me, he arches his head and releases a long belch followed by an immense fart that sends me running out of the room clutching my nose.

Four weeks later the United States intensifies its antiterror campaign in eastern Afghanistan, dropping bombs on suspected al-Qaida and Taliban hideouts. Since December the region has been a constant target of U.S. bombers. Local residents say fugitive Taliban leaders could be hiding in the area. Banditry and fighting across Afghanistan continue to hinder efforts to deliver food and other supplies to freezing, starving, and ailing Afghans. One relief worker was killed when he was caught in cross fire between feuding Afghan factions near a refugee camp on the Pakistani border. Two others were wounded. About thirty-five thousand refugees have entered Kabul since the end of November, and the city is teetering on the edge of a humanitarian crisis.

Security remains threatened by the presence of armed soldiers on the streets, despite Karzai's order that they return to their barracks. The deployment of an international security force in Kabul will do nothing for cities and villages outside the capital where Northern Alliance soldiers use their weapons to kidnap suspected former Taliban for ransom.

Vice has returned with a passion. Women peddle sexual favors, gambling dens are commonplace, and the sale of alcohol, as I fully expected, is a thriving business.

Maggot grows. At night we play fetch. Then in the morning we drive through the rubble of this ruined capital to speak with more people about reconstruction. Day after long day, seven days a week, until it seems I have done nothing with my life other than speak with Afghan officials.

Peter and I feel increasingly alone. More and more journos leave as Afghanistan slips off the news radar. The Taliban were routed, and the war seems all but over. The United Nations no longer holds nightly press conferences. The mundane details of international aid projects can't compete with the faint but persistent rumblings of impending confrontation between the United States and Saddam Hussein's Iraq.

One morning while I heat water for instant coffee, Bro runs into the kitchen and grabs me by the arm. The man who organized the cockfights is at the door, he says. He wants Maggot.

"Someone must have seen you take him," Bro says. "It is too easy to find foreigners in Kabul."

I ask Bro to take Maggot to my room, but he won't touch him. Instead he chases him through the house until finally he herds him up the stairs. When I hear my bedroom door close, I walk to the front of the house. A man in a heavy green coat stands behind the front gate.

"You have my dog," he says.

"The dog died," I say.

"I want three hundred dollars."

"No."

"One hundred then."

"The dog is dead."

"I want fifty dollars."

"The dog is dead. You can have its bones."

"I have other dogs you can have."

"How much?"

"Thirty dollars."

I give him a twenty-dollar bill.

"I will bring you another dog."

"No. Go please. I don't want to see you again."

American reporters often drop by to see Maggot. They live in hotels or houses nearby. We refer to the houses by the news organization renting them: USA Today House, Knight Ridder House, BBC House, AP House. The list is long. When new reporters arrive, we search their bags for booze and additional computer equipment. One reporter likes to make desserts. When two apples she bought for an apple pie disappear from her kitchen, she accuses her Afghan translator of stealing them.

"This is not just about apples!" she screams. "This is much bigger than apples!"

"For Afghans, we are used to fighting, used to difficulties," Bro says after she storms out without further explanation of the importance of the apples. "For me it does not matter. I don't like apples. But for others, Afghanistan is a stressful place."

Many of us have been here three months and longer. We have grown accustomed to limited bathing, intermittent electricity, no central heat. We throw sticks and crouch on the ground, playing with Maggot as he barks around our feet. We sit in the dark, smoky oil lamps our only illumination, and share photographs of our families. Smiling husbands and wives with their children and often a dog look out at us. Trimmed lawns, flower beds, lawn chairs, mailboxes, clear skies.

I tell stories of growing up on the North Shore of Chicago. I had been a restless suburban kid, itching to leave home ever since I could walk. My father helped scratch that itch. He liked to make up stories. When I was four years old, he told me we had a lion in our attic. I ran upstairs to the attic and listened for the lion but didn't hear anything. For days I asked my father to show it to me. He always had an excuse. I never did see the lion, but at night I dreamed of it growling and roaring at the locked door until finally it would escape and I'd follow it outside.

After school I played in our yard. I was forbidden to go beyond the driveway on the street. My mother watched me from the kitchen window. I would wait until she was distracted. Then I'd run into the street and race around the block, past sculpted lawns and two-story brick houses separated by narrow driveways, past side streets leading to a forest preserve and beyond that an expressway thrusting toward the horizon. I ran back into our yard and sat with my back to the kitchen window so my mother would not see me gasping for air. I dreamed of the day I could walk out of the driveway and keep walking.

In high school my friend Paul and I would catch the El into Chicago, rattling along the worn tracks to the skid row of south Michigan Avenue. We hung out in dimly lit bars thick with cigarette smoke, a couple of rich kids, rebels without a cause. We saw old women wearing stiff wigs and men whose sad eyes stared off into space and saw things

I couldn't imagine. Their tattoos were faded, teeth gone. They teased the rim of their wet glasses with tired fingers, and spoke in hoarse tones when they hustled us for change.

One man gave me his mottled real estate business card, which he still kept in his wallet. What drew us to these lost souls? All these years later I still don't know. Maybe it was the forbidden fruit syndrome: Don't go there, our parents warned us. It's a bad neighborhood. So of course we went. Perhaps it was the lure of danger, something to get the blood pumping that an evening at Dairy Queen could never do.

Our Afghan translators don't believe poor people live in the United States. They show us photos, faded and torn at the edges. Families grinning shyly at the camera. After awhile we stop talking. Pictures are returned to wallets, memories shelved for another time. A sat phone rings. We consider one another for a moment, the lives we lived before all of this.

The journos pass Maggot around one final time before they leave. He licks their faces, squirms to be put down, chews our shoes, jumps against our legs demanding more attention. I look forward to taking him out mornings, wrestling with him in the yard, and putting the day on hold for a few minutes. Bro sometimes joins me, throwing Maggot sticks to fetch.

I tell my colleagues of this routine as if it were unusual. As if no one other than me has ever had a puppy.

"Does he eat kabob?" a Fox Television reporter teases.

We laugh, talk of home. Like prisoners we ask each other, "When are you getting out?"

I'm often asked what I'll do with Maggot when I leave.

"The Afghans give us a hard enough time taking rugs out of the country," a *Chicago Tribune* reporter says. "They'll be thrilled with a dog."

"I'm here for the long haul," I say and dismiss the question.

"You going to the Powell presser tomorrow?"

I nod. Secretary of State Colin Powell is scheduled to arrive in the morning to meet Karzai. I'm part of a pool of reporters selected by lottery to attend a joint press conference.

"Don't forget to give me your notes," the *Tribune* reporter reminds me.

■ ■ ■

In the morning Maggot follows me to the head of the stairs. He greets Bro with a bark and whimpers when we leave. The streets shine from a morning rain. I raise a cupped hand to my forehead against the glare waxing the windshield. Bro swears, swerves hard to the right.

"Inshallah!" Bro shouts. "God help us!"

I roll on top of the gearshift, catch a blurred glimpse of the front of a bus looming toward us. It strikes our sport-utility vehicle, tossing us forward and then back against the seats.

We spin to a stop by an open sewer, showered in a wave of water kicked up from a deep pothole. Cold air and sunlight fill the vehicle. I peek through my arms, flicking broken glass off my legs.

"Why do you have an accident with me, you crazy man," Bro shouts at the bus driver, wiping blood from his nose. He gets out and stands on the street, the suit his father loaned him half off his shoulders.

"We have had an accident, yes," the bus driver says, leaning out his window.

The bus has smashed our vehicle, shearing off the headlight, side mirror, and part of the passenger door, exposing the seat where I sit. A boy shoves a hand at me through the damaged door, begging.

"How are you going to pay for this?"

"I am a poor man," the bus driver says.

Both of our left tires are flat. Glass speckles the cracked pavement like tossed dice. Beggars collect scraps of shorn metal from around the tires, examining each piece. Only the left headlight on the bus is broken.

Women and men descend from the bus and surround us, tilting their heads like birds. Taxis honk. Mules drawing wood carts supported by truck tires and stacked with firewood roll their eyes and bray through reedy teeth.

"I think you drink some alcohol," Bro tells the bus driver. "You're not a good driver."

Bro bought the 1991 SUV recently. He drove it home and jacked up the wheels until he felt like a giant in traffic. He sealed the side windows with plastic to block the sun. No one could see into the car. The interior was cool and mysterious. Bro borrowed a suit his father wore in college and drove downtown each day, believing that those he passed on the road would think he drove for ministers.

A traffic officer hurries toward us, a handheld stop sign hanging from his belt. Bro grabs him by the arm. A growing crowd follows, shuffling through the glass and skid marks of the accident. Street vendors hawk fruit, bread, raisins, and nuts as Bro harangues the traffic officer with his version of the crash.

"You see he hit me, he hit me," he says insistently.

"I am a poor man," the bus driver says. "We both hit each other. Why should I pay for him when I'll have to pay for my bus?"

The traffic officer runs the toe of his boot against the road. The wet street steams under the sun, and water jells around garbage rotting in the sewers. The officer wipes his forehead and asks for a cigarette.

"Tell me what happened," he says.

Before anyone can speak, two battered pickup trucks barrel down the street, stopping abruptly a few feet from us. About twelve Northern Alliance soldiers sit in the back of each truck. A man wearing green military fatigues, a prayer shawl around his neck, and a pair of shiny black lace-up boots jumps out.

"What happened?" he asks the traffic officer, who quickly explains.

"I know this man," the Northern Alliance commander says, shaking the bus driver's hand. "He is from my village in Panjshir."

They huddle to one side. The Northern Alliance commander pats the bus driver on the back. They look in our direction, then look away, staring at the ground.

"I am going to get two more police, and then we will investigate," the traffic officer says.

"You stop," the commander says, turning around. "I am police also."

"You don't have this job. This is my job."

"Shut up," the commander says. "I'll speak with them."

He turns to Bro.

"You pay for the bus."

"Why I pay? He hit my car."

"Where are you from?"

"Kabul."

"Kabuligoc," the commander laughs. "You little man from Kabul."

"I am from Kabul," Bro says. "I spit on Panjshir."

Some of the soldiers jump out of the trucks and approach us, loosening their rifles from their shoulders.

"Come here," the commander tells Bro, grabbing him by the coat. "We'll speak in the police station."

"There is no need for a big problem," the bus driver says. "You fix your car, and I'll fix mine."

Bro stands on his toes, jerked up on one side by the commander.

"Yes. You fix your car," Bro says in a high voice, "and I'll fix mine."

The commander looks at the bus driver.

"If he pays for his car, I'll pay for the bus," the bus driver says.

"I have to investigate this accident," the traffic officer says.

"Shut up," the commander says. "Do you agree to this?"

"You have a gun," Bro says. "When you not have a gun, I'll speak to you again."

"Go. Go, you stupid Kabuligoc."

The commander walks back to his truck, followed by the soldiers. They race by us and pass the sport-utility vehicle, tilting to the side, spattered with drying mud.

"You are fortunate," the bus driver tells Bro. "If you went with him, you would have lost your car and would have had to pay to get released from jail."

Beggars sit on the sidewalk, already selling broken parts they have collected from the sport-utility vehicle. Bro approaches them, reaching into his pockets. He doesn't look at his car. The bus driver joins him. I open my wallet. It is an Afghan custom to give to the poor when you have been lucky.

This evening Maggot greets me at the door. For the first time, I notice how he has grown. He has long gangly legs, wide brown eyes, thick white fur. We go outside.

"How was your day?" I ask him. "Mine? I was in a car accident. Then I attended a press conference. The secretary of state is pleased with progress in Afghanistan. He announced that the United States has restored its embassy to full diplomatic status. He told Karzai, 'We will be with you in this current crisis and for the future.' Impressed?"

Powell promised that the United States would not abandon Afghanistan. He spoke in a joint appearance with Karzai at the presidential palace, where an uncertain electrical system aptly symbolized the perilous state of the country: just before the news conference the lights went out.

Later Powell appeared at the reopened U.S. embassy, which badly needs renovation. About thirty members of the U.S. staff sleep in a bomb shelter on the embassy grounds, five to a room. But Karzai's administration is far worse off. He is urgently asking for a hundred million dollars to run the government and pay the salaries of 270,000 longtime government employees. Of an initial twenty million pledged by the international community, only four million has actually arrived, including a million from the United States. So much for "being with you," Mr. Powell.

Maggot sniffs my feet. I follow him outside as he marks his territory. Beyond our house I hear the shouts of beggars, the bells of scared goats, the calls of muezzins. Maggot listens as I do, dimly aware—despite our proximity to everything around us—that we live separate lives and therefore live alone.

FEBRUARY 2002

Snow falls. Ice glazes my bedroom window. I nestle deeper into my sleeping bag when I hear Peter shout from across the hall. Maggot pricks up his ears and runs into his room.

"I'm going to the Caribbean," Peter shouts after he hangs up his satellite phone.

"What?"

"I'm going back to Miami. Washington's sending me home. I just got the call."

Peter starts sorting through piles of winter clothing, deciding what to leave behind so he will have room in his duffel bag for the Afghan rugs he bought on Chicken Street, a two-block stretch of carpet vendors, Kabul's version of a tourist trap.

"Take what you want," he says of his clothes. "I won't need them."

Maggot carries off a dirty sock. I kneel by the growing pile and sort through it. I realize that if Peter is leaving, then soon I will too. I always knew I'd go of course but in an abstract kind of way. My Kansas City home had assumed the character of a distant pleasant memory, much like childhood. Suddenly it has resumed a presence in my life that verges on threatening when I think of abandoning Maggot. I need a plan for my dog.

Peter pours himself a glass of vodka mixed with mango juice. Maggot sits on my lap, gnawing on the stolen sock. The pile of discarded clothes has grown almost knee-deep. Peter's space heater lights up his five duffel bags. Darkness covers the rest of the room. A sliver of moonlight reveals the empty street outside the window.

"We'll have him shot," Peter says, the vodka bottle poised precariously on his laptop computer.

"If I can't get him out?"

"Better than turning him loose on the street."

"He'd starve."

"The commander next door could do it."

"What?" I say.

"Shoot him. If it comes to that. One of his men. We'd have to pay him."

"I'm not paying anybody to shoot my dog."

"You've given him a good life, cowboy. Listen, when I go through Islamabad, I'll find a hotel that takes dogs. If you get him that far, you'll have a place to stay."

Maggot squirms off my lap onto the floor. He chews on one of Peter's rugs. Peter nudges him with his foot. Even if I get Maggot out, I'll have to find him a home. My landlord will never allow me to have three dogs.

Peter pours himself another glass of vodka, oblivious to my increasing complications.

Peter has been gone two days. Fighting continues in the Gardez region between supporters of the local tribal council and the acting governor appointed by Karzai. Returning refugees flood Kabul, as many as fifteen thousand a week, overwhelming aid organizations. I keep up with the news and file stories once a week.

I adapt to living alone by taking walks with Maggot. On an unseasonably warm afternoon that strongly hints of spring, I walk Maggot no more than a block when I hear someone running up behind me, feet slapping noisily in muddy puddles of melting snow. I pick up Maggot and turn around.

"Mister," a grubby-looking shoeshine boy shouts.

I know him. He always sits outside the house. Peter paid him a dollar to shine his shoes twice a week. He stops to catch his breath.

More shoeshine boys spread out across the street asking cigarette-smoking Northern Alliance soldiers for money. One soldier takes off his scarf and snaps it at a boy. It makes a loud crack, tagging him on the cheek. He holds a hand against his face, more perplexed than hurt. Still, the tears flow. I look away. The boy who ran up to me tugs my jacket.

"Where is Mr. Peter?" he asks.

"He flew home yesterday," I say and point at the sky.

"B-52?"

"No."

"You are holding a dog. Why?"

"I like him."

"My mother has no money. Mr. Peter said he would buy me some shoes."

"That's between you and Mr. Peter."

He grabs my left arm and points at his rubber shoes, torn at the toe. Maggot growls, and the boy steps back. Mud has seeped inside his shoes and onto his feet. I put down Maggot, who tries to sniff the boy's shoes. The boy steps back again. I give him some candy and wave him away.

"Mister, give me six bills. I need shoes."

Six Afghani bills comes to about three dollars. I could afford that, but with the other children around, I'm not about to give this kid a dime, or I'll be mobbed.

"No," I say.

I continue walking Maggot. The boy follows. We reach an intersection, and I turn toward downtown. The boy follows, shoos away other children who ask me for money.

"Mister, I will be your bodyguard."

"No."

"I shine shoes. I'll brush your boots."

"No."

I walk around piles of mud thrown by two men who stand in a trench trying to repair electric cables with tape.

"Mister, my mother is very sick. I have to work, but my feet hurt."

I unzip a jacket pocket where I have a wad of Afghanis and pat the inside as if I'm looking for money.

"See? I have nothing."

Dogs skirt a group of soldiers down a rock-strewn side alley and snap at scraps on the road. One dog runs away from the pack with something hanging from its mouth. Nearby children scatter away from it. Maggot strains at his leash. I pull him back.

"You have a father?"

"My father was killed in the bombing."

"American bombs?"

"Does it matter?"

I look at his feet.

"Mr. Peter was going to buy shoes for me."

"I'm not Mr. Peter."

We pass small shops squeezed together with lopsided signs: HAMID STORE, HAMTYON WORKSHOP, NOORINE PHOTO STUDIO, NANI OVID PHARMACY, FAHIM'S SHOE SHOP. The boy watches me. I have my hands full taking care of a dog. I don't need this boy. I look around and see other kids hustling passersby on the sidewalk. None of them notice me. Let's get this done, I think.

"I'll pay six bills for your shoes. No more," I say. "Now walk away from me so the other boys don't know what we're doing. I'll meet you in the shop."

He runs into Fahim's Shoe Shop. I continue walking about a block. Then I turn around and retrace my steps. Maggot draws looks from the crowded sidewalk. When I am in front of the shoe shop, I pick up Maggot and duck inside.

A bare bulb hangs by an exposed wire from the ceiling, offering feeble light. I wait for my eyes to adjust to the dark. Stacks of shoe boxes lean to one side near the door, shivering when a truck rumbles past. The shopkeeper stands behind the counter, rubs his hands together against the cold.

"How are you, mister?" he says. "Is that a dog?"

I put Maggot down and keep him close to me. The boy tells the shopkeeper I am buying him shoes. The shopkeeper looks at me and smiles. He collects several boxes of shoes under both arms and places them on the counter. He offers me a piece of chocolate and a cup of tea. He shakes my hand and smiles again. I feel something behind me and turn around. Boys on the street crowd the doorway. They block the light, and I lose sight of the shopkeeper. The shopkeeper yells, and the boys run away and gray light filters through.

The kid ignores the commotion. He tries on a pair of black shoes, square at the toe with thick heels and silver buckles. Too big. He kicks them off and slips on shoes made in a similar style but without the buckles. Too big. The shopkeeper offers him another box. Brown loafers. He holds them up to the bulb. He rolls them to one side, then the other, shining them in the pale light. He grins at me, puts the shoes on, and walks in a circle. He slips them off carefully and wraps the shoes in the tissue paper from the box. He closes the box. He folds the box under his arm. He looks at me and nods.

I count out six bills and put the money on the counter. The shopkeeper looks at the money for a long moment. Maggot whimpers, impatient.

"I am sorry," he says, then speaks to the boy in Dari.

"What's the matter?" I ask.

"He needs three thousand, one hundred and thirty-five Afghani," the boy says.

I do a quick calculation.

"That's sixty bucks, man," I tell the boy. "You said six bills."

"Mister, please."

Sixty bucks. The shopkeeper has doubtlessly seen Western journalists, diplomats, and soldiers dispense money without a thought. He assumes I am no different. I feel the money inside my pocket. I have it. Goddamn it. The boy and the shopkeeper know I have it. I count money out on the counter. Darkness closes in. I know without turning around that street kids have converged at the door again.

"Boro," the shopkeeper tells them. "Go."

I stop counting. I can't buy the shoes. Those kids will be all over me if I do.

"No," I say. "No."

The boy looks away. He has given up. I wonder how he knows when to push and when to quit. In a life of reduced expectations it may not be that difficult for him to judge his moments. He returns the shoes to the shopkeeper, watches him put the box back on a shelf.

"I'm sorry," I say to the shopkeeper.

He shrugs. While we shake hands the boy grabs the money I left on the counter and runs out of the store.

"*Sai koo!*" the shopkeeper shouts, coming around the counter. "Hey!"

I spin around but can't catch him. I see the other boys chase after him. Maggot barks until I give a sharp tug on his leash. The shopkeeper stands in the door, hands on his hips. He shakes his head.

"I am sorry, mister," he says. "Crazy boy. Six bills—that's impossible for shoes."

"Of course," I say. "I know."

One morning toward the end of February when I check my e-mail, as I do every morning, my editor tells me I'm to be sent home in two weeks. Afghanistan is slipping off the news radar, he writes. The Taliban are gone and the war all but over. The mundane details of reconstruction can't compete with the escalating rhetoric between the United States and Iraq.

I lie in my sleeping bag staring at the ceiling, Maggot curled in the crook of my arm.

"Leaving," I say out loud.

Maggot sits up, looks at me.

"What am I going to do with you?" I ask him.

On September 11, 2001, I fended off my two border collies as they woke me for their morning walk. It was still dark, the sky beginning to fade at its edges. I heard a car, the thud of the morning newspaper landing on the stoop.

The sound of my feet, the rattle of the dogs' leashes slapped the still morning. Small, one-story brick houses shouldered heavy shadows cast by trees blocking the line of sunlight that slowly tinged the sky a pale pink. Full plastic garbage bags squatted haphazardly beneath street-lamps like boulders loosed from their moorings. The lights in the Blue Bird Cafe were on, and a janitor swept the floor. Joggers ran past with reflectors around their waists. The dogs squatted, did their business. I scooped it up in a plastic bag and dropped it among some leaf bags piled along the street. My dogs sniffed at the bags and I tugged them and we moved on as we always did.

After walking the dogs I ate some cereal and then walked to work. A homeless man stopped me. He held a radio bound with duct tape against an ear.

"Hey, d'ya hear about the planes that crashed in New York?" he said.

I assumed he was crazy.

I stopped at a gas station for coffee. No one was behind the counter. I leaned over it, looked around the cash register toward the back room.

Two men sat huddled around a small television with their backs to me. I saw "Special Report" flash across the screen but didn't know what it was about.

"Excuse me," I said. "I want some coffee."

The men ignored me. Perhaps they hadn't heard me. I cleared my throat. They didn't move but remained glued to the TV. Then I saw an airplane veer across the sky toward what appeared to be a skyscraper, and I didn't care about coffee anymore.

Maggot paws my face, pulls me back to Kabul. Time for his morning piss. I let him out and wait by the door until he runs back inside. I feed him. While he eats, I throw my winter clothes on the floor to see how much room I can make for rugs and other souvenirs. Another reporter, who moved in about a week after Peter left, sees the stack of clothes and knows without asking that I'm out of here. He falls to his knees and grabs long underwear and heavy socks.

"When do you go?"

"Couple weeks."

"Can I have these?" he asks, holding a pair of gloves. He pushes Maggot aside, who waddles away with a pair of underwear, tail pointed triumphantly in the air.

"Yeah."

"I did something I shouldn't have yesterday," he says, examining a shirt.

"What?"

"I was doing this story on refugees in Kabul. I gave the leader of this one group of refugees one hundred dollars. I shouldn't have, but you should have seen how they were living."

I don't say anything. Good for him. Cry me a goddamned self-indulgent river, pal. May you win the Mother Teresa Award. I'm saving a dog. We do what we can, and the rest—I don't know.

"What are you doing with Maggot?"

"Taking him."

"Good luck."

He has been in Afghanistan two weeks, his second time through after a three-week break. On his first two-month tour he followed the Northern Alliance into Kabul. He survived dust storms and floods. He saw men shot and die, ripped to shreds by mines. He likes to pose with

AK-47 rifles procured for him by his driver, a former Northern Alliance soldier, and have his translator snap pictures.

"When this place falls apart, I don't want to be caught standing here with a butter knife in my hand," he shouted one afternoon when other reporters were at the house for their routine dose of Maggot.

"What's he talking about?" a woman whispered to me.

"He's talking Alamo, baby," I said. "He's talking Pearl Harbor, Bay of Pigs, Gulf of Tonkin, you feel me? He's talking and ain't going down for nobody, dig it?"

"You're both crazy," she said.

I toss him a pair of waterproof pants. So what if he's mental toast? That's no reason to let him get wet.

In the days leading up to my departure, Steve, an American reporter with the Berlin bureau of *USA Today*, tells me that German people love dogs. "They take them into restaurants, theaters, supermarkets, you name it," he says. I should fly back to the States through Berlin. No one there would give me a hard time about Maggot. Steve offers to travel with me; he needs to return soon for his wife's fiftieth birthday.

I assume I'll need papers to get Maggot out of Afghanistan and into Pakistan and Germany. Bro suggests we drive to the Ministry of Agriculture. They have health certificates for farm animals. Why not for dogs?

At the ministry we're led to a man sitting in a room, empty but for his desk and chair. I tell him I need veterinary papers for my dog. He doesn't blink, behaves as if this is a perfectly normal request. "Has Maggot been vaccinated for rabies and distemper?" he asks. I hand him twenty dollars and tell him Maggot has had all of his shots. I just need the documentation. He signs a piece of paper and hands it to me.

Next we drive to the Ministry of Foreign Affairs.

"What do you need?" an aide to the foreign minister asks.

"Papers authorizing me to take a dog out of the country."

The aid to the foreign minister tugs his coat around his thin chest. He runs a hand over the papers from the Ministry of Agriculture.

"Maggot," he says, fingering the papers. He covers his mouth, looks away. Eventually, he stops laughing. "Where do you want to take this Maggot?"

"The U.S."

"He lives in America," Bro says.

The aide shakes his head. "When the Taliban came into Kabul, I was a shopkeeper," he says. "I lost much money because women were not allowed to shop. My neighbors had a wedding party and were arrested for playing music and spent eight nights in jail. The Taliban are gone, but I have not been paid for six months."

He asks my name and rolls notebook paper into a manual typewriter.

"Something should get out of this damn country," he says, typing.

I find another journalist to employ Bro. She also works for Knight Ridder and will replace me.

"A woman reporter?" Bro says.

"Yes. She's cool. You'll like her."

"When will you come back?"

"I don't think I will. The war's over, Bro."

"Silly war," he says.

Steve and I hire Wahob, an acquaintance of Masood, a translator who had worked with a Knight Ridder colleague. Wahob will drive us to the Pakistan border for two hundred dollars. It will take us at least eight hours on the one bomb-cratered road running east from Kabul. We will spend the night in Jalalabad, a former Taliban stronghold. Four journalists were killed in November outside Jalalabad near Srubee Village shortly after the war started. We don't want to be out after dark.

From the border we will catch a bus to Islamabad. Then we will fly to Berlin.

On an overcast morning, Steve and I load the car with our bags. Masood and Bro help. Masood will stay on with Bro to help my replacement. Everyone has a job. Everyone is taken care of.

Wahob sits stoically behind the wheel and waits for us. I put Maggot in a wicker basket I bought at the bazaar. I heft him into the backseat, fussing with the latch. When I'm done, I turn to Bro.

"Remember what I told you. Save your money. Go back to school. Working for journalists won't last."

"Inshallah, it will last."

I shake my head but give in. "Why not?" I say.

Bro embraces me. "I am your driver," he whispers in my ear.

"Yes," I tell him, "you are."

I get in the car with Steve and rest my arms on Maggot's basket. Wahob starts the engine. I look out the window, but Bro has already left. Just like that. After so much time together. Gone.

Wahob maneuvers through traffic into downtown Kabul and toward distant snow-covered mountains. I tap my coat pocket, making sure I have the papers from the Ministry of Agriculture and the Ministry of Foreign Affairs.

It starts raining. Bicycle riders hug the sides of the road, holding umbrellas over their heads. Cars douse them with water. Disconsolate mules haul carts of wood and charcoal, their ears flattened against the rain. Traffic bogs down from an accident. We skirt the pandemonium of the bazaar, where vendors' stalls sag under the weight of water collected in tarps.

I take a final look around. A misshapen pillar stands upright in the middle of the street, looking like a gnawed bone. A lone doorway rises from the rubble of a former office building. A boy stands in traffic with his hand out.

Wahob follows the road as it dips into a valley beside the Kabul River, swollen and muddy from winter rains. Kabul sinks behind us with each twist and turn that carries us farther east until I can see only one downtown building. Then it too disappears.

Two hours later, armed men in the ruins of several stone huts stop us at a checkpoint in Srubee Village. They ask Wahob to follow them inside one of the huts.

Steve and I wait for Wahob.

"So, I interview this banker," Steve says, talking more quickly than usual. "He owns the only private bank in Afghanistan. And I tell him I work in Berlin, and he asks about the euro and I give him one, a five-euro note. 'Keep it, it's my gift to you,' I say. Then he tells me, he says, 'Oh, I have to get you a gift.' I can't take a present from a source, but I don't want to offend the guy, so he gives me this package. What am I going to do? You don't accept gifts from a source."

I tell him it's not a big deal. I'm more interested in graffiti on a nearby boulder. I have seen no graffiti in the time I've been here, and I wonder what it says. Soon villagers surround our car, peer inside at us. They put their fingers to their mouths indicating they want money for food. Rainwater runs off their hands. Maggot, asleep on my lap, puzzles them. I smell wet clothes, the sweat of unwashed bodies.

"So, if I come back here, and I'm sure I will on another assignment, I'll give him something," Steve says, his voice pitched a little higher. "I'll get his gift valued and give him something of comparable worth."

"What did he give you?"

"I haven't looked yet."

A man with a rifle walks up to the car, followed by Wahob. He looks inside, letting the muzzle of the gun rest on the open passenger window.

"Smile," Steve whispers.

The man reaches in and shakes my hand. He waves Wahob forward and opens the door for him.

"He wanted to see if my ownership papers for the car were good," Wahob says.

He shifts into gear and we roll forward, sinking into deep muddy holes that threaten to swamp the car.

"What does that say?" I ask, pointing at the graffiti.

"Don't collaborate with the Western enemy."

In minutes, we're driving out of the village. We open our windows and the stuffy air inside the car clears, and I breathe easier.

"Anyway, about the banker," I say after a moment.

We stop for the night in Jalalabad and take a room at a run-down hotel. We have a bed, a mattress on the floor, and a gas lamp. A generator grumbles outside, but the lights in our room don't work.

No cars or people on the street. The air has a sullen heaviness to it that inspires me to do nothing more than slump against a wall and pet Maggot. Mud huts across from the hotel sink into expanding shadows except for one dilapidated shop, where a tailor sews by candlelight.

We call it a night. I'd like to bathe, but the one shower is in a rancid-smelling room, the floor wet and slimy. The odor of mildew rises out of corners. I look forward to a shower, drinking tap water again, using a toilet that's more than a hole in the floor, having power at the flip of a switch.

"And real toilet paper," Steve says.

"And real coffee," I say.

"And something to eat other than kabob."

I close my eyes. The lamp spits and sputters, slowly burning itself out.

"Hey," I say, rousing myself. "What did the banker give you?"

"A rug. I checked while you were in the bathroom. You want to see?"

"No."

Maggot curls up at my feet. I close my eyes, listen to the steady drizzle outside. The rug and whatever else I want can wait.

In the morning we begin the two-hour drive to Torkham, a border town where we will catch our bus to Islamabad. Without warning, Wahob stops the car halfway there and shuts off the ignition. He insists the fee we had agreed to pay him was six hundred dollars, but we all know it was really two hundred dollars. He dangles the car keys outside his window. I take out my wallet and he starts the car.

"We cannot let you take the dog," a soldier tells us at the border.

"Wait a minute!" I shout.

"We've got all the documents," Steve says.

"A note from the Foreign Ministry."

I reach into my pocket for Maggot's papers.

"I'm only joking," the soldier says and laughs. "What do I care about a dog?"

After a five-hour journey through the Khyber Pass, the bus drops us off in downtown Islamabad. We take a taxi to the Marriott Hotel, where Steve rents a room. I cannot stay there with Maggot. The driver takes me to a guesthouse Peter had found for me; a ramshackle compound next to a foul-smelling garbage dump. Thanks, Peter.

The owner has no problem with Maggot. The odor of mildew overwhelms my room, and I sleep in the hall, holding Maggot in my lap. I eat with Steve at the Marriott, wrap food for Maggot in my napkin.

I spend the next two days haggling with merchants until I find one who will build a cage for Maggot. I give him specific measurements, but he follows his own ideas and constructs a waist-high, heavy wood box that resembles a chicken cage.

To my surprise the airline flying us to Berlin accepts Maggot without question, despite his nonstandard pet carrier. We leave at midnight. Maggot stares at me from the luggage conveyor belt rolling him out to the plane.

Steve was right about Germans. Customs agents don't ask about Maggot despite his howls of indignation at being cooped up for so many hours. Steve leaves for his apartment, while Maggot and I catch a taxi to the Hotel Palace where I had made an Internet reservation. The hotel manager coos over Maggot without commenting on his outrageous cage. He gives me a key to a second-floor room. I play with the light switches and thermostat, thrilled to have power again. I run my hand over the pink sheets, the soft red quilt.

Suddenly I feel exhausted. I pick up Maggot and crawl into bed and crash for the next twelve hours, Maggot sprawled across my chest. When I wake, I find that Steve has left a message for me. His English neighbors, Duncan and Jackie, want Maggot. I had asked Steve if he could find Maggot a home, but a part of me had hoped he wouldn't.

The next morning, Duncan comes over and waits for me outside my hotel. I hold Maggot, pressing his nose against my face. I look in the mirror to have a last image of us together, but he wriggles out of my arms. He yaps at my feet, ready to play, dodging around my backpack and boots. I hold him by his new collar until he calms down and then carry him outside.

"Hello Maggot," Duncan says.

Maggot sniffs his shoes.

"I appreciate your taking him," I say.

"No, thank you for giving him to us. We're going to change his name, of course. To Harvey, I think."

"Harvey," I say.

I hand Duncan the leash. Maggot sits on the sidewalk and stares at me, eyes wide, ears alert. Then he cocks his head, stops wagging his tail. I turn away to leave Maggot and Afghanistan and everything I've known for the past four months. Duncan says something, and I don't hear him clearly. My eyes are tearing. I dread returning to my room alone, but can't stand here any longer or I'll lose it.

PART TWO

Maybe the Killing Has Finally Stopped

CHAPTER SEVEN

The Man Comes from Outside

MARCH 2002
Kansas City

I wake up early from jet lag and walk to a Starbucks. A clear day, yet indistinct somehow, as if I'm not really back. The same people who retrieved their morning newspapers from their porches when I left in November say hello, still in their bathrobes as before. Flags hang everywhere, faded from months in the sun, rain, and snow. Peeling bumper stickers boasting patriotic slogans plaster mud-spattered cars. Teenagers wear T-shirts mocking Osama bin Laden. The nineteen-year-old son of a friend tells me he enlisted in the army.

"Did you see any kills?" he asks me.

A colleague takes me out for beer.

"They kept you out there longer than you needed to be," he says. "Afghanistan has been off the front page for months."

I want to talk about Afghanistan, but no one seems interested. Most people have read enough about it and don't need to hear my stories. I give up trying to say anything about it.

At night I fall asleep reading and wake up in the dark, unaware of the time. Groggy, I call my dogs, and together we walk down empty streets. A few joggers disturb the silence. I hear the wheeze of commuter buses gathering volume. The humid aroma of dew-dampened lawns hovers around me. Inside some houses, I see people moving around in their kitchens. The chatter of evening news programs coming through open windows with the latest reports on Afghanistan distracts me, and I hurry on.

The street twists around dense wooded areas looming out of the dark beneath cloudy streetlights, and shadows cling to me from far away as my dogs and I submerge ourselves in the tall grass and shrubs and weeds, tramping a path toward some trees. We walk beyond the fringe of lights, hear only the crush of dry brush beneath our feet, and escape the constraints of the world around us.

My second week home I attend a Saturday softball game of the daughter of a friend. We sit on bleachers and several people ask me about my trip. Before I can answer, they say, "You must be so happy to be back," and turn around to keep watching the game.

Nine-year-old girls swing limply at the ball. Their fathers tell them to choke up. "C'mon! Hit that ball!" Moms and dads challenge the umpire's calls and in their frustration shake their water bottles in the air. "That's not a strike! What does he mean that's a strike?" I hear in their angry voices the shouts of Afghan soldiers leering in my face—"You go, what do you want, get out. Go or we shoot you!"—when I stop them from striking a street kid with the butts of their rifles for begging outside the presidential palace, the boy screaming for his mother.

"I can't take this shit," I say.

"Shh! My God!" my friend says.

I get up and walk away. My friend calls after me, but I keep walking, her voice and the voices of parents around her still mixed up with the Afghan soldiers shouting inside my head. I cover my ears and run.

When I return to my apartment, I open the door and stop. I notice the rug needs vacuuming. I notice dishes in the kitchen sink. I notice a painting on the wall that needs to be straightened. I notice I'm losing my mind.

I think of Bro. How is he? What is he doing?

I think of the boy who wanted me to buy him shoes. Where is he now?

And Maggot. I remember how he waited for me at the head of the stairs. How I took him outside and cringed from the gunfire while he peed. I haven't heard from Duncan. How is my dog?

I recall seeing a woman fending off feral dogs in a garbage pit as she searched for food. What month did I see her? How long had I been in Kabul then?

I saw a man with an amputated leg. When was it? January?

His crutch broke, and he fell down on a crowded sidewalk. He tried to get up but was trampled by an onslaught of desperate sandaled feet rushing toward the office of the World Food Programme for free bags of rice. Who was he? Why can't I forget him?

I see them all so clearly. They burrowed into my mind and lurk in my memory, assuming the collective weight of ancient ghosts that I have carried all my life, wearying me to sleep.

Every week I hound my Washington editors to send me back. Finally they ask me to cover the *loya jirga,* "grand assembly," a tribal delegation of fifteen hundred men that will decide who will lead an eighteen-month transitional government. They will gather in June in an air-conditioned German beer tent on a disused soccer field in Kabul.

The plans for the jirga were drawn up in the UN Security Council and sanctioned at a handpicked conference convened by the United Nations near the German city of Bonn in December 2001. The selection of the jirga delegates was presided over by a committee, appointed and supervised by UN officials. The committee not only held the power of veto over elected delegates but chose five hundred businessmen, clerics, and others to represent special-interest groups.

As far as the United States is concerned, the loya jirga's main purpose is to rubber-stamp Karzai's rule. But the whole process has been wide open to manipulation, vote buying, and intimidation. One Western monitor told the *Washington Post:* "In dozens, perhaps hundreds, of local elections, militia leaders and regional strongmen have muscled their way into the loya jirga by spreading money among voters, marshalling blocks of support among their followers or simply dominating their old political turf."

I ask my editors about Bro. All they know is that he had a falling-out with Masood. They aren't clear on what happened and don't care. Masood and Wahob are watching our house in Kabul. I haven't forgotten how Wahob shook me down on the way to the Pakistan border. I want Bro. I'm determined to work with him.

JUNE–JULY 2002
Kabul

As my UN flight from Islamabad taxis to a stop at the Kabul International Airport, I see Masood and Wahob waiting for me behind the wire gate of the parking lot. Lines of heat weave above the surrounding scrub brush and desert. I walk off the plane and board a new German-made air-conditioned bus to the terminal. I'd heard that foreign aid had begun to trickle in. The sounds of hammers and drills echoing from unseen construction sites reverberate through the cool air.

The bus driver points out the traffic-clogged streets. He blames the congestion on foreign entrepreneurs, dashing from one appointment to the next as they try to take advantage of the flow of aid dollars.

"Kabul is the yellow pages of aid agencies," he says and smiles.

He stops beside a row of Afghan soldiers standing at attention in new green uniforms and lets us off. I step off the bus at the terminal gate. Thoughts of my long flight recede as if I dreamed it, as if I am slowly coming awake and the dream is drifting out of focus, sinking to the bottom of my memory, diffusing into this vast expanse of sky, sun, wind, and desert.

A man unloads our luggage onto a conveyor belt. The belt doesn't work, and the bags pile up at the opening to the baggage chute. I grab my backpack from the pile and pass a tourist information booth with a faded 1970s promotional poster for Afghanistan.

Outside taxi drivers swarm around, offering me a ride. Everyone appears to have cell phones. Cell phones! My God, how long have I been gone? A few months, right? Damn.

I fend off the taxi drivers with my backpack as they clutch at my arms. I feel a tug on my shoulder, turn, and face Masood. He has on a new leather jacket, new blue jeans, and new black boots. His black hair is slicked back from his forehead, and a goatee enhances his chin. He grins and embraces me. He takes the backpack from my hand. Wahob smiles too and reaches for my hand. I ignore him.

"Nice," I say, touching the new leather coats worn by Masood and Wahob.

Masood laughs.

In some ways I can't blame them for shaking me down. He and the other Afghans we employed saw us throwing around hundreds of dollars on things other than salaries. We bought carpets and antiques and asked them to sign "receipts" for us so we could pass off the purchases as legitimate expenses. We had our scams. Wahob showed me that Afghans had their own.

Masood tosses my backpack into Wahob's new Jeep. Rain begins to fall. Masood holds his hand out the car window and laughs. He insists that a seven-year drought has finally come to an end. "It has been raining for weeks," he says. I open my window. The cool air rushes against my face. The damp streets sizzle beneath our tires.

We pass freshly butchered lambs hanging from vendors' stalls, the rain-soaked meat a deep, runny red. Slopes of wet grass cover towering mountains. New wood benches encircle small gardens close to the airport. Water drips off trees and forms pools on the dark asphalt of newly paved roads, and birds splash in puddles scooped into the muddy earth. Lightning forks across patches of black clouds, revealing green valleys. Distant villages slicked in rain emerge for seconds in the jagged light, then sink into shadows.

We drive through a hive of vendor stalls in the fetid, sharp-elbowed chaos of Kabul, to our house in the Wazir Khan, where we unload my bags.

The cook, Daud, and the housekeeper, Zabib, introduce themselves. Where did they come from? Peter and I never had house staff. They take my bags up a flight of stairs to my second-floor room. Water runs off the roof in long, beady streams, splashing the leaves of waist-high sunflowers and ankle-deep ferns below my window.

We walk back downstairs. I see two men on the couch. Who the hell are they? I look for Masood. He hovers in the kitchen, inspecting boiling pots on the stove. He wrinkles his nose.

"I do not want this," he tells Daud. "Make me kabob."

Daud walks to the refrigerator without questioning him and lifts out a plate of beef.

"Wait a minute," I say. "You don't decide what you'll eat in my house."

The two men remain on the couch watching us. Masood looks at me, his face red because I am dressing him down in front of the others. I look at the men on the couch and then back at Masood. His posse, I think. Masood's cronies. The big man with the hangers-on. Time to take him down.

"Before you come, the other journalist left. I kept the house for you. I was in charge," Masood says.

"You're a translator. You don't tell people what to do. I do that. You work for me."

He smiles, tight-lipped, and shrugs. "Of course. It is no problem."

"Who are these guys?" I ask, pointing to the two men.

"The driver and translator for the photographer who worked with the reporter who replaced you."

"What have they been paid?"

"One hundred dollars," Masood says. "As before."

"A day?"

"Yes."

"And you?"

"The same. All of us."

"My budget allows me to pay you fifty dollars a day."

Masood looks at me. "I told them you were a good guy and would continue paying them."

"I am a good guy, but I can't pay a hundred dollars a day. How many foreign reporters do you see in Kabul? The story's not what it was last year."

Masood looks away. If I'm not careful I could wind up with dozens of hangers-on who insist on being paid because Masood promised them, because they had sat around all day "watching the house." It's another desperate plea of "Mister, give to me money."

"What's Bro doing?" I ask.

"I don't know," Masood says.

"I want to talk to him," I say. "Tonight we'll drive by his brother's pharmacy and find him. When will dinner be ready?"

Masood turns to Daud.

"An hour."

"Let's go," I say. "I'm starved. All I've eaten is airline food."

"Daud has to cut the vegetables."

"You weren't too happy with what he was cooking a minute ago."

Masood says nothing.

"Tell him we're going out. Tell him to save what he's doing for to-morrow night."

"He wants to cook every night. He is very happy to have a job."

"Tomorrow," I say to Daud in a slow, loud voice, as if that way he'll understand me. "Tomorrow you cook. I pay you fifty dollars."

I turn to Masood.

"Fifty dollars. The same as you."

Wahob drives us to the Herat Restaurant, where I ate my first night in Kabul. He jumps out at intersections and wipes mud off the hood, his hand moving in slow circles. His new car shines in the glare of bare bulbs hanging along the street from sagging wires, and the light catches his smile and the proud shine in his eyes.

Traffic jams the narrow streets around new construction sites, where signs promote the aid organizations behind the new buildings. Bakery fires glow, as the night wind refreshes the air with the aroma of fresh beef kabob. Boys emerge from alongside the road and shovel dirt into potholes. Wahob drops an Afghan bill worth about twenty-five cents out his window, and the boys scamper after it, swinging their shovels at each other. One boy's head jerks sideways, his twisted face spraying blood. Gusts of wind tease the bill until it bounces and spins out of sight.

We pass long lines of vacant factory buildings not yet touched by reconstruction. Ancient-looking men and women and children watch us. No sound comes from their mouths. No wave of the hand. Only the slow turning of their heads as we jostle past. These people will never be hired by correspondents or aid agencies. They have no education, can't translate, and have no skills useful for reconstruction.

The blue wooden tables in the Herat have been replaced by glass ones with new brown, cushioned chairs redolent of lemon-scented furniture polish. The old furniture, now piled in broken pieces behind the restaurant, is being used to fuel the wood-burning stove in the center of the floor.

A waiter, wearing a red polo shirt with a decal of HERAT ironed crookedly on the back, pauses at our table with a menu. I recognize him from before.

"Hello, my friend!" he says, raising his arms to hug me. "Do you have my pants?"

"Of course."

I had promised, should I return, to bring him a pair of blue jeans—"cowboy pants," he called them—from the States. I had not remembered. Anything from the United States has almost a mythical quality, especially blue jeans, which Afghans associate with the free-spending U.S. journalists and aid workers. His pockets would be lined with cash if he could only own one pair of jeans.

"In the car," I say. "The pants are in the car. Let me eat first."

"Kabul is better, but I need cowboy pants from America. America very big friend of Afghans."

"The war has been good to you," I say, glancing at the menu. Prices have doubled in my absence.

"We do what we can with what God has given us," the waiter says. "I am still a poor man and can't afford pants. What will you have?"

"Lamb kabob, two orders," Masood says, glancing at me. I give my approval. "Salad, chips, and what? Three Pepsis?"

"No. Orange drink for me," I say, referring to Fanta.

"And a pair of pants," the waiter says and laughs.

Rain starts falling again. A man cooks kabob on a grill beneath a tin overhang near the front door. Orange flames snap at the meat when raindrops strike the grill.

Our waiter brings us salad, chips, and flat loaves of nan bread, shaped like sandals. Masood tears off a piece of bread and scoops up tomatoes and onions from the salad plate with his fingers.

I tell him, "Wait until the rest of the food gets here."

He mutters under his breath.

"What?" I say.

Masood shakes his head, and I let it go. The waiter places a platter of sizzling lamb squarely on our table. I fold bread around two pieces of lamb and stuff it into my mouth. Masood watches me. I motion toward the plate with my chin. He and Wahob reach for the bread.

"The other driver and translator, we're not going to need them," I tell Masood between swallows.

"They have families," he says.

"So do you."

Christ, I'd hire them all if I could and give away all my cash. But I can't. And if I did, the money would run out and they wouldn't believe me. They'd think I was lying and hate me for abandoning them.

When I was a social worker, I stopped carrying cash. When a homeless person hit me up for bus tokens, diapers, food, I'd pull out my empty pockets.

"I don't have it. See?" I'd say. "I don't have it."

They never believed me. I knew where my loose change was: at home in the right-hand corner of my desk drawer, where I'd deliberately left it. I could see it in my mind, and I hated myself for leaving it.

"I need one translator and one driver," I tell Masood. "No more."

"You have Wahob and me, yes?"

I hear the worry in his voice but say nothing to reassure him. Wahob turns to Masood at the mention of his name. Cars plunge into potholes and spray the restaurant with bursts of water.

"You know I will help you get good carpet this trip," Masood says. "All journalists like carpet."

"We'll talk about that later."

"Do you want me to tell them they are no longer needed?" Masood asks of the two men at the house.

"You'll have to translate, but I'll tell them."

"What about the cook and housekeeper?" Masood asks.

"We don't need a cook and a housekeeper," I say.

"The housekeeper's good. Someone to watch the place when you're out."

"The cook would be convenient, I suppose."

"Yes."

I scoop up more meat.

"When we travel outside Kabul, I'll let the cook go," I decide. "Bring him back on when we return. No point paying him when we're not in the house."

I watch the man outside fill his grill with fresh coals. It has stopped raining.

"I'll need you to translate until I find Bro," I tell Masood.

"And what happens when you find him?"

"Then we'll talk again. Bro prefers driving to translating."

"Wahob is driver."

"Tell Wahob we'll need him tomorrow. We'll take him day by day."

"What is wrong?" Wahob asks Masood.

"Nothing's wrong," I say after Masood translates. "We don't need that many people."

"But you need a driver."

"Yes, and I said we'll use him tomorrow."

"And after?" Masood asks.

"Wahob should have thought of that when he drove me out of here and took me for four hundred dollars more than we had agreed on."

"If there is sadness between you and Wahob?"

"There is no sadness."

"And you and me?"

"We have no problem."

I finish eating and push the platter of meat to the edge of the table.

I don't care if Masood and Wahob are done. I am. I'm finished talking. I want to find Bro. The waiter removes our plates, and I pay at the counter.

"My pants," the waiter reminds me at the door.

"Tomorrow," I tell him.

"You said after it stops raining."

"Tomorrow."

He opens an umbrella and walks with me to the car. I tell him I'm fine, and he offers it to Masood, who lets him hold it over his head. Mist beads up on it. We walk to the car, and the waiter runs back inside. Masood opens the passenger door for me. I get in. He closes it. Wahob slides behind the wheel. Masood sits behind me. We pull away from the curb. The waiter watches us leave and waves.

We pass a new hotel with a sign outside promoting an indoor pool. Masood stares out the window. Fires from construction sites reflecting against the glass illuminate his worried face. Wahob says something to Masood and then glances at me. Masood raises his hand for him to be quiet.

"How long will you be here?" he asks.

"Two months."

"And then? Who will come after you?"

"I don't know. I don't know if anyone will come."

I won't think about that. It's not my call. I suppose I'll go back and stare at the four walls of my apartment and wait for war in Iraq. Masood too will wait, hoping for more journalists. I think I'll get satisfaction before he does.

"Save your money," I tell him.

"Inshallah," Wahob says.

I glance at him. Wahob ignores me, stares straight ahead. He can't possibly have understood me. Lost in his own thoughts, he had wished for something, and inshallah, "God willing," it will happen for him.

Masood closes his window against the rain. The wet streets glisten. I feel okay. A little jet lag. As long as I keep Masood in check and find Bro. I need someone I can trust. We drive back to the house amid the limitless possibilities, resonating out from the noise of hammers and drills, of a revitalized Kabul, pulsing deeply into the night.

CHAPTER EIGHT

Drop by Drop

MAY–JULY 2002

The next morning, I tell Wahob I no longer need him. He gives me a hateful look but says nothing. I stand in the open door and watch him leave. I have no regrets. I have reasserted my control. The smell of fresh manure from a herd of water buffalo lumbering past assaults my nose. I listen to the shouts of the boy driving them to market and then notice the shine of Bro's parked van behind the bulk of their lumbering bodies. He steps out of the van, jumps over a water-filled sewer, and wraps me in his arms, lifting me off my feet.

"Welcome back to Afghanistan!"

I slap him on his back to put me down and then we hold one another at arm's length, neither of us able to stop grinning. Kansas City is somewhere behind me, wonderfully indistinct as a half-forgotten memory. The troubled thoughts I'd had those two months at home vanish in Bro's grip.

We walk into the house, arms draped over each other's shoulders. Bro can barely contain himself. "Look," he exclaims, "look around."

The downtown market sells washing machines instead of laundry baskets. An Italian restaurant opens next month, two doors from a new Chinese restaurant. Commercial airlines fly into Kabul's airport. More and more women show their faces and wear makeup, high heels, and black fishnet stockings. And best of all, Bro's wife is expecting her baby any day now.

■ ■ ■

The cook brings us tea.

"Where do we go now?" I ask him.

Bro fidgets on the couch. He can't work with me, he explains. He wants to be with his wife when she goes into labor.

"I am sorry, Malcolm."

No worries. Masood will help me. I know he's pissed I fired Wahob, but I also know he's not so pissed he'll quit out of principle. Money trumps loyalty.

Besides, covering the loya jirga will be tedious duty. Only a few reporters will be allowed in the large circus tent below the InterContinental Hotel, where the jirga will gather. The rest of us journos must watch the proceedings through a video feed in the hotel's auditorium. We may even follow it on TV.

Yes, television. Kabul has functioning TV and radio stations. And cell phones. No towers have been erected outside the capital yet, but within Kabul we all chatter on palm-size phones like children with new toys. The phones often die, and we curse them and Afghanistan when they do. Still, no matter how flawed its electronics, Afghanistan is catching up with the rest of the world.

Not that I will have much to follow. We all know Karzai will win. The former king, Mohammad Zahir Shah, has already announced he is not a candidate. His appearance with some American officials raised questions of whether the United States had interfered to assure a Karzai victory. Of course they had. It's an open secret no one admits. Deposed Afghan president Burhanuddin Rabbani has also bowed out under American pressure.

"An election should never be confused with democracy," a UN worker on my flight had reminded me.

I tell Bro to stay with his wife. In the new Afghanistan, inshallah, I can always call him.

At night a woman picks through garbage outside the house. She can speak a little English, learned, she tells me, when she cleaned the house of a Russian diplomat in Kabul who had English-speaking guests. Her husband was a teacher but now is jobless. He suffers from a "nervous problem." Sometimes her mother and father feed them. She has no hope, nothing. Since September 11th, her life has not changed. Every night she sits with her husband. "He is very sick," she says.

I fill a bag with rice. I put twenty dollars in an envelope and put it in the bag so she will find it later and not open it on the street. She thanks me for the rice and waits as if there might be more. I shake my head. She turns away and walks into the dark, finished for the night, a bag of rice proof of a successful evening that cut short the need to scrounge in filth.

She will be back. Word will get out about this night, this house, this khaarijee, and other beggars will join her. At some point I will spurn all of them because I cannot take on dozens of beggars. They'll wail outside the house, enraged by my rejection. They may take out their frustrations on her, a woman promising false hope. Then they will move on, and so will I. But she and I will remember this moment of limited relief that has allowed us both a temporary peace.

I listen to BBC reports on Iraq. The Americans command Saddam Hussein to do this and that, knowing he won't. Knowing options other than war decrease with each demand. Most journos assume a war in Iraq will start before the end of the year. I try to follow the politics, the reasons for another war, but am distracted by the jirga and its endless debates. I file stories: arguments among jirga delegates delay efforts to choose members of a national assembly; tribal fighting in northern Afghanistan, including the gang rape of an aid worker, causes some NGOs to pull out; a massive influx of refugees could further destabilize the country.

I return every morning to the auditorium to update myself on the jirga. Without air-conditioning, among all the journalists, photographers, Afghan officials, and agency heads vying for space, it becomes unbearable. People vomit from the heat.

Bro calls me. He is stir-crazy, sitting with his wife day and night. He does not understand her moods and often sleeps on the roof of his house to get away from her. His mother-in-law lives with them, and when both she and his wife get on him, all he can do is stare at the stars and dream about Miami Beach.

"Where do we go?" he asks.

He picks me up at the InterCon during a lull in the jirga, and together we drive to an old part of Kabul where the changes sweeping the country have not reached. We stop by a vendor cooking kabob and buy lamb and bread and sit beneath a straw overhang. The damp ground smells of chicken and cow dung in the thin shade. Flies dart above our heads, drawn to our sweat. Vendors squat on the ground, smoking by the road.

Thick smog from hundreds of taxis and buses bringing refugees back to Kabul stretches across the horizon. Trucks and more buses overflowing with people rumble past us on the broken road running through Bini Sar toward Lowgar, Paktai, Khowst, and other provinces in the southeast. A sharp stench rises from open sewers and fills our lungs like soup. Conversations rise and fall in the valleys of silence between traffic. Everything but the air moves.

"In the morning I wake up and have tea," one man tells us. He points to his stall where he repairs hunting rifles and also sells gasoline. "I open my shop and then change clothes and organize my materials. In the evening I go home and sit with my family. We have dinner. After that we sleep. There's nothing to do. I am wasting my time with my shop, but I can't find another job."

"Does he know what will happen in our country after Karzai becomes president?" a vendor asks, looking at me.

"I don't know what he knows," the first man says.

He splits open an apricot, tosses the pit into the road, and watches it bounce through the wheels of a mule-drawn cart. He introduces himself to Bro as Nasir. Flies hum in clouds and swarm the pit. A few feet away stand the shattered walls of the mud brick compound where Nasir was born.

During the civil war Afghan factions destroyed the compound. Pashtun and Uzbek forces pounded Bini Sar with mortars and rocket-propelled grenades. Nasir evacuated with his wife and family and moved to a house on the outskirts of the village. A padlock holds shut the massive front door of the compound, where peeling wood curls into clumps the size of fists. Dogs ramble out an open side door, leaving wet paw prints in the dirt. Outside, chickens scatter ahead of them on the hot stones.

Nasir remembers as a boy building snowmen inside the courtyard. He expects the compound to be torn down for new housing as part of an expected reconstruction effort following the loya jirga.

"My family's house here is one hundred ninety years old. This was where my grandfather died, and my father and mother and two cousins. I do not live here now. I will die in a different house. It was cheaper to build a house than try to repair this one. There is no room for sentiment."

I ask him how homes built from mud withstand rain.

"These walls are very strong and tough," Nasir says. "We stomp the mud with our feet and cook it and make bricks. After one, two years, you might have to patch the roof, but that is all. We have an expression. When somebody asks, 'How long will your house stand?' we say, 'As long as people don't destroy it.' Rain did not destroy this house."

A vendor offers Bro and me a cigarette. He asks if I know what Karzai will do about education, health, and poverty.

"How would he know?" Nasir asks.

"I'm sure they have talked about all these things," Bro says.

"What is the United Nations?" Nasir asks.

"Representatives from countries all over the world who meet and discuss the problems of the world."

"This is not my fault I ask you these questions. I didn't go to school. I know nothing."

"The fix was in," another vendor shouts at me. "Everyone is angry at the Americans for supporting Karzai instead of the king."

Bro tells the man to stop acting silly. "He," Bro says, lifting his chin toward me, "did not make Karzai president."

Nearby a generator starts and I don't hear what the supporter of the king mutters to himself. Bro ignores him and waits to see if I have more questions. Flies collect on our arms and knees. I give up swatting them. The flies mill around, a black churning mass, seeming to be uncertain what to do without the threat of a hand hovering above them.

"Be very careful," the supporter of the king says. "As an American you are a target of people's anger."

"Please," Nasir says, "he is our guest. There will be no more fighting. Maybe the dying has finally stopped."

The supporter of the king walks away. Shadows retreat up a rocky hill, exposing an old graveyard where Nasir's parents, grandparents, and great-grandparents lie buried beneath nameless slabs of stone shaped like large arrowheads. Above the graveyard, boys dig rocks to fill the foundations of new houses.

Bro's mobile phone rings. After a moment he shoves it in his pocket and gets up. "It is my uncle," he says, walking toward the van without waiting for me. "He is very sick."

■ ■ ■

Bro drops me off at my house. Later he calls to tell me that his uncle has died of a heart attack. I listen to him weep on the other end. "I'm so sorry," I say. "I'm so sorry." He stops crying after a moment. The silence in my ear stretches over miles, and I feel lost in the vacancy of his grief. Bro asks me to attend the memorial service in the morning.

The next day Masood and I catch a taxi to Haje Yaqob Mosque. Bro's uncle was fifty-two. I catch myself counting sometimes. Most Afghans don't live past the age of forty-six. Bro is twenty-four. Statistically he has about twenty-two years left to live. If I were Afghan, I'd have four years left. His uncle beat the odds by six years—not bad in a world of such reduced expectations. Easy for me to say. He was not my uncle.

"This is no way for you to show respect," Masood says when we arrive at the large, blue-domed mosque, surrounded by beggars. "It is disrespectful for non-Muslims to enter a mosque."

"Bro asked me to come," I say, shouting above the blasts of car horns.

"They won't let you in," Masood says.

"Then we won't go in. Who will be there?"

"The men of his family."

"Where do the women go?"

"They stay and mourn at home," Masood says.

Goats covered with dried mud and herded by children wind their way between stalled cars. Along the roadside, boys with straw switches swat flies off slabs of red meat hanging from hooks in the sun.

"Why don't the women come to the mosque?"

"Because it is right for them to stay at home. Stop asking these questions."

I had not realized Masood was so pious—and so resentful. In part because of Wahob, sure, but it's more than that. Although he wears a leather jacket and blue jeans, he draws a line at how far Western culture may intrude. And as far as he's concerned I am intruding. But I'm here for Bro, not him.

The centuries-old mosque rises in shadows beneath huge trees. It somehow lived through all the fighting and stands defiant above other buildings broken down from war. The blue tile of its dome undulates beneath the wavy outline of leafy branches. Beggars, shoeshine boys, and women cluster at the broken gate with their hands out. Other women in long dresses with scarves pulled back from their foreheads skirt around them and look away, some walking with men in business suits and ties.

Masood stays in the car, won't look at me when I invite him to follow me in.

"This is wrong," he says.

Bro stands outside the mosque greeting the men of his family. His eyes film with tears when he sees me. He holds my outstretched hand in both of his and leads me into the mosque after I remove my shoes.

I kneel on the carpeted floor among a circle of men. They hold their hands out, palms up in prayer, making sidelong glances at us. Bro's family sits against a wall. A mullah recites verses from the Quran. His voice rises and falls, echoing off the cool concrete walls until it fades like a whisper. He stops and takes a deep breath after each verse, and the men around me brush their faces with their palms in prayer.

The service lasts two hours. I leave after bowing to each member of Bro's family, my right hand over my heart. Outside the sky has darkened with clouds, but it remains hot. Bro walks me to the gate. A man sits on the sidewalk selling used Reebok sneakers. The taxi driver waves at us. Women in business suits pass us, hold my look when I glance at them. I don't see Masood. To hell with him.

I open the door to the taxi, making room for an elderly man who squeezes past pushing a cart filled with faded blue jeans, donations discarded to the street by some NGO.

"I'm sorry about your uncle."

"He lived a long time. He is with God. I hope my children, inshallah, live as long as my uncle."

Two weeks later, on June 13th, Karzai overwhelmingly wins the election. Some of the former king's supporters grumble, but none of the delegates raises serious objections. Karzai will lead a new government for eighteen months, to be followed by Afghanistan's first presidential election in October 2004.

The assassination of a new Afghan vice president outside the Ministry of Public Works three weeks later on July 6th casts a pall over his victory. I catch a taxi to the ministry to report on the shooting. No police tape cordons off the area. Reporters mill around a bullet-riddled Toyota

Land Cruiser, and Afghan soldiers pose inside for photographers shifting around the blood-stained seats without expression.

Haji Abdul Qadir, one of three vice presidents under Karzai, was murdered just hours after a senior U.S. commander admitted for the first time that U.S. bombs apparently killed civilians in southern Afghanistan. Later the same day, U.S. and Afghan officials admitted killing dozens of Afghans in an air strike in southern Afghanistan. Afghans claim the villagers died celebrating a wedding.

The attack on Qadir came about 12:30 p.m. when two gunmen stepped from behind bushes outside the Ministry of Public Works in downtown Kabul and riddled his Land Cruiser with more than thirty rounds from assault rifles. The vehicle skidded fifty yards and crashed into a stone wall. Qadir's driver also was killed.

Omar Samad, spokesman for the Ministry of Foreign Affairs, tells us that poppy growers may have been behind the assassination, angry about Qadir's efforts to crack down on their profitable crop, which is used to make opium and heroin. Or members of al-Qaida or the Taliban may have sought to disrupt the fledgling government.

"This is an unfortunate, isolated incident, but no one in Afghanistan is under the illusion that there is no risk in Afghanistan," Samad said. "But the process for reconstruction continues. The goal is to bring peace and stability to Afghanistan."

I have my doubts. Earlier in the day I covered a joint press conference with Lieutenant General Dan K. McNeill and Afghan Foreign Minister Abdullah Abdullah. McNeill acknowledged that 48 Afghan civilians were killed and 117 injured in and around Deh Rawood village in Oruzgan Province in a U.S. air strike six days before. U.S. planes bombed Deh Rawood late Sunday night and early Monday morning because, McNeill said, of antiaircraft fire coming from the village. Afghans said that villagers were celebrating a wedding with a traditional firing of guns into the air, and that the bombs killed and injured scores of civilians, including women and children.

"We will initiate all formal investigations to determine what caused these civilian casualties and what we can do or implement to make sure they do not reoccur," McNeill said.

Assassins on the one hand, military blunders on the other. I feel unnerved and question the progress around me. Then I shake it off.

Of course there will be problems after nearly thirty years of continuous war. It's nothing but an unfortunate blip on the radar. Still, I tell Bro, something doesn't smell right.

"Smell right?"

"It feels strange. Like being scared of the dark. You know you're okay, but you continue to have a little chill in your neck for the rest of the night."

"That's how it was in the Russian time," Bro says, taking out his notebook to write *smells right.* "Kabul was very dark."

After I file my stories on the assassination and the air strike, Bro drives us out of Kabul for no other reason than to leave the congested capital for a few hours, where summer temperatures exceed one hundred degrees. We pass the road to Bagram Air Base and drive into leafy, tree-filled mountains, where streams cut lines through the soft soil and farmers planting rice wade ankle deep in muddy water. Stone houses rise up on the rocky ledges darkened by deepening shadows. Birds surf a sharp wind.

It's the kind of scene that makes you swear you'll never live in a city again. You'll invest your life's savings in some out-of-the-way place, and leave traffic and pollution and stress behind. You'll get up in the morning and sip coffee on the porch by the hammock and watch the sun rise over fields alive with squirrels and rabbits. You're going to stay in one place this time and never leave. You swear you will, and for a moment you actually think you might.

Bro asks me to take his photograph. He puts on sunglasses and adjusts his vest jacket. He shoves one hand in his pants pocket and rests his other hand over his stomach. He stands with his profile toward the camera, head turned to the horizon, chin up. Then we get back into the car and continue driving.

Minutes later we see cars pulled over to the side of the road, people milling about. Bro stops behind them. A man's body lies on a blanket. It appears that the cracked pavement had broken and sent a bus crashing down into a river. Foaming water twists through its shattered windshield and over displaced rocks. Beside it an overturned Russian tank and a rusted antiaircraft gun jut through the bubbling water.

A surprising scratching sound comes from the bus, and boys slide down the cliff and break open locks on the luggage compartments. Sheep bolt out, tumbling into the foaming water, hooves slipping on rocks.

I am told the bus crashed about an hour ago. Two men were the only ones inside, the dead man and another who was taken to a hospital.

"Hamid Karzai says as president he is going to repair our roads, but it is too late for this guy," a man says.

"Who is he?" Bro asks.

"We've never seen him," someone says behind him, peering over his shoulder.

"I don't know either," another man says. "I just think of food. I think of where I'll get something to eat today."

Ants mill at the edges of the dead man's blanket. Thick black hair slides across his forehead to the ground. Stubble marks the beginnings of a beard. A purple bruise spreads beneath his right eye. Ink and grease stains darken his loose clothing. His small, dirty hands curl against his legs. I guess him to be about thirty, but in Afghanistan people often look older than their years. He may be eighteen.

"We should take him to a hospital," a man tells Bro. "We can't leave him here."

"Why didn't you take him with the other man?" Bro asks.

"We did not have enough room on the cart."

Wet sheep wander onto the road and huddle together, turning in aimless circles.

"Would you take him?" someone asks Bro. "The hospital is only ten miles from here."

Bro looks at me. We don't want to be stopped at a military checkpoint with a dead Afghan.

"I'm sorry," I say and shake my head.

"What should we do?" another man wonders aloud.

No one answers. The boys herd the sheep up a path into the mountain. Wind blows off the river, ruffling our clothes. The dead man's hair flutters.

Bro and I get back in the van and drive toward Kabul, our urge to get out of the capital shaken by this unexpected death. Something will be done, I'm sure. By tonight the body will be gone, and the bus will look like another bit of war debris instead of the empty coffin of an unknown man who did not die in the wars.

■ ■ ■

This morning I notice Daud limping. His right leg, he says, has hurt on and off for years. Sometimes a slight twinge, other times an intolerable pain. Today it's somewhere in the middle.

I offer to take him to Mark Timlin, a British doctor who lives down the street from my house in Kabul. Referring people for help comes naturally to a former social worker. Mark, known as Doctor Mark by Afghans, helped my housekeeper Zabib rid himself of kidney stones.

Daud, in his early forties, has never been to a doctor. The idea scares him, but he understands a doctor could help him. Recently a German-financed clinic set his wife's broken arm. It had been broken for four months before Daud told me about it. He did not have the forty dollars needed to have it set. I gave him the money.

When her arm healed, Daud placed a scrap of the plaster cast on my fireplace mantel below a faded map of Afghanistan. He held it gingerly. "It made her well," he would repeat again and again as if the plaster possessed magical charms.

Daud and his family live in the Shomali Plain north of Kabul and have suffered through many battles between the Taliban and Northern Alliance. During one bombardment, shrapnel tore through Daud's buttocks.

"There is no dignity in war," he says.

I make coffee and pour Daud a cup. I encourage him to see Doctor Mark. He thinks about it while sipping his coffee. He prefers tea but has learned to drink coffee in part, I think, to please me. I add milk; he adds sugar. For a brief moment we sit side by side, two guys awake at 7:00 a.m., rubbing sleep from our eyes.

As a social worker, I liked to think that I treated the homeless as my equals, but I didn't. They had nothing to offer me. I didn't need to learn the intricacies of Dumpster diving to eat, but they needed the shelter referral slips I had in my drawer to sleep inside. Daud and I both know I can prepare my own food if I must, but he won't get paid unless he cooks for me. We know I will leave Afghanistan and still have a job, but he will be unemployed when I do. So at least I should take him to Doctor Mark if he will let me.

Daud finishes his coffee, then walks to the kitchen to scramble my eggs. He warms the coffee and pours me another cup. He puts his cup and saucer in the sink. He washes my cup when I finish, although I offer to clean it myself.

Zabib shuffles through the living room to the bathroom, as thin as Daud but with a thick head of black hair, in contrast to Daud's bald crown. He carries a towel over one shoulder and an empty plastic bottle jammed in the back of his pants. He won't drink coffee. Bad for his kidneys, Doctor Mark told him. He uses his fifty-dollar-a-day salary to pay his younger brother's tuition at Kabul University.

"One day," Zabib told me, "there will be jobs besides working for journalists, and all Afghans will need to have gone to school."

I hear children outside herding goats past our house. I like mornings. I like the quiet and the sounds that slowly emerge: chants from a nearby mosque, the crying of cats, children pumping water from a well, goats bleating.

"Look," Zabib says, coming out of the bathroom.

He places his plastic bottle on the fireplace mantel beside the piece of plaster. He has expelled more kidney stones, he says, grinning. Daud and I stare at the bottle filled with cloudy urine. I'm more than a little disgusted at having it in the living room, but how can I respond to the joy in Zabib's face other than "That's great"?

Daud looks at Zabib's bottle and takes a deep breath.

"I will see Doctor Mark," he says, as if accepting a weight as great as the unwashed men and donkeys carrying loads outside our door.

We walk to Mark's house, a block away on a narrow street. Children run to us and offer to sell cigarettes. When that fails, they hold out their hands for money and twist their faces into silent pleas.

I stop at a gate and ring the bell to Mark's white stucco house. Thin trees cast sketchy shadows across the walk, and a cat minces across the sun-dappled roof. Mark's housekeeper leads us to a living room furnished only with a torn couch, a chair, and a medical dummy Mark uses to teach CPR to Afghan medical students.

"Morning," Mark says from the top of the stairs. He walks down and looks at Daud and me as if it's the most natural thing in the world for us to be in his house.

"Morning, Mark. Sorry to barge in…"

"Not at all."

"Thanks. If you have a moment, this is my cook Daud. He's complaining of pains in his legs."

Mark is a tall and lean man with a tenor voice. He towers over Daud and places a hand against Daud's face, tips his head back, and looks at his eyes. Daud stiffens and pulls back, but Mark keeps a strong grip on his face. He works his hands down Daud's body, squeezing his arms and legs.

"Anemic," he mutters. "Joint pain?"

The English-speaking housekeeper translates for Daud.

"Ankle to thigh," Daud says.

"How long?"

"Four years."

"Have you seen a doctor before?"

"No."

"Tests might show him to have rheumatoid arthritis," Mark says. "We can give him tests, but the equipment is primitive. Can't be sure they'll be done right. Taken any medicine before?"

"No."

"I don't specialize in joints, but normally the meds you take for this sort of thing are always the same. Problem with people not used to taking medications are the side effects. We can start him on smaller doses and then go on to stronger ones. We'll start with a cream he can rub on his joints three times a day and then go on to tablets if that doesn't work. Giving them loads of meds at first is generally problematic. They sell them instead of taking them."

Mark reaches for a blank sheet of paper, writes a prescription, and hands it to Daud. The housekeeper translates. Daud smiles, pats his face, arms, and legs where Mark touched him, trying to determine what secrets his body released.

"I have a regular contingent of Afghans who come by the house," Mark says. "Quite nice really. Sort of the reverse of house calls. Patient calls. The mentality is, I can write a prescription and the pain will be done away with. Not quite, but at least they come, you know. They get some treatment."

Mark has practiced medicine since 1995, the same year I left social work to pursue journalism. He had considered architecture but left that to his younger brother.

"I prefer being with people," he says, straightening some of the clutter in the living room. "Trying to figure out what's wrong. In London, you've got, like, hundreds of patients all with the same problems— lonely, depressed. You were a social worker, weren't you?"

"Yes," I say. "Fourteen years."

"Then you know what I mean. Why'd you stop?"

"It was time. I was tired."

"I'd dish out tablets in ten-minute slots and shout, Next!" Mark says. "That kind of thing. I didn't feel useful."

"What are you complaining about?" his wife Vickie asks, walking up behind him.

"Feeling useful. Hi, sweetie."

Vickie appears half asleep, her curly hair sprouting in different directions. She was born in Australia. They met on a charity walk in London in 1998 and married a short time later.

"Coffee?" she offers.

"No, thanks," I say. "Had my fill."

"Tea?"

"I'll pass, thank you."

"Did you eat breakfast, Mark?"

"No, I didn't."

"The cook made eggs."

"I know, with onions. I don't like onions in my eggs."

"So fussy."

Mark turns to me. "We're going to Cheltan School," he says. "Everyone's been asking us to help build more schools. We do mainly health care, but wherever the need is we try to help. We tend to be flexible. So we got a grant to help rebuild this school. Come along if you like, Malc."

"All right."

"Use our bathroom before we leave," Vickie says. "There's only one dodgy dirty toilet at the school."

I tell Daud I'm staying. He holds his right hand over his heart, bows to Mark, and leaves.

"How is Zabib?" Mark asks. "He hasn't come by for awhile."

"Whatever you gave him works. He pisses in a bottle every day and shows us the stones he's passed. He places it on the fireplace mantel."

"Lovely. You don't confuse it for mineral water do you?"

We drive south out of Kabul to Cheltan School, Mark chattering behind the wheel.

"I always wanted to go to Afghanistan," Mark says. "Then I heard someone lecture about the desperate need of the place, and Vickie and I started looking into it."

"Mark was always talking about it," Vickie says. "He asked me if I'd go there, and I said I'd go so long as it was hot. I had no idea where it was, let alone that it had winter."

"I didn't want to marry someone who didn't want to go to Afghanistan."

"He wanted to marry someone totally daffy."

"Look at that," Mark says, pointing out the window at an isolated patch of greenery. "I love the brightness of everything. . . . Say, did you notice how our driver poured water over the engine this morning? 'Gives it more of a chance to charge,' he says. I think that's rubbish. What do you think?"

Before I can answer, we turn down a dirt path to a broad field filled with rusted shipping containers. Boys and girls run out of the containers and swarm around us.

"Salaam, salaam," we say, tapping their outstretched hands.

The bullet-riddled containers stand near the construction site for the new Cheltan School and serve as classrooms to eight hundred children between the ages of five and fifteen. Some walls of the school have already been erected. Heaps of stones and sacks of concrete lay scattered about. We enter one of the stifling containers.

"In the summer, these containers are ovens," Mark says. "In the winter, they're freezers."

Children fill the small desks and chairs inside the cramped, stifling space. The air clings to my skin like blown seed. The temperature inside rises with every step forward. I don't know how they stand it. Mark walks the length of the container and sketches several figures on the dusty walls.

"In English," he says to the children, pointing at the wall.

"Dog!" the children shout.

"In English," he says again, pointing to another drawing.

"Cat!"

"In English."

"Mouse!"

"In English."

The children stare at a triangular shape Mark has drawn.

"What is that?" Vickie asks.

"A house," Mark says.

"Don't give up your day job."

Headmaster Amir Mohammad Ebrahami watches us, bemused. He has been a teacher for eleven years. Since the Taliban fled Kabul, he has enrolled 290 girls in the school.

"Every day I get notes," he says. " 'If you register girls, we're going to kill you,' these notes read. The other day, I went to a funeral, and while I was gone some people burned my house. I come to work every day, but now I don't stay in Kabul at night. I move every night so no one knows where I am. My daughters come to school every day. This is where I see them. In the afternoon they go home without me. They could be hurt if they're with me."

Mark reaches for his shoulder.

"Be a bit sad, wouldn't it?" he says. "Leaving your children?"

"What can I say? It's difficult, of course. But I am proud. Even if I am killed in the process, I have done well. I am here to serve for the younger generation."

"Everything else okay?" Mark says. "Supplies?"

"Yes, yes," Ebrahami says.

We walk back outside, where I see workmen carrying buckets of cement up rickety wood ladders to a partially built classroom. Other men hammer wood planks together into wall frames. Boys shovel sand into wheelbarrows.

"Over there," Vickie says, "that bit of rock will be fourteen toilets. They won't know what to do. Imagine. They just have one now."

We walk back to the car, a gaggle of boys and girls following us. Ebrahami raises a hand. His arm protrudes above the small faces beneath him as he waves vigorously, almost desperately, and I wonder if he thinks he might not see us again.

"He's got to be careful," Mark says. "This antigirl thing. Many families are afraid they'll lose their daughters if they go to school. We have to talk them through it. We have to show them that when we educate women, we educate the whole nation. Create opportunities."

We stop at Karte School Medical Hospital where Mark sees patients and acts as a consultant. Men suffering from diarrhea fill tents outside the crumbled walls of the hospital. No room inside, Mark explains.

"All infectious diseases," he says, looking inside the tents at the wasted patients sagging in flimsy army cots.

"Meningitis, diarrhea, typhoid. Then there's the dust. Their lungs are wasted."

Vicki has a meeting with nursing students downtown and flags a taxi. Mark leads me to the director's office, where a group of doctors sit around a table, passing a pot of tea.

The director, Sayeed Hassan Kamal, waves us in.

"The Japanese are giving money to the hospital. But they are giving it to us through the Ministry of Public Health."

"Not good," Mark says.

"Not good?" I ask.

"My concern," Mark says, "is that the ministry may not pass it on. Mighty tempting to keep it for themselves since they don't have any money."

"You mean we'll never see it?" Kamal says.

"We need to go to the Ministry of Public Health and make sure the money comes here," Mark says.

Kamal passes him a cup of tea. Mark hands it to me, and Kamal passes him another. Afghans always offer tea to guests. I appreciate the thought, but few buildings have functioning toilets. At some point I know I will need to piss in the ruins of one of the many bomb-blasted buildings that serve as public toilets in Kabul, standing in the rubble with other passersby.

"I heard you all got your certificates," Mark says.

"The examiners were very impressed," Kamal says.

"We didn't think many would pass," Mark says to me, "considering they hadn't done the course before. Things like putting a tube in someone, putting someone on a ventilator, emergency techniques is what I'm talking about."

"I thought they were doctors," I say.

"Yes, but they never had this kind of training before. They didn't have mannequins to practice on. They'd never seen one before."

"I don't understand."

"In medical school, we couldn't see female patients," Kamal tells me. "We couldn't use mannequins because they all had breasts. That would have violated Taliban law. So we knew nothing."

We walk rounds with them, down a long corridor to a twelve-bed room filled with infants. The once yellow walls have been blistered white from the sun. A nurse draws blue curtains across the open windows but a hot wind thrusts them aside. Flies swarm the ceiling.

Mark stops at a bed and looks at a baby brought in three days ago with chronic diarrhea. The baby sleeps; his mother looks at Mark with a long, sad face.

"Oh, so tiny," Mark whispers.

He waves his hand above her face.

"A lot of flies. We don't have money for screens. Patients get most of their food from their families. We have to be better about clearing the dirty dishes. We need to do more."

"What more can you do?" I ask.

He doesn't answer. I wanted to do more too, but came to understand there would never be just one more family to help. There would always be more and more and more.

Mark stops at another bed where two boys sleep, one four years old, the other seven.

"One has meningitis, the other typhoid," a doctor tells Mark.

"How long have they been on the IV?"

"Three days."

"Good to see those in properly," Mark says.

I follow Mark across the hall to the Chronic Care Unit. A man stares at us from his bed, eyes blank. A partially filled glass of water, a roll of toilet paper, and a teapot rest on his nightstand.

"He has cirrhosis of the liver. Not from drinking, mind you. Malnutrition. Hepatitis too. Can't do anything for him. Just reduce swelling. Make him more comfortable and alleviate symptoms, pain."

"Then what?"

"Wait until he dies."

The prognosis for the patient next to him is equally bleak. "Leukemia," a doctor says to Mark.

"Can't do anything," Mark says.

"Can't that be treated with radiation?" I ask.

"We don't have that equipment," adds the doctor.

"They have it in Pakistan," Mark says.

"Does he have money to go to Pakistan?" I ask.

"I don't know. I'm hoping he goes into remission, then maybe Pakistan," the doctor says.

"And this one?" Mark says, stopping at another bed.

"Typhoid fever."

"He's responding?"

"Yes."

A lizard scuttles across the floor and over Mark's boot as he moves to the next bed, which is completely covered by a rumpled sheet. Mark draws the sheet back slowly and jumps when an elderly man opens his eyes and shouts.

"You scared him," the doctor says.

"I always worry when they have a sheet over them," Mark says. "What's he have?"

"Pneumonia. He had typhoid, but it went on to pneumonia. He's responding well."

The next patient is only thirty yet has the kidneys of a seventy-year-old.

"He's stable," the doctor says.

In the last bed lies a small, shriveled girl. She stares at the ceiling without blinking. One night when all the shelters were full, my girl-friend offered to take in a homeless woman and her daughter, who had wide blue saucer eyes like this girl.

"You can't," I told her. "What if they don't want to leave in the morning? How will you get them to go? Where will you take them? What if the mom robs you while you're asleep?"

"But she's sick," Sandy said, listening to the girl's cough. "She's sick."

This Afghan girl has meningitis. She is extraordinarily thin and already paralyzed.

"Her parents are very poor," the doctor says. "She was in several hospitals, but they didn't have medication."

"Are we giving her the drugs she needs?" Mark asks.

"We have one or two being brought over from Pakistan."

"Her prognosis is very bad. Her paralysis won't improve."

"I think she'll die," the doctor says.

Mark shakes his head.

Standing there I recall another mother and child in San Francisco. I gave the mom shelter referrals all the time while she was pregnant. She had a baby boy and proudly showed him to me days after he was born. His eyes were shut tight, hands balled into minute fists. Later I learned he had a deformed stomach and heart because mom smoked crack during her pregnancy. He died a few weeks later.

Crack, booze, speed. Only one percent of the more than one hundred people who came through our doors every day entered substance abuse programs. We had no statistics on how many actually completed the programs.

Most were illiterate. Those who found jobs signed up for shelter because their minimum-wage salaries couldn't cover rent even for a cheap welfare hotel room. But they were working and weren't eligible for shelter. They had money and therefore should be able to find someplace to stay. That was the thinking, a rationalization. We didn't have enough room to shelter everybody.

If they drank, however, they could get into detox. Income didn't matter if you were drunk. Many tried controlled drinking, just enough to get into detox, have a roof over their head for the night so they could work the next morning. They were back on the street in no time.

One percent. At best we offered homeless people a safe place to spend their days and nights as they slowly killed themselves. We held memorial services under highway overpasses where they died, to honor them, and to let God know they were worth remembering. Traffic rushed by, and we stepped around discarded bags of fast food. Some prayed. Others of us just closed our eyes so those who did pray felt comfortable. I felt the space in the crowd at the front door when a regular was gone.

Many of my colleagues, guys who had trained me, fell off the wagon after two, three, five, even ten years of sobriety, never to pick themselves up again. Most died on the street in grim doorways buried under cardboard boxes. One guy I knew, Gypsy, fell off. For weeks he had been frustrated that he hadn't been promoted to supervisor. Then he disappeared. When he came in weeks later asking for detox, he sat in a corner in his soiled clothes reeking of booze and crying bitter tears.

I found another coworker, Lyle, dead in his hotel room, arms splayed out to either side, eyes and mouth open, a surprised look on his face. He was in my volunteer orientation group. We all had name tags, except for one woman. Lyle made sure she got one. Looking at his pale body, I remembered how he slid the blank tag to her across the table and asked gently if there was anything else she needed. I sat next to him and waited for the coroner.

I prayed at Lyle's memorial service, searched for answers as the fragile world around me shifted because a colleague—friend—had died from an addiction I thought he'd beaten. I didn't understand. Over the years, the shock grew less.

"Bobby," I had once said to a homeless man I hadn't seen for some time, "where you been?"

"San Jose."

"Shit. I thought you died."

"No," he said. "Not yet. How are you?"

Not yet. I used to feel for the pulse of men and women I saw passed out on the street, to make sure they were alive. I stopped that after awhile. Stepped around them like everybody else.

"What are you doing in my world?" a homeless man we dubbed "Too Tall" because of his lean seven-foot frame, asked me when he started drinking again. "What are you doing here?"

I didn't answer. I didn't know anymore.

Before visiting another hospital, Mark takes a break at the Sultani Gym in downtown Kabul, where he meets another doctor he knows. Dr. Bashir was a professional bodybuilder before the Taliban outlawed gyms and most sports. He persuaded Mark to join the gym.

A faded red-and-black-striped carpet covers the hard concrete floor. Movie posters of Sylvester Stallone as Rambo decorate the walls. After thirty years of conflict, athletes use war debris for weights—broken wheel hubs, brakes, axles, and other vehicle parts. Bashir is stripped to the waist, glossed in sweat, and straining to deadlift a small car engine.

"How was that woman with gastrointestinal shock?" Mark asks.

"Good," Bashir says. "We pumped her with fluids."

"I think we can get more bed frames from that Japanese NGO."

Bashir smiles. He helps Mark fit two carburetors to either end of a metal pole.

"My wife says I'm fitter," Mark says, stretching out on a bench. He raises his arms, and Bashir hefts the bar over Mark, who lowers it to his chest. Breathing deeply, he does a series of bench presses.

"You're supposed to do three sets of eight of everything or it doesn't work for some reason. I have no idea why."

His face pales with the strain. When he finishes he wipes his forehead with the back of his hand.

"It relieves stress to a certain extent, but I think about work because I find this quite boring. But it's companionable. Everyone calls you brother and hugs you."

He stoops, picks up a bar, and curls it toward his chest eight times. "Two more sets to go."

Bashir nods. Mark notices another Afghan doctor from the clinic.

"Hey, what? How was the night?"

"Not so bad," the doctor says. "But early this morning we had a hysterical patient. Twenty years old."

"What did you give her?"

"Nothing. I think it was some problem in the home."

"Beating?"

"Yes, her husband hits her."

Mark nods. He takes a deep breath, stares at the ceiling and curls the bar to his chest.

"One . . . two . . . three . . . four . . ."

An hour later we drive to Factory Clinic outside of Kabul on Jalalabad Road. At an intersection, a policeman recognizes Mark and waves him to the curb.

"My mother is sick. Shakes like a chicken. I think she had high blood pressure," the policeman says.

"Lower her salt," Mark says.

"In Afghanistan, what you say is difficult."

"Yes, too much oil, too much salt in the food. What's her blood pressure?"

"I don't know."

"I could measure it for you."

"If you want, I bring her to your house?"

"Okay. Tonight."

Only a few patients sit in the waiting room of Factory Clinic. Doctors sweep the clinic floor. Dust swirls around the brooms. Mark examines the expiration dates on medicines. He advises the doctors to give patients only three pills at a time. When they finish them, they can come back for three more, otherwise they might sell the pills for food.

"Under the Taliban people died all the time," Mark says. "Got bad when you knew you couldn't do anything. At least now we have a hope to get meds. Good things came out of September eleventh."

We watch a beetle hurry across the cracked floor.

"I used to think what I was doing was a joke," Mark says. "Today at least there's a chance they'll get medicine."

We walk outside and sit on a bare steel cot and wait for my taxi. The cot was tossed out with other hospital beds to be repaired, but no one is working on them. We put a long piece of cardboard over the rusted springs, yet they still dig into our thighs.

"I'll reach my limit," Mark says, "but when I leave Afghanistan, I want to look back and say I helped a bit."

We spot a taxi and Mark flags it down. The driver's small daughter lies asleep in back, curled into a ball. Mark touches her forehead and examines her hair.

"Brittle," he says. "Dehydrated."

I jog across the street to a vendor and buy bottled water. Mark wakes the girl and holds the bottle to her mouth. She grips it in both hands and drinks. She can't be more than six years old. I offer another bottle to the driver. He talks to Mark.

"He has no place to leave her," Mark explains. "He has to feed his parents and take care of his little girl. His wife was killed in the wars."

Mark watches the father drink. He almost drains the bottle dry before he puts it down and screws the cap back on and sets it in the backseat by his daughter. He looks at her. She watches us wide-eyed.

"*Tasha core*," the man says. "Thank you."

"A river is formed drop by drop. Do you know who said that?" Mark asks me.

I shake my head.

"I don't have a clue either," Mark says.

A plane flies high overhead. I can't tell if it's a military aircraft or a UN flight. Mark gazes after it, and I wonder what he is thinking, knowing he won't be on a plane out of Afghanistan anytime soon. He offers me a wistful smile. He helps the girl sit up, and I slide in beside her, putting the bottle of water on the floor. Mark taps her father on the shoulder and the driver puts the taxi in gear. Mark shrinks in the rear window, his arm raised in good-bye. When he is too small to recognize, I turn around and offer the girl more water.

CHAPTER NINE

For Now You Are Here

The buildup for a U.S.-led war against Iraq appears unstoppable. I expect to be sent to Kuwait, but my editors have different plans. They believe Afghanistan may erupt in jihadist outrage once American soldiers topple Baghdad. Now, four months after I left Afghanistan for the second time, I am being sent back for an embed with the 82nd Airborne Division.

I arrive in Kabul right after the new year, put my name in for an embed at Bagram Air Base, and get a room at the downtown Mustafa Hotel, where I meet Bro. Knight Ridder no longer has a house. The bureau stopped sending reporters here in the fall. I will have to fend for myself—with Bro's help.

"Welcome back to Afghanistan!" Bro shouts as I get out of the taxi.

He gives me one of his gravity-defying bear hugs and then holds the door for me as I lug my gear into the hotel.

The Mustafa is about thirty years old. In 2001 the owner turned it into a money exchange. He tore down rooms and converted rooms into offices. Laborers bolted metal grilles over the windows. Then September 11th happened. The sudden influx of foreign journalists into Kabul made it more profitable for the owner to maintain the Mustafa, named after his brother, as a hotel.

A dark stairway leads to the second floor of the building where I live behind the main office. My room has a space hollowed out of the wall for a safe. I look out my window between the bars at a junkyard piled with scrap metal and the stripped shells of cars. The thin plaster walls crack from the cold, revealing broken wood slats and no insulation.

My windows rattle from frigid winds. Ice forms on my ceiling and in the corners on the floor, despite my space heater. Lying in bed, gathering the desire to get up, I see my breath rise to the ceiling. Back to the no-shower-until-I'm-desperate routine. Cats howl and dogs bark outside. Old men sip tea in the feeble light of a fire in the stone oven of a bakery across the street. A small boy curls up against the warm stones.

I get up and drink lukewarm Nescafé coffee for breakfast while Bro eats a biscuit. We shiver together in the gray overcast winter morning and plan our day.

Every morning we check in with the United Nations and various ministries about the security situation. Rival warlords continue to fight, and al-Qaida and Taliban sympathizers remain in the areas bordering Pakistan in the southeast. A U.S. soldier was injured in a grenade attack in Kabul. Soldiers with the international security force regularly confiscate weapons hidden in the capital.

"Afghans have become discouraged with the government," Minister of Higher Education Sherief Fayez tells me. "They believed it would solve a lot of problems. It can't."

From his office we drive to the aid organization Women for Women International in north Kabul to sit in on a support group for Afghan war widows who follow the news in Iraq and relive their own losses.

"When the Taliban came here, they took my husband and killed him," says one woman with a deeply lined face. "They killed my older son. They said he had a gun. He didn't."

"I'm very sorry," I say.

"We suffer," she says. "We can't work without men in the house. I am very worried that if there is war in Iraq, the United States will forget about Afghan women."

I guess her to be fifty.

"I'm thirty-nine," she tells me.

A woman moves toward a wood-burning stove in the center of the room to warm her hands. She keeps her back to me so I don't see her face.

"When the mujahideen took power, a rocket exploded inside my house," she says, referring to Afghan fighters who resisted the 1980s Russian occupation.

"The rocket killed my child and brother-in-law. All the property was stolen. I have nothing."

She shifts back to her spot, face averted.

"I'm very sorry," I say.

"It's not your fault, mister."

"When the Taliban took power, they burned our house and all our property," another woman says. "They killed my husband. I have five children I'm worried about. I have no money to spend."

"I suffered during the Russian period," a woman next to me says. "I lost my husband. Now I have one son-in-law who is disabled from a rocket explosion. I wash my neighbor's clothes. Sometimes I sew blankets to make money."

"I'm sorry," I say.

"It's not your fault, mister. We just want peace."

To the first woman who spoke, she says, "I don't know why you're worried about Iraq. I'm still trying to survive the wars in Afghanistan."

"I lost my husband," another woman says. "I work washing floors. My eldest son goes to school. I cannot afford stationery and other school expenses."

"I'm sorry."

The women sit quietly watching me.

"I lost a husband and one son," another woman begins.

I lean against the wall and listen to her story. Her words fade in my head, and I feel as if I've assumed a great weight, but not nearly as heavy as what all of them must carry.

Six war orphans sit outside the Mustafa on shoeshine boxes and hustle Westerners for change. I smile and shake my head when they ask for money. These boys, however, are not as persistent as other street kids. They don't clutch at my clothing and follow me for blocks with their hands out demanding money. They induce guilt with their compliant acceptance of my repeated rejections, and it breaks me down. I begin giving them candy. No cash, I rationalize. Candy won't attract the attention of other street kids who would swarm me.

"Thank you," they say in unison and return to their shoeshine boxes without a backward glance.

I ask their names but can't pronounce them. Instead I resort to my social work days and give them "street" names. There is Ayaz Gol, Mr. Bakhsish, an expert at begging for free tips; Moheb Ullha, Mr. Ten Dollar; Ahmad Jamshed, Mr. Meat; Jahed Ahmad, Mr. Gigolo (because of his cool sunglasses); Jawed Ahmad, Mr. Nike (he had a windbreaker with the company logo); and Abdul Sabor, Mr. Chocolate, because of his love of Snickers bars. They thought they were about thirteen but could not say for sure. They did not know their birth dates. Their parents died in the civil wars.

After a few days all the boys except Mr. Chocolate stop accepting candy from me. The sweets upset their empty stomachs, they explain. I had not considered that and take them to lunch instead at the Herat Restaurant. This one time, I tell them.

We enter the restaurant and sit at a new glass table. Bro takes the boys to a corner sink. I watch them, small, thin youngsters in baggy, filthy clothes and tattered sandals, patiently waiting behind grown men to wash their hands. I watch them shake their hands dry and walk back to our table. I watch them sit down. They look at me expectantly. Through Bro, I order beef kabob and rice for us all. Uneasy at first, the boys begin talking among themselves. Laughing, they puff out their cheeks as if their mouths are full.

"What are they saying?" I ask Bro.

"They are debating who will eat the fastest when the food comes."

I suspect the humor hides how hungry they are. They will be this hungry again tomorrow and the next day, and will look at me and wonder, Will he feed us again?

"Just this once," I tell Bro.

"Yes, of course," he says.

A large circular tray arrives filled with plates of beef, rice, and salad. Sitting ramrod straight, immobile except for their widening eyes, the boys watch the waiter distribute the plates with abandon across our table. When the waiter leaves, they look at me to start.

"Eat," I say and motion with my hand to my mouth.

They scoop the food with the fingers of their right hands, left hands on their lap. Rice flecks their mouths and occasionally they cough from eating too fast. Finally Mr. Gigolo looks up from his plate and lets out a long sigh. He tells Bro he feels guilty eating so much when others are hungry.

"He doesn't look all that guilty," I say and slap him on the shoulder.

"Your fathers would want you to eat," Bro tells him.

After lunch we drop them off at the Mustafa, and they resume their

positions by their shoeshine boxes, where they huddle against the cold
and the rush of legs moving past them. Once a week, I decide. Once a
week I'll take them to lunch. No more than that. I walk up the cracked
staircase to my room with Bro beside me. "We should get them coats,"
I tell him.

"Just this once?" Bro says.

"Shut up."

"In Islam, if anyone helps poor children, God will give him everything. If you help any of those children you will go to Mecca."

I snap open a warm beer I'd stashed beneath my bed. The cost of
beer has dropped to three dollars a can, a sign of progress.

"You should have children," Bro continues. "I can get a wife for you
if you become Muslim. It will take three days of study. You'll have to
swear on the Quran to Allah and swear off gambling and drinking."

I take a long pull from my beer. As a social worker I avoided poor
kids. They broke my heart. It was one thing to deal with some grizzled
dope fiend pleading for a shelter referral; it was another when grimy,
wide-eyed kids stood beside the dope fiend staring at you.

"I don't work with kids," I tell Bro.

January merges into February. My paperwork for an embed snakes
through the army's arthritic bureaucracy. I wait for e-mail from a public relations officer approving my request. Any day, the military assures
me, any day.

Tensions between the United States and Iraq intensify. As the troop
buildup in Kuwait continues, Kabul police stop and search vehicles at
major intersections, knotting up traffic for miles. Coalition soldiers
maintain a heavy presence on Chicken Street to protect Westerners.
Ragged pieces of paper, bearing scrawled denunciations of Americans,
appear nailed to the doors of mosques.

"You know Iraq and Afghanistan are Islamic," an Afghan traffic cop
tells me. He holds a Ping-Pong paddle with STOP on it. "This is a call
for jihad for us. Iraq doesn't want war."

The situation in the south deteriorates by the day. A gunman
wounds an associate of President Hamid Karzai; men in vehicles firing
rocket-propelled grenades ambush an 82nd Airborne Division convoy;
a mine meant for their father, a deputy police chief in Kandahar, kills
two children.

I try to fill my time at the Mustafa writing and filing stories and wait for my embed, enjoying a beer at night with other hotel guests, mostly aid workers, security firm contractors, and entrepreneurs seeking a fast buck in reconstruction projects. One contractor tells me he fought in the Balkans. He has guns and grenades in his room and plans to defend the Mustafa once the Iraq war "goes down."

"The hotel is like a maze," he says, sketching it out for me on a napkin. "Difficult to defend." He needs more grenades. "You can never have too many," he says. He is convinced that violence will sweep Kabul because of all the booze and whores coming into the capital in violation of Islam.

Bro removes his headphones and turns to me. "Shock a lock baby. Is that really the name of an American song?" He offers me the headset of the CD player I brought him from the States so I can listen.

"What do you think? Did God create man or did man create God so that God could create man to honor God with war?" the contractor wonders aloud.

"Wow," I say and open another beer.

A British reporter coughs and sips deeply from his own beer. "Fucking fecal dust, mate," he says.

"What?"

"You heard me. You don't see anyone scooping up after these donkeys, do you?"

"Wow."

"I got to go boom-boom," an Indonesian videographer says. He tells me that once when he covered a riot in Jakarta all he could think about was how bad he had to piss.

"Why do I have a bad feeling about you?" the contractor says to him.

Boom-Boom dashes to the bathroom as Wais, the hotel owner, bursts into the bar waving his 9-mm Glock. The Afghan security guards who normally man the front door follow behind with AK-47s.

"We got word from the U.S. embassy that the Mustafa is a target for terrorists," Wais shouts. An Afghan by birth, he was raised in New Jersey and talks like he's fresh out of Newark. "You can be pussies and leave, or you can stay with us!"

He turns around and runs up a staircase without waiting for an answer. I stare after him and order another beer.

"Wow."

"We should probably tell the boys to move their shoe boxes across the street, in case this place blows," Bro says.

"Shock a lock baby," I say and laugh.

"Did Wais call us pussies?" the contractor asks me.

"Yeah."

"If he can call me a pussy, then I want him to serve some fucking American food. I want a grilled cheese sandwich with pickles. Grilled cheese. That's all I want."

He looks after Wais.

"I want a grilled cheese, motherfucker!" He stares wild-eyed until his breathing steadies. "Sorry," he says. "Sometimes I miss the simple things."

"Shock a lock baby."

The boys, Bro, and I meet outside the Mustafa in the morning and get into Bro's van. We make the rounds of ministries as I had on my first trip. The boys sit beside me openmouthed, stunned to be in the presence of ministers. Never mind that the ministers wear clothes that haven't been washed in days and occupy windowless offices with broken furniture. For the boys, these weary men represent the epitome of authority.

If I'm to continue taking them around with me, however, they will need shoes. What they wear on their feet amounts to little more than strips of torn cloth held together by threads and laces. Bro and I walk with them to the bazaar. We all make our way down a muddy alley, taking large steps over deep puddles until we come to a shopkeeper selling used, Western-style sneakers.

"Good morning, Uncle," Bro says to the old man sitting near a wall of Adidas. The light of a BBC broadcast from a U.S. base in Kuwait relieves the gloom of the shop and illuminates holes in the walls.

"These boys need shoes," Bro tells him. "Together you and I can help them."

Bro raises his chin at me. I set the range of bargaining at three hundred Afghani, about six dollars. Bro explains my offer but lowers it to two hundred Afghanis, about four dollars. He winks at me. We are about to engage in sport.

The old man points to the back wall where small shoes hang from nails. I am distracted by a tank rolling across the television screen. Bro calls my attention to the shoes. I pick out a pair of white sneakers with thick rubber soles.

"What do you think?" I ask the boys.

"Very good," Mr. Gigolo says and looks at the other boys, who nod eagerly.

"How much?" I ask the old man.

"Six hundred Afghani," the old man says, about twelve bucks.

"No, Uncle," Bro says. "These shoes are not for the foreigner. They are for these boys who have no mothers and fathers."

"How much do you want to pay?" the old man says.

"Two hundred. I told you. For five pairs. One thousand Afghanis."

The boys listen. They look as if they expect to be disappointed.

"No," the old man insists. "Two hundred eighty for each pair."

"Uncle, you give to us for two hundred each. The boys will be happy. This foreigner will be happy. God will be happy."

"I won't be happy," the old man says.

"If God is happy, you'll be happy."

Bro offers him a cigarette and lights it for him.

"Marlboro. From America."

"Very good," the old man says and closes his eyes.

"Okay, two hundred each?"

"Okay," the old man says and exhales slowly with satisfaction.

The boys beam as he places the five pairs of shoes in a pink plastic bag. The image on the TV screen turns grainy. Soldiers fire rockets in a military exercise and the picture shivers. I watch the broadcast until I feel a tug on my pants leg. A man without legs sits on a skateboard and holds his hands up to me. A mine victim, I think, stepping around him. What money I have, I have spent on the boys. I am sorry for this man, but I won't dwell on him. I can do only so much.

"You all have your shoes?" I ask the boys on our way out.

One afternoon at the Herat, I ask the boys why they don't attend school. "We can't afford it," Mr. Gigolo explains. They need to earn at least one dollar a day to help feed their families. Bro knows of a school supported by the government that they can attend. Aschiana School for Street Children is a few blocks from the Mustafa. Its half-day classes are scheduled for the students' convenience. Those who make money hustling the streets in the morning have afternoon classes. The reverse is true for those children who prefer to work in the afternoon. The boys smile, liking the idea. They look to me to make a decision.

I don't like it. We'd have to buy them supplies—paper, pencils, book packs. I'm not here a social worker. I have responsibilities to my editors. And I will leave as soon as I complete my embed. What about the boys then? These boys aren't Maggot. I can't take them with me. We're getting too deep.

"Lunch is not enough," Bro says, noticing my hesitation.

I know that. Nothing is ever enough. "The boys understand I'm going home after my embed, don't they?"

Bro shrugs. "That is the future. For now you are here. You should not disappoint them."

"Okay. But remember I'm going. I always go. Where is this school?"

In the morning I buy the boys new socks. They raise the socks to their noses and then press the soft fabric against their cheeks, eventually deciding not to wear them so as not to ruin the fresh smell. They wear clean white shirts and brown pants. Their hair is slicked to one side and still wet. I give them green book packs that they sling over their shoulders. Then we all walk to the school, the boys strutting like sailors.

Children play soccer in the courtyard of Aschiana. Water drips from a rusted pipe that protrudes from a cracked, sun-bleached cinder-block wall. We follow an unlit hall to a small office. The director waves us in. I explain why we are here as Bro translates. He considers the boys, their solemn faces. He folds his hands on the warped table that serves as his desk.

"I have a plan to show you about study," the director tells them. "The challenge here is how to study. There will be no fighting, no bad words. When we feed you breakfast, you clean your plate. When you go to class and you're given a textbook, you put it back on the shelf when you are finished. When you are given an assignment, you complete it."

In another room I hear BBC radio reporting that the United Nations has issued a security alert to its personnel as the likelihood of war between the United States and Iraq increases. The director pauses and listens too. Then he continues.

"You are here for each other. You work together like brothers. You don't bring the bullet or the grenade to school. You don't write on the walls, carpets, or doors. If you work on a computer, you use the machine like it is your own. Okay, an important point I must make: If you miss three days of school, I will go to your family and ask what happened. If they give me no good reason, you will be expelled. Do you understand all that I tell you? Tell me about yourselves."

"Our fathers died in Russian time," Mr. Gigolo says.

"I am sorry. What do you like to study? Do you know how to write?"

"I know a little," Mr. Chocolate says.

"I like sports," Mr. Bakhsish says.

"Sports are good for your health. You give me your promise to attend school?"

The boys nod, still looking very serious.

"Here is an application form. I will help you to fill it out."

Bro and I leave to eat lunch while the boys complete their applications. We wander down Butchery Street where vendors sell slaughtered meat. Slabs of red meat hang from rusted hooks above bloody pools and heaped carcasses of recently killed sheep and water buffalo.

"All of this comes from Pakistan by truck," Bro says, pointing at the meat. "It's not good. The water is bad in Pakistan. The grass is not good. Sheep are not good. We should eat elsewhere and talk. I have a good story for you."

"What?"

"A friend of mine knows a former Taliban," Bro says. "This Talib, he's with the Northern Alliance now. My friend says this Talib can arrange an interview for you with one of Gulbuddin Hekmatyar's commanders."

"Hekmatyar? Where?"

"Lowgar."

Hekmatyar is thought to be behind renewed fighting in the southeast and the recent killings of a Red Cross worker and two U.S. Special Forces soldiers. He has aroused strong passions among Afghans in part because he is Pakistani. Many Afghans despise Pakistan for its prior support of the Taliban. Some think the Pakistani government continues to support them by ignoring Hekmatyar and other rebel fighters operating along the border.

Last week the hotel manager, Wais, asked a man who represented an aid organization and wanted to rent rooms for his staff, "Where are your people from?"

"Germany," the man said.

"Okay," the hotel manager nodded, shifting the handgun in the back of his pants to one side. "If they were Pakistani, I wouldn't let them stay here."

Support for the Taliban increases the farther south you drive from Kabul toward Kandahar, their spiritual birthplace.

"You know, at the start of the war here, Hekmatyar called for jihad against Westerners," I say. "He's offered a bounty for Westerners."

"I know this," Bro says. "Twenty-five thousand dollars for Westerners and sixteen thousand for Afghans working for Westerners."

We walk on silently, stones crunching beneath our shoes. Candles light up some of the vendor stalls. I watch a man sawing a knife against the throat of a wide-eyed chicken.

"All of Pakistan hates Afghan people," Bro says. "Why does Gulbuddin offer less for Afghans? I know as much as you. More. I am no different from you. It's because they hate Afghan people."

"If we do this, we'd probably go alone to a mud hut in Lowgar," I say. "Your friend and his Talib friend would stand to make forty grand. I don't know how they'd split it, but they'd kill us. Forty grand. We'd be dead."

"What is life? If they take our lives, so what? Then they can take nothing more."

"That's because we'd be dead, Bro."

We stop by a vendor, and Bro buys cigarettes. A boy plucks dead chickens, tossing the bloody feathers into a gutter.

"So we won't do this thing?" Bro says.

"No. I appreciate the idea, but no."

"We have to make a decision."

"We have. We're not doing it."

"It would be a good story for you."

"No. Let's get something to eat and go back for the boys."

Bro scowls, but then his face brightens at the sight of a small group of sheep scavenging in a pile of garbage. An old man taps them with a stick, urging them forward. Bro talks to him as we pass.

"He's from Parvān Province," Bro says, referring to an agricultural region north of Kabul. Melting winter snows have turned the farm fields there dark green.

"Those sheep, especially the lambs, make the best kabob. Not like Pakistan."

In March, UN weapons inspectors are withdrawn from Iraq, making war all but certain. In the mosques around Kabul, mullahs increase their calls for jihad against Westerners. The international peacekeeping headquarters in Kabul sustains a rocket attack. It's all the talk among the vendors and shoppers in the downtown bazaar.

The boys meet Bro and me at the Mustafa for our morning walk to school, as we have done since they enrolled. This morning, however, I tell them our routine must change. In the future they are to stay away from the Mustafa. It's a target for terrorists, I explain, more now than ever. Beginning tomorrow they will meet us farther down the street.

A thin tension begins insinuating itself throughout Kabul. An invisible moat surrounds the city. On this side of the moat a degree of order and an emerging Western influence—commerce, restaurants, bars. On the other side are the bandits and the fighting that still rack the country. In the south the situation worsens. An Afghan Military Forces water tanker is blown up, costing a soldier his legs; another 82nd Airborne Division convoy is ambushed; five employees of an aid organization are robbed at gunpoint.

So we wait. Not for war. No one thinks there will be war. Not in the traditional sense of the Taliban opposing the Northern Alliance on the battlefield. No, we wait for something else. We don't know what, but we feel it draw nearer each day as the war in Iraq becomes inevitable.

Bro tells me that when he prays at the mosque, the people around him chant, *Al jihad fe sabeelillah:* "For every person it is a duty to join jihad for God." Maybe what we're anticipating will happen on Chicken Street, where Westerners can order American-style club sandwiches with french fries.

"Conflict is good for us," Wais says above the sound of a U2 disc playing in the basement cafe. "I was full when there was fighting. It's good for reporters, it's good for egos. Think of the money hotel owners are making in Kuwait."

His Afghan staff listens to war news on NBC. They talk bitterly when they hear about civilian casualties near Kandahar, stopping when they see me. "How may we help you, boss?" they ask.

A humanitarian aid worker I know starts an exercise group in the Mustafa. She and five other Americans and British walk a mile each afternoon. But lately unseen assailants have been pelting them with rocks, and they begin exercising inside.

"Hear anything about Iraq?" we ask one another every night, often in the dark because power is erratic. "Anything?"

Nothing. Not today.

"We fight," traffic cops tell me when I walk the boys to school. "We are not afraid of war. Iraq and Afghanistan are Islamic together. It is jihad for us. If not Iraq, we'll fight for something else."

The cops hold my hands.

"Friend, today you are our guest. Tomorrow, trust in God, you will still be our guest. Who knows? Only God. Come, don't be afraid. When you come back from the school, drink tea with me."

Some days after school we drop the boys off in south Kabul where they live with relatives in mud brick huts off dirt roads swamped with sewage and pools of melted snow and stagnant rainwater.

One afternoon, Mr. Gigolo's uncle, afflicted with polio, invites us into his house. He asks us to sit on a heap of mildewy carpets. When his wife enters the room, she pulls a veil over her face and hurries out. I tell the uncle she can stay, but he shakes his head.

"She does not need another husband," he says, looking hard at me.

"I don't want to marry her."

"You have so much. Look at this," he says of his house. "She does not like it, but it is not up to her to like it. We can't afford better. She does not need you to tempt her."

Mr. Gigolo walks Bro and me back to the car. In the rearview mirror I watch him return to his house.

"I have five uncles," Bro says. "All of them are doctors. My father was a police officer and under Russian time was sent to Czechoslovakia and Russian universities. He has a diploma. The same can be for these boys. Every NGO needs people like this. With a job they would not live like this."

"That will take a lot more schooling than Aschiana can offer."

"We tutor them. After school. I will buy notebooks. I'll write a mathematical problem. One plus three plus one equals what? After this we'll start with the alphabet. I'll write small letters and big letters."

He suggests we give the boys kilos of rice and beans when they do well on tests to provide them an incentive to stay in school. Not bad, not bad at all, but what can I do? I don't speak Dari. We agree that I will critique their English lessons.

Shops close and voices fade, leaving only my dreams to intrude on the long, silent night ahead. The war starts sometime in my sleep. In the morning I walk downstairs for my worthless cup of Nescafé. On the kitchen TV I see smoke billowing out of Baghdad. Bro, hotel staff, and hotel guests alike huddle around another TV and watch the same footage replayed over and over. According to the news bar at the bottom of the screen, nearly one thousand U.S. soldiers have descended on villages in southeastern Afghanistan. All UN offices and embassies in Afghanistan are closed. International flights into the country have been canceled.

"I wasn't leaving anyway," a contractor says.

"Our Afghanistan is all destroyed," Bro says. "Now Iraq will become like Afghanistan."

We hurry downstairs and look for the boys. People pause on the sidewalk at stores selling televisions and watch the news reports. Others press radios to their ears. The boys run over from across the street and all talk at once. They don't have school. What do I want them to do?

"Go home," I say, watching police stop cars and search them. "There's nothing we can do today."

"If it stays quiet come back tonight, and we will have a class," Bro says.

"But there is no school," Mr. Gigolo complains.

Bro shakes his head. "You should not miss school," he says.

At night Bro and I meet them in a back room of his brother's pharmacy next door to the Mustafa. Bro helps them write composition assignments, which they then read aloud to us. He corrects their math and science. He asks them history questions he thinks of at random. I go over the English alphabet and simple phrases.

"What does this word mean?" Mr. Gigolo asks, showing me a slip of paper with "pizza" scrawled across it.

"Where'd you get this?"

"I find on the street."

He hands me a tattered Dari-English dictionary he has from school.

"I can't find."

I know pizza won't be in the dictionary, but I thumb through it anyway, reeling off words in Dari for him to repeat in English.

"*Tarafik.*"

"Traffic."

"*Kuchi.*"

"Nomad."

"*Sasej.*"

"Sausage."

I try to explain what a pizza is. He asks me if I'll buy him a bicycle.

"Wow, where'd that come from?"

He laughs. I tell him perhaps, if he does well in school. Then the other boys ask me. I wave them off.

"First, your studies," Bro says.

A girl stops outside the pharmacy and stares at us through the window. I ignore her until I realize she isn't going away. I look at Bro and tell the boys to keep reading their lessons while we go outside.

"What is it?" Bro asks the girl. "Those boys are Aschiana students. They are studying. Don't disturb them."

The girl tells us she was in Aschiana but not now. She lives with her mother and goes with her to do laundry. She had completed Aschiana, but her reading and writing skills were not strong enough to attend high school. Instead Aschiana enrolled her in vocational training at a beauty salon. She studied there for two, maybe three months, but she had no money to buy a makeup kit to start her own business. Her mother would not let her look for work anyway because she does not believe a woman should work. So the girl stays at home. Always with mother. Never alone on the outside.

"I was happy in Aschiana. I hope to have a good time in the future, but I don't know the future."

A woman calls to her, and the girl steps away from us. The woman walks quickly to her side and grabs her hand.

"She has a nervous problem," she tells Bro. "I spent all my money for a doctor, and still she is sick. Don't listen to her."

We watch them walk away. I know that girls were banned from schools under the Taliban regime. Fewer than one million Afghan children attended school under Taliban rule, and most of those were boys. Roughly six million Afghan children, including two million girls, attend school now. But not this girl. Many conservative families still keep their girls home.

"I should have done something."

"Like what?"

"I don't know, but she wanted help."

"There is nothing you could have done if her mother did not want it," Bro says. "Even without the burqa, some women continue living under the Taliban."

Above a shelf of vitamins, a television provides the latest war news. Earlier tonight Wais and a contractor got drunk and shot up the hotel after they convinced themselves that insurgents had somehow infiltrated the lobby. They fired their guns whenever they heard someone walking up the stairs. So far no one has been hurt.

Bro and I and the boys take a break and watch news footage of exploding bombs, tanks rolling through deserts, guns blazing. My thoughts are on Mr. Chocolate. He has started skipping classes to earn more money. Tonight I tell him I will no longer buy him lunch. He storms out of the pharmacy and stares through the window at us, arms crossed, and watches us complete the night's lessons.

Afterward I invite the boys to my room, where I have some peanut butter cookies. We creep up the stairs. Wais and the contractor have left. I check my e-mail as the boys share cookies. I have a message from a U.S. Army public information officer. I am to report to Bagram Air Base in forty-eight hours. I will then be flown to Kandahar for an embed with the 82nd Airborne Division. Finally! I pace the room thinking out loud about what I should pack.

"What about the boys?" Bro says.

I look at them and they stare back at me. The boys ask Bro what's wrong. He tells them. They put down the cookies. They turn to me. Mouths crumb-smeared and full but still.

I give Bro money to buy them lunch and replenish their school supplies while I am gone. I don't know how long that will be.

"Stay on Mr. Chocolate, Bro."

"And then you'll leave Afghanistan when you come back?"

I close my laptop.

"We've talked about this, Bro. I told you and told you. How many times did I ask if the boys understood I'd go?"

"They are boys. What do they understand?"

"For now I am here."

Bro smirks. I pop open a beer.

"Take me with you," Mr. Gigolo says in his halting English.

"Stop it."

"Please."

"Stop."

He leaves the room. The other boys look after him and back at me. I wave them away, and they follow him out. Mr. Bakhsish pokes his head back in and hands me the tin of cookies. I finish my beer.

"They are only boys, Malcolm," Bro says again.

"Bro, this is exactly why I didn't want to do this. I told you. Stay on Mr. Chocolate."

"He'll be back in school," Bro says. "He is no different from the other boys. He likes you for the lunch but also for you too. Why is that such a problem for you?"

To take my mind off the boys, Bro suggests we drive to the house where he was born and lived almost twenty years. It was destroyed in fighting between feuding Afghan forces in the mid-1990s. He likes to visit the house once a week, he tells me, because it still feels like home to him. I agree to go and follow him out of my room to the van.

We drive only a few blocks when his mobile phone rings and he is soon caught up in heated conversation. I stare out the window at sheep standing in the shadows of bombed buildings and pawing at the ground. Bro slows on a dirt road. He clamps his phone between his right ear and shoulder while he parks at the foot of a rutted alley. Lines of sewage slice veins into the hard, dry ground. The refuse gathers in a gutter beside the road, and I turn away from the stench blowing through my window and unlock my door.

Bro shouts into the phone, stepping hard on the parking brake as if he would push it through the floor. I get out of the sliding side door, stepping over dank puddles, and wait. I immediately miss the van's heater. The cold afternoon air blows down my back until I am chilled and humbled, my hands clasped tightly under my chin.

Kabul is divided into fifteen districts. We have stopped in Shasha-
hid District, better known as District Eight. It is an area of Kabul that
remains heavily damaged after almost thirty years of war. District Eight
has received scant attention from international aid organizations, despite massive reconstruction projects in other parts of the city since the
Taliban fell from power. Broken walls of two compounds line the sides
of a pitted alley and stretch toward a street far ahead of us. A black mule
at the opposite end stares at me, its back heaped with a bundle of dry
wood. Bro slams his door shut and walks up beside me. He wipes dirt
off his blue jeans. He crosses his arms stiffly against the tight leather of
his jacket and scowls, tugging at his mustache.

"What's going on?"

"That was my father," Bro says, sounding angry and hurt. "He
wants to know why I make my mother-in-law sad. My mother-in-law
is angry with me because she says I don't talk to her. We all live together.
Why do I have to talk to her? There are too many people in our house.
My father, mother, uncle, cousins. I have two sisters, four brothers, my
wife, my two girls, my mother-in-law. We lost our first house in the
civil war after the Russians left. My uncle and mother-in-law lost their
homes in the civil war. It is too many people in our house. Last night
I slept on the roof, and my wife now is mad with me because I left her
alone with our two daughters."

"Sorry."

"It is not your fault."

Bro lights a cigarette. I look at my watch. I leave for Kandahar
tomorrow and need to buy supplies. We are near a bazaar where I can
buy bottled water, toilet paper, food, and other things I need for the
trip. We walk down the alley, stopping at a neglected wall of one of the
compounds. A rusted scrap of tin hangs from a strand of rope barely
covering a large hole.

"It was a big door here," Bro says, tapping the tin with his fist. "Our
front door. When we left here we locked this big door to prevent stealing. But this area was being bombed with rockets, so what good is a
locked door?"

"Habit to always lock a door when you go somewhere," I say.

"Yes," Bro says, "silly habits."

Two barefoot girls peak out through one side of the hole. Their eyes
widen at the sight of me.

"My name is Khalid," Bro says. "I lived here when I was small. I'm showing this American journalist my old home. Let us in."

When I hear Bro say his given name it hits me that, although I have known him for three years, I don't know his last name. Small talk about our families marked our early days of driving around Kabul together. Slowly we revealed enough bits and pieces of ourselves that eventually conversation flowed and awkward silences filled with trust.

We have been working together long enough that our drives through Kabul spark mutual random memories.

Malcolm, remember this road is where I flat the tire on my old van? Look, it is paved.

Bro, wasn't this the checkpoint where we had tea with Northern Alliance soldiers after they stopped us for being out after curfew? It's been torn down.

Malcolm, remember all the UN briefings you had in this hotel? Today they have art exhibits here.

Bro, look, they've turned our old lunch joint into a movie theater.

So after all this time how could I not know his last name?

"Sarwary," he tells me when I ask. "Khalid Ahmad Sarwary. Why?"

"Never knew."

Bro pushes the ragged piece of tin aside and ducks through the hole. I follow him, emerging into a large courtyard filled with rubble. I hear myself breathe and feel stones crunch beneath my boots. The girls stare at me, hands to their mouths, and step away. The remains of a wall divide the courtyard in half. Empty rooms stand exposed. Scrawny chickens run in circles and leap into the exhausted air, talons outstretched as if clawing at some invisible menace. The girls watch us without speaking, sentient waifs marooned in this desolate place.

"Here was our house. I was born here. Here was one wall," Bro says. "My brothers and I had rooms on this side, my sisters and mother and father on the other side."

Bro steps through a gap in the wall and walks toward the crumbled remains of one large room. Splintered beams slant to the floor from the broken roof. Straw hangs from the ceiling and shrieking birds drop out at our approach, snapping the air with their wings. A cat scrambles through a gaping hole in the back wall.

"This was our sitting room. We always stayed here. That night when the rockets came, we ate in the downstairs right below this room. One rocket came here where you see the cat. It was eight o'clock at night, June second in 1995. Afterward we left this place and went to my grandfather's house."

Silence settles over us, disturbed only by the wind. I think of the many times I have joined Bro's family when he has invited me for dinner. On those occasions, I usually arrive at his house in downtown Kabul at sunset. I take my shoes off at the front door. I follow him into a brightly carpeted living room where I join his father, Aziz, and four brothers. His mother and two sisters stay in another room. We sit on the floor and Bro's father unrolls a black rubber mat. Then his brothers carry platters of pasta, bread, rice, carrots, chicken, and lamb into the room from the kitchen, arranging the food on the mat. We eat with our fingers, scooping food with the bread.

After the meal we drink cups of green tea. Then I excuse myself. I have work to do before I sleep. I put my shoes on, and Bro hands me my jacket. His father shakes my hand and kisses me on both cheeks.

"You are a member of this family," Aziz always says. Then, smiling, adds, "We thank you for being so good to Bro."

Never during the countless meals I've shared with Bro and his family, amid all the banter about politics, questions about America, and the laughter that follows my efforts to speak Dari, had I ever considered what it must have been like to have a rocket crash into their home while they were enjoying a meal together.

My excuse is I didn't know. But as I look at the smashed walls of Bro's boyhood home, I feel I should have. I think of them here giving life to these disintegrating ruins.

"There was a big tree there," Bro says of a vacant spot near the destroyed living room. I'm not sure where to look. The area he points at doesn't have even one brick left to define it. "I played hide-and-seek. You know this game? It was a very thin tree and not good for hiding, and I always got caught. My father pretended not to see me. Then he would grab me. Now the tree is gone."

He walks to a well. I peer over the side. Dead branches and bricks fill the cracked bottom.

"After six months, when the fighting was stopped we came back and saw all was destroyed," Bro says. "There was a dead body by this well. There was another dead body in the kitchen. We took them out and put them in the cemetery."

We wander over to a square patch of bare ground. Feces lies in piles and a pair of torn black shoes fill a hole.

"This was my room," Bro says. "Now it is a bathroom for refugees."

We move to the center of the compound. The two girls stand a short distance away. Smoke rises out of a room that Bro says was the bedroom of one of his brothers. A blanket covers the door. Pots and pans have been stacked to one side. I see fingers wrap around the edges of the blanket, pulling it back slightly and revealing a narrow oval shape of pitch-black darkness. Neither of us can see who is watching us.

"Hello," Bro says. "How long have you lived here?"

"We've just come," a woman's voice answers.

"Where are you from?"

"Parvān Province," she says. "But we came here from Pakistan."

"How long were you in Pakistan?"

"Since the Taliban."

"How long will you stay here in this house?"

"At least four months."

"Do you have a man?"

"Yes, but he is crazy in the head."

Bro approaches the blanket and holds out some money worth about two dollars. A soot-blackened hand reaches around the blanket, hesitates in the light, and then takes the money.

"We do not have the money to rebuild here," Bro says, walking back to me. "After all was destroyed, we moved to Gabolsarag one hour from Kabul. There we stayed until war in our village between the Taliban and the Northern Alliance. So, my father returned us to Kabul and rented the home of another family. Then my uncle and his family come. Then my mother-in-law. We take them all in because they lose their homes in the fighting."

"I'm sorry."

"It's not your fault."

I don't know what else to say. I look at my watch. I tell Bro I need to buy things for my trip to Kandahar.

"I'm disappointed I not go with you to Kandahar," he says.

"I am too. I don't have the money to fly you down. Another reporter I know recommended a translator there, so even if I could afford to buy you a ticket, I couldn't justify the expense to my editors of paying you with somebody already down there."

Bro shakes his head and smiles sadly. "Malcolm, it is not about money. You are my friend. I look around me, and then I think of going home tonight with too many people in our house. I think it would be better to go to Kandahar with my friend. I think tonight if it's not too cold I'll sleep on the roof again. I don't care what my wife says."

He looks toward the demolished sitting room and his eyes redden, and I feel tears in my own eyes. Annoyed, I wipe them away. "Sorry," I say.

Bro looks at the ground, raises a hand, waving me off. I pull the hood of my coat low over my forehead against the wind and walk to the hole in the wall. The two girls flee to either side of me, creating an invisible aisle that draws me forward as if I am some spectral force threatening to engulf them. I pause at the hole, begin to look back at Bro, hesitate, then push the scrap of tin aside and step through.

I see so much devastation every day in Kabul that the numbness I feel is not so much painful as business as usual. It won't be the same working with Bro or eating dinner with his family after today. Their lives have assumed a modest yet incomprehensible strength that dwarfs and intimidates me. I look at my watch again. Bro walks up beside me.

"Where do we go?"

CHAPTER TEN

The Lord's Army

MARCH 2003
Kandahar

A swing dick Florida cop, now a reservist with the army's 82nd Airborne Division, who to his everlasting goddamn regret has been put in charge of me, leans toward my face.

"You'll experience all the fears, concerns of being a combat soldier," he says. "Just be ready to run when you hit the ground."

Blond hair, lean, eyes aflame. A corporal. Twenty-eight, engaged to a gal back home. "Can't leave a widow if you ain't married yet," he says and laughs. All gung ho, ready to burn, baby, burn, burn, burn! He points to a brown desert map overlaid with tangled blue flight lines, wind patterns, and other swirled graphics. The 82nd hopes to route Taliban insurgents in Helmand Province to a mountainous area called Bagrama. Means nothing to me. Swing Dick says we should be moving out in the next twenty-four hours.

"When we're loading up in a bird, I'll fill you in," Swing Dick says. "This is going to suck—cold, wet, and miserable. Be situationally aware. As a cop, I go into dark buildings and know there's some shit in there trying to kill me. That's bad enough. But I'm more nervous about this op. Way more."

He is right to be. Kandahar has become an increasingly dangerous place. Attacks against Afghan army units are commonplace. Humanitarian aid organizations retreat in spite of the dire need for assistance. The roads are unsafe. Banditry is epidemic.

I follow Swing Dick out of the tent into a light rain. An army soldier pauses and stares at me.

"Is there something wrong?"

"They don't see American civilians very often," Swing Dick explains.

He wonders what we will do with all the enemy dead. Bring them back to Kandahar? Bury them where they fall? He shrugs, doesn't know.

"We'll be spread out so we all can't be taken out in an ambush by snipers. Make yourself as short as possible. Get out of the kill zone. It's harder to kill a moving target. The enemy will have the tactical advantage. Questions?"

"I need to make a call," I tell him.

"That's not a question."

"May I make a call?"

"Your wife?"

"I'm not married."

"Divorced?"

"Manner of speaking. We weren't married but lived together and then separated."

"Kids?"

"Manner of speaking. I'm helping out some orphans in Kabul."

"Little hajjis? You shitting me? How old?"

"I'd guess thirteenish."

"Old enough to shoot."

I kneel in the dirt, twist the antennae on my satellite phone until I get a signal. I don't know why I told Swing Dick I was checking on the boys. None of his business who I'm calling. They've done well. I'm proud of them. Let him think they're my kids.

I had considered writing a note to them with some final words of wisdom. Behave yourselves, work hard, attend school. But I thought somehow I'd jinx myself if I did that and get myself killed in the field.

So I said nothing.

"I think we go out tomorrow or the next day, Bro," I shout above the static-filled line. "How're the boys?"

"The boys ask about you," Bro says. "They miss you. They want to know where you are and are very worried for you. Should I tell them anything?"

"Tell them to do their homework."

"What else?"

I don't say anything. I remember one hot afternoon we played soccer. We bumped against one another, laughing, kicking at the ball. Finally the heat drove us back to the Mustafa, and we stopped for kabob. The boys teased me for my use of an asthma inhaler. I thumped my fist against my chest, the Afghan equivalent of giving them the finger. They howled with laughter and my unexpected taunt, holding their stomachs, unable to eat. When we finished, we stopped by the pharmacy, and Bro and I went over their homework. We gave them bus fare and waited with them until a bus stopped. They got on and waved, and I waved back and then turned around feeling suddenly empty at the thought of going to my room alone after such a full afternoon.

"Tell them I miss them," I tell Bro.

Swing Dick awakens me at midnight. I hear a Humvee idling outside.

"It's on," he says.

He drives us to the tarmac. Soldiers run in from every direction. They throw bulging backpacks on the ground and load pallets with boxes of ready-to-eat meals and jugs of water. Trucks and Humvees spit dirt and stones from beneath their wheels as they swerve past me. Commanders shout against the wind. Their faces turn red in the cold; their words are blown away behind them. Dogs are yipping at the confusion.

"When we land, you run out of the bird and stay down," Swing Dick tells me. "When I get up, start moving. If we receive fire, we'll flatten them. You see something no one else sees, you need to let me know. Things get real exciting, real scary, real fast. Just think, we were drinking Cokes last night and it might have been our last night on earth. You reach those kids of yours?"

I shout yes, but he can't hear me above the noise. I can't stop shaking in the frigid desert air. Soldiers examine their weapons: Vietnam vintage M16 rifles, mortars, .50-caliber machine guns.

"Everybody on the mountain is bad," an army chaplain rails at us. "Shoot them in the face and keep moving. When we go into a village, use common sense. You were trained to shoot. If you shoot make sure it's a well-aimed shot. The guys on your left and right need to go home. Everybody understand?"

"Ooh-rah!"

"The Lord is looking at you! He's telling you one fucking thing: Don't forget what they did to three thousand innocent Americans in New York. The enemy is not innocent. They should be fucking dead. We owe the Lord some hajji bodies. You don't have to kill everybody, but if you shoot, kill them! Kids included! When you jump off, think of those twin towers falling. The Lord said blessed are the peacemakers. We want to bring peace to these knuckleheads, but they want to keep fighting. Holy Father, you are deploying us, and we are ready to respond!"

The blades of a dozen Chinook helicopters begin rotating, slowly picking up speed until they blur and we are consumed by swirls of grit and stone amid the *thump, thump, thump* of the spinning blades.

"That's an awesome display of firepower," the chaplain shouts. "Now imagine you're a Taliban and you hear this. Knowing thirty or forty guys on each bird belong to the Lord's Army, and they are coming to kill you."

Swing Dick hefts his pack over his shoulder and grips my hand.

"If we don't come back . . ." he begins, but the noise around us consumes the rest of his words, and I can only nod. I am confident that beneath the gruff talk, he will cover my ass if he can. If he wants to talk to me like a pissed-off football coach, that's all right. Neither of us wants to die.

We run together toward a Chinook loading ramp, the chaplain still raving behind us.

The Chinook lands in a green wheat field, and the propellers fill my ears with wind. I hear the hoarse, indecipherable shouts of soldiers running out of the bird. Swing Dick looks at me and bolts out, and I follow, throwing myself on the ground beside him. The sixty-pound flak vest I wear crushes my chest. Black Hawk helicopters circle above boulder-strewn mountains and loose bursts of gunfire. The Chinook rises into the air behind us. The aroma of damp grass reaches my nostrils. Insects hum. Donkeys graze. My ears feel plugged with cotton. An officer tells us to walk on the dirt ridges that separate the fields instead of tromping through the flattened wheat. I pick up my pack and the soldiers grab their rucksacks and military rifles and I follow them, the ground crumbling beneath our boots.

"Follow me," Swing Dick says.

Soldiers fan out, some stopping to piss. Every noise is amplified—the crunch of gravel, the splash of urine, the gusts of cool air.

"What's that hajji doing?" a soldier asks, and points to some Afghan farmers and their children watching us from beside a stone wall.

"Eating a fucking rock looks like," Swing Dick says.

The farmers leave the wall and follow a path into the sheep-speckled mountains. The Black Hawks cut loose with another blast. The children look up and duck and then turn their scared eyes toward us.

"Most of the people we see will say they don't know nothing," Swing Dick says. "They offer you tea and smile. Then we'll look in a woodpile and find a weapon. Your hajjis'll be no different."

Hours have passed since the Chinooks landed, and the grunts are no longer animated by the pastor's rallying cry to kill, kill, kill the enemy. We've walked miles in the open on desert land spotted with scrub brush and have seen nothing. Not one thing. Not a lizard in the sand, not a bird in the sky. Not a Taliban insurgent. Nothing but our shadows on the ground. Finally we stop at a mud brick village compound.

"Johnson, file up the gully to the door."

A sergeant, followed by a handful of soldiers and me, pounds on a towering green metal door. The rest of the battalion remains on a ridge above us. The sun glints off their weapons pointing down at the village.

A stooped village elder pulls open the metal doors. Children cluster around him.

"We were asked to come here to make sure your village has no weapons," the sergeant says. "If we find any, we will confiscate them. With your permission we'd like to go through the houses of this village."

The old man looks at the guns pointing at him from the ridge.

"We do not want to involve ourselves in trouble," the old man says. "This is our request; we need a well in this area. We just have buckets. In each house, but no water."

"I can't promise, but I'll put it in my report. We're here to support the government and make sure things are safe," the sergeant says.

He steps aside. A few grunts stay with him while others move to some thatch-roofed huts. They shine lights from their guns along sagging wood shelves packed with tin plates, bowls. Worn carpets cover the mud floors. Sacks of rice slump against the shelf posts. Goats run out of a hut. The old man spits, watches the soldiers break locks with the butts of their guns. Their Afghan interpreters kick in doors.

"Stay the fuck back!" a soldier shouts above the noise of wailing babies.

"Anything?" the sergeant asks.

"We found two AKs."

"Some families keep weapons for security," the old man says. "I don't know who they belong to."

"We have to confiscate any weapons we find. We'll have to take those."

"Vehicle coming, Sarge. Got multiples in it."

"We need to search it. Tell them if they don't stop, they get shot."

The soldiers stop a car riding low on its wheels. About a dozen children fill the open trunk, legs dangling over the bumper. They stare out at us, puzzled. One girl begins to cry.

"Anything?"

"No, Sarge."

"Tell them fucking thank you."

"Where do we go next?"

"The other side."

We look across a dry riverbed at a series of compounds, hazy in the afternoon heat. Bald, cave-pocked mountains rise up behind, their shadows slowly advancing.

Four soldiers ask to test fire a .50-caliber machine gun.

"Take the tree on the right," a soldier says.

"We got permission to test fire this bad boy?"

"I radioed in," the first soldier says. "Waiting to hear back."

An old man leads a donkey along the riverbed. He wears the black turban often associated with the Taliban. He walks slowly on the uneven sun-bleached stones, keeping one arm out for balance.

"I think these folks live the way people lived in Genghis Khan's time," a soldier tells me. "I don't think much has changed."

"Command says hold off," the soldier with the radio says. "Too close to the village."

"Too bad," the soldier behind the gun says. "It's a good weapon to fire."

A long line of villagers watches us, hands cupped over their eyes. We try to pick out the old man we saw moments ago but cannot distinguish one person from another. Children run every which way toward other compounds.

"They're warning everybody," Swing Dick says. "We won't encounter the enemy today."

We search villages for another day, but the enemy never appears. We find some military rifles but encounter no resistance.

"Helen Keller would have heard our birds," a soldier complains on our flight back to Kandahar the next morning. "Why would the hajjis have stuck around? They wait until we go. Figured out a method to this madness?"

"No," I tell him.

"I don't think there is one. Fucking hide-and-seek."

In the morning we fly to Orgun-e, a desolate spit of a forward operating base near the Pakistan border routinely subjected to rocket fire. So frequent are the attacks that the soldiers refer to them as JARA: just another rocket attack. For reasons no one understands, Thursday nights are particularly active.

I consider a plywood mural dedicated to a Sergeant Steven Checo in the mess hall while I wait to go out on a night patrol. The mural depicts a fire-strewn orange landscape roiled in flames, merging into black, snow-capped mountains under a red sky. Black birds form Vs in the sky, and a diminutive Humvee carrying a helmeted soldier drives up one of the mountains.

The world is a lesser and lonely place with you gone, begins a dedication to Checo, written in tight black script on the hot orange paint. *It is also a better place overall for you having been here.*

Soldiers seated at rickety, picnic-style tables spoon mashed potatoes and beans off cardboard trays. The dim interior provides relief from the desert heat outside. A television drowns out conversation with the latest news on the battle for Baghdad.

"Do you remember when he was killed?" one soldier asks another when I ask about Checo.

"Yeah, same night one of our other guys got hit in the head."

"December?"

"I think you're right."

"They flew his body out in a Chinook. I know that."

Everyone who knew you for the wonderful person you were cried when they heard you were gone.

"There's Camp Vance, one of the tent cities at Bagram Air Base, named after a guy who died. Then you got Disney Drive. I think Disney was the first soldier at Bagram to die."

"Some of the guys are angry everyone's talking about Iraq. I'm happy no one's paying attention to us. Iraq keeps my family distracted from what's really going on over here. It keeps them from worrying about me."

"There was a CIA guy. What's his name? He was killed in Mazar."

Those of us who knew you, knew you died doing what you loved and wanted to do.

"They're naming a school after a Special Forces soldier that was killed in Helmand Province."

"South Helmand?"

"Maybe."

"When was that?"

"Don't know."

Guys file out of the mess hall, toss their trays in a trash bin. A few pause, squinting before they step from the shade of the door into the sun.

You will always be remembered as a great leader, a great soldier, and most of all a great friend.

"These names, the memorial to Checo, they're tombstones really. Reminders. After the past two weeks, with all the rocket fire going on, I wouldn't be surprised if there were more memorials. Newly arrived guys don't even know who Checo was."

"I remember when it happened."

"December."

"I think you're right. I think so."

Swing Dick comes up behind me.

"Put your helmet on. You ready?"

Night patrol.

I sit in the back of a Humvee dubbed "Cock" with Swing Dick and two other soldiers. Swing Dick scans the horizon with night vision goggles. He hands them to me. The night is transformed into a green lunar landscape. Rocks, sand, birds. I see everything. A lunar landscape head trip.

"We own the night," Swing Dick tells me.

In the morning a Chinook will fly me back to Bagram Air Base and Kabul.

"I just want to go to Outback," Swing Dick says. "I'd get a rare, rare steak and those mashed potatoes with skin."

"I want a milk shake from Dairy Queen," I say.

"Shit, you'll get a beer."

"And then another and another."

We laugh, drive on a dirt trail. No headlights, seeing in the absolute dark only by the goggles. We stop at a mud hut sentry post. Afghan soldiers offer us tea. Grunts call the Afghans by the acronym FEW: fucking early warning system. They radio in when insurgents launch attacks.

"See nothing?"

"No, everything good," an FEW man says.

The silent night creeps up on us in small gusts and loose rocks rolling down inclines. Stars hang in the sky like ornaments. A grunt takes out a deck of cards. Candlelight shadows dance against the walls of the mud hut. The grunt shuffles the cards. I hear them snap and slide until a sound like a high-pitched whistle penetrates the hut, and I look outside as if this was nothing more than another natural aspect of an Afghan night.

A grunt throws me down.

"We got a rocket coming in!" he shouts.

"Shit, shit, shit!"

"From the ridgeline!"

Feet scramble behind me. The rocket lands wide of us, but the explosion sends waves beneath my chest. I don't move. The earth below me slowly settles. I hear a trickle of stones falling somewhere.

"Bad shot," the grunt says, getting off me.

"We got more!" another soldier shouts.

I stumble up and lurch back toward the hut, arms out for balance, suddenly dizzy and unable to control my legs.

"Four incoming!" a grunt shouts into his radio. "Two from the south, two from the north!"

"Those fucks!"

We drop to the floor of the hut, hearts racing. Wait. Wait. The sound of our breathing, clouds of air from our mouths. Shit. Nothing. Shit. Wait. Nothing. I am aware only of how still everything is.

Slowly one soldier at a time stands up. Still crouching slightly, we walk carefully as if we're afraid we might awaken someone. The grunts fire an illumination mortar to light the valley below us. A lone dog flees from the expanding light, a boy running behind him. Swing Dick aims his gun but doesn't shoot. After a moment he lowers his weapon.

"Whoever's doing this is rolling, dude," he says.

In the distance, a mullah begins chanting. An FEW man offers me another cup of tea. Swing Dick waves him away.

"The FEW probably collaborate. I hate the United States, want tea? Fuck them."

He raises his gun again, but the boy and dog have vanished into the dark. Shouldering his weapon, he sits down. He glances over at me. "You going to see those hajji boys of yours?"

"Yeah."

"Remember. Anyone above the age of six, dude, is a potential enemy."

We return to Kandahar the following day with the intention of catching a flight to Bagram the next morning and going from there back to Kabul.

While I wait for our plane to Kandahar, I fumble with my sat phone until I get a signal. I dial Bro but he doesn't pick up. Soldiers wander past and nod at me and duck into their own tents. Humvees rumble off beyond the dust. I try Bro again, and this time he answers.

"I'll be back in Bagram in the morning," I tell him. "Can you get me?"

"Yes," he shouts into the phone. "The boys will be happy to see you."

"It will be good to see them. And you."

"But they will be sad because they will know you will be leaving."

"I'm sorry."

"It's not your fault."

My military flight back to Bagram is delayed twenty-four hours. I use the wait to accompany a civil affairs patrol to an elementary school near

Kandahar. We stop on a dirt road overlooking the school. The sergeant leading the patrol steps out of a truck with her rifle, and the children swarm toward her. I watch them and wonder how my boys are doing.

"*Salaam alaikum,*" she says brightly, "Peace to you."

American soldiers in the two trucks behind her strap on black goggles. One of them sits behind a machine gun, turning his head left and right.

"Hey, smile," the sergeant says to her troops. "I'm doing some hearts and minds stuff."

"What?" one of the soldiers says.

"Smile," she says, smiling.

The soldier shrugs, faceless behind his opaque goggles. He starts unloading small blue shoulder packs filled with notebooks, pens, and pencils. About 170 boys attend classes here.

"Wait, wait, wait!" the sergeant shouts. "I have to make a speech."

The soldiers hesitate, urge the children to form two lines, and motion them to stand still. Dust settles on their hair, faces, and clothes as they wait for the sergeant to speak. The air is thick with grit.

"American children about your age donated a dollar each to their schools so you could have these packs," she says, facing them. "So you could have a chance to be whatever you want to be. Good luck."

The principal of the school, Mohammad Yousuf, translates. The children approach the trucks two at a time for their packs.

"These will just end up in the bazaar," a soldier mutters.

"I'm here to help people," another soldier says, waving the children into a group. He tells them to hold their packs and smile.

The sergeant snaps a photo. She then follows Yousuf along a narrow path to a partially charred building. Faded rugs cover the cracked patio. The empty storage room we enter smells of stale smoke. Blackened wood beams lie broken on the dirt floor.

Recently six rural schools for boys outside Kandahar have been vandalized by suspected Taliban and al-Qaida sympathizers, a departure from the more common attacks on schools for girls. Storage rooms at some of the schools like this one were torched. No one seems to understand why the schools became a target or what the attacks meant.

With Yousuf sitting beside her on a faded rug, the sergeant takes out a scrap of paper from a pocket on her flak vest and asks him what happened.

"They came at night, March ninth or tenth," says Yousuf. "They stole biscuits donated to us by the World Food Programme. They stole copies of the Holy Quran and our registry books with the addresses of all of our teachers."

The sergeant nods, taking notes. I think of my boys, grateful they live in Kabul away from this madness. An Afghan guard fingers his Calvin Klein cap, looks off at the dust storm racing across the desert valley below.

"There have been threats to teachers," Yousuf says. "Night letters that say our noses and ears will be cut off if we continue teaching."

"Have any students dropped out?" the sergeant asks.

"No. When they are not here, they spend the rest of their time harvesting poppies."

She makes a face, shakes her head, writes.

"Where do they put the night letters?"

"In front of the school on the wall," Yousuf says. "They are the result of ignorant thinking. If the children don't get the opportunity for education, the ignorant thinking will continue."

The sergeant closes her eyes as if she is pained by the thought. Dust rises out of the valley, obscuring one of her soldiers who is standing guard on a rock ledge.

"What would you like us to do?" she asks.

"When soldiers are assassinated, there is an investigation," Yousuf says. "If many teachers are killed, no one knows. Nobody will ask why they kill teachers. Teachers are the foundation of the country."

"My job is to put in wells," the sergeant says. "I can't promise anything."

"We are even afraid of men who lead animals when we bicycle home," Yousuf says, referring to the shepherds who herd goats and sheep along village streets. "We don't know who to trust."

"I can put in wells," the sergeant says again. "But I can't promise I'll find water."

"These guys don't have respect for schools. They are doing this all over Afghanistan. They are a big problem. These guys don't want a new generation with new ideas. They want to keep us in darkness."

"The best I can do is forward your concerns along," the sergeant says.

She stands up and walks to the trucks, gets back inside. A few children stand on the path with their dust-covered packs. The sergeant smiles, waves out the truck window. Clouds of dust billow from the lurching trucks, shrouding Yousuf in an abrasive mist. I am aware that soon I will leave my boys behind just as we are leaving him behind. But at least they are in Kabul, I comfort myself. At least they are in Kabul, and they'll have Bro.

Alone with the children on the rocky road, Yousuf raises a hand one last time before we lose sight of him.

I return to Kabul late the next day. The following morning, I reorganize my backpack for the flight back to the States. Bro grabs my duffel bag, and I get ready to leave the Mustafa for the last time. I give him four hundred dollars to feed the boys and provide for their schooling. In Afghanistan that should last awhile. I heft my backpack over a shoulder. Afghanistan's only airline, Ariana, departs Kabul International Airport for Dubai in an hour. From there I'll fly directly to New Jersey and then to Washington, D.C.

Before I close the door, I look back into my empty room. Cot, desk, chair. Red rug, dirty white curtains. Two broken space heaters. Not one indication that I've been here four months. Nothing but dust and dead flies. I know the boys wait for us outside by their wood shoeshine boxes. I have all sorts of fanciful schemes in my mind for when I come back. Opening a school of my own. Getting the boys into a university. Flying them to the United States. I don't ponder the practical problems I would face if I put my plans into action. Simplify, I tell myself. Tell them you'll return in August. I could say June, July, September. It doesn't matter.

"It's all crap," I tell Bro without letting him in on my thoughts.

I close my door and walk downstairs, running past Bro a few things I want to tell the boys: stay in school; study hard and you'll have a shot at becoming doctors, lawyers, even the president of Afghanistan. The choice is yours.

Bro shakes his head.

"Their future is no longer your worry," he says. "Your leaving was never their problem. It was your problem."

Outside the Mustafa, Bro gets in his car and unlocks the passenger door. He turns on the radio. The BBC reports that a minibus has been destroyed by a mine, leaving eighteen dead in Kandahar. I squint at the spring sun glancing off the freshly washed sidewalks.

Gazing across the street and then to my left and right, I look for the boys.

Nothing but merchants and a glut of honking taxi and bus drivers.

"Where are they, Bro?"

"Get in. You'll miss your plane."

"Where are they?"

"For them, you are already gone," Bro says. "Come, you will miss your plane."

PART THREE

Inshallah

CHAPTER ELEVEN

Looking for Mr. Big

MARCH–APRIL 2004
Islamabad, Pakistan

I wake up, television's on. CNN special report.

I look at the clock—4:00 a.m. Damn. I crashed at eight thirty last night. Must've forgotten to turn it off. Jet lag sucks. I arrived in Islamabad two days ago. Once again Iraq has eluded me. My editors instead asked me to report on the growing presence of the Taliban in Pakistan.

I wipe my eyes, prop myself up on my elbows, struggling to focus on the TV.

" . . . key al-Qaida leader may be surrounded in the stark, mountainous border region separating Pakistan and Afghanistan . . ." The anchorman continues, ". . . possibly Osama bin Laden . . ."

The words sink through the foam of my half sleep, ". . . possibly Osama—"

What!

I leap out of bed, grab my wallet for a phone number. Dial. Pace. Roll my press ID in my hand. Pace.

Possibly Osama bin Laden. Jesus!

"Yeltsin?" I shout into the receiver when I hear someone pick up. "Yeltsin, that you?"

"Yes, sir, but that is not my name, sir."

Yeltsin drives for me. He is old school, his work ethic influenced by the British Raj. Only I call him Yeltsin. His real name starts with a *Y*. When we met, I considered some nicknames that would remind me of his actual name should I forget it. I decided the last name of the first post-Soviet Russian president, Boris Yeltsin, would be a good prompt. But now I remember only Yeltsin.

"I'm sorry to wake you, brother."

"No problem, sir," Yeltsin says. "You are our guest."

"CNN says they might have found Mr. Big."

"Mr. Big, sir?"

"Osama."

"Bin Laden?"

"The same."

Mr. Big. A character from the television series *Sex and the City*, whose name has somehow been applied by journalists to bin Laden. He'd be pissed if he knew. I doubt *Sex and the City* fits his criteria for jihad-family values friendly television.

I look at the TV again. The smirking anchor can't help himself. "Exclusive," he keeps repeating. He likes that. Bastard. From one journo to another, screw you. Cut to an interview with Pakistani president Pervez Musharraf, the army general who came to power in 1999 in a bloodless coup. "In the mountainous tribal regions between the Pakistan and Afghanistan borders," Musharraf says, "Pakistani troops have surrounded—"

"Osama?" the interviewer interrupts.

"A leader," Musharraf says, voice soft, flirtatious. Eyes passive behind his round glasses. He knows we know who he means.

"Mr. Big, you bastard," I say for him.

I imagine thousands of reporters streaming onto the street outside my window and, like me, screaming at their drivers and translators on static-filled mobile phones to pick them up. Listen to them running. Their car engines rev, rev, rev. I see them peeling out of stone parking lots into the quiet Islamabad night for a glimpse of the monster in chains. The sequel to part one of the story of the century: *September 11, 2001: America Attacked;* part two: *Osama bin Laden: The Perpetrator in Chains.*

God will read that story. Careers will skyrocket from that story. No more humble freelancing for me. Straight to the top, baby!

TERRORISM DIED TODAY, the headlines will scream.

WE GOT BIN LADEN.

SWEET, SWEET REVENGE.

Everyone but me. I am dead to the world. I cradle the phone against my ear and check my e-mail. Dozen of frantic notes from my editor:

Have you seen the CNN report?

Where's your story?!

What are you doing?

Sleeping, dude. But I'm moving now.

"Yeltsin, how close can we get to . . ." I squint at the television where an arrow points to a red dot on a map north of Islamabad where Pakistani troops have surrounded Mr. Big. "South Waziristan?"

"Peshawar."

"Pesh what? Where's that?"

"Near South Waziristan, sir."

"Where?"

"South Waz—"

"Okay, okay. Is that close?"

"Yes."

"Good. We'll go there. How far?"

"Two-hour drive, sir. You want to go?"

Let me think, let me think, goddamn it! Leave now, get there at six. Who'll be around? Nobody. Military checkpoints will stop us. Some areas have curfews. We'd be stuck on the road, sitting in the car for hours. Not me. Rather deal with this when it's light out and the checkpoints have closed. Christ, I'm tired. Leave here at seven, get there at nine and find somebody to talk to. Makes more sense.

I sit on the bed, feel woozy. Too early for this adrenaline rush.

"We'll leave at seven. Go back to sleep Yeltsin."

"Thank you sir, but that is not my name, sir."

"Sorry," I say, closing my eyes and falling backward onto the bed. "Go to sleep, brother. Bye. Oh, Yeltsin?"

He has hung up. No matter. Nothing important. I am wondering again where the hell is Peshawar.

Three hours later I see Yeltsin in the stone-strewn parking lot across from my hotel. He waves and hurries to his taxi to pick me up. Very proper, this Yeltsin. Very deferential. The strictures of a defunct British colonial ethos imbued in his soul. By the time I reach the street he has pulled up to the curb and opened my door, ushering me in with a hand. The whole nine yards.

"Good morning, sir," he says.

"Morning. Did you have a good night?"

"Very good, sir. And you?"

"Good. Sorry to wake you."

"No problem, sir."

This *sir* business has got to go. However, I have priorities to consider before I deal with his formality. Yeltsin and I met two days ago. I got here about 6:00 a.m. after a twenty-four-hour flight from Washington, where I had stopped to get my visa at the Pakistan embassy.

A guard there had taken me into a small, brightly lit, bare room. A short fat man walked in seconds later. I showed him my passport.

"What do you want?" he asked me in the curt voice of an officious bureaucrat.

"I came to apply for a visa. I'm here to see…" I dug into my pocket and handed him a slip of paper with a name that a colleague had given me of a guy who could expedite the process. The bureaucrat led me into another room. A photograph of Musharraf hung on the wall.

A man wearing a turban stopped us. He ranted at Bureaucrat in a language I didn't understand. After a hot exchange, Turban turned to me.

"You should not be in here. This is a sensitive room. An intelligence area. But it is too late. You are here."

He hurried me into yet another room where I was introduced to a woman who gave me several visa applications to fill out.

"You will have to sign in with the External Publicity Department when you arrive," the woman said. "They will advise you about your security and give you details about where you can travel within Pakistan."

I nodded, answering questions on the forms: name, purpose of trip, where I would be staying, passport number. The previous day I had met with a man who once worked with former Pakistani prime minister Benazir Bhutto. He had advised me about the EPD.

"They'll tell you the purpose of the EPD is to help you with your trip and to provide you information for your protection. That is not true," he said, standing up from his desk and looking out his window at the nearby park. "It's so they know what you are doing. Pakistan has the outward look of a democracy, but you should know it is a military dictatorship. Nothing is what it seems."

When I finished filling out the visa applications, I handed them to the woman, who sorted through them and then tossed them into a tray without further thought.

"Come back tomorrow. Your visa will be ready then."

Bureaucrat, seated in an outer office, showed me to the door. He stopped me as I was about to step outside.

"You can pick up your visa here because you have seen this room. This door will be closed. Knock like this," he said, tapping the door twice with his fist and then tapping it twice again after a brief pause. He asked me to try.

Tap-tap. Tap-tap.

Satisfied, he let me go.

The next morning, Bureaucrat met me at the door.

"You're late," he snapped.

"Sorry."

I remained by the door, determined to knock the secret knock. I tapped twice before he waved a hand in my face.

"No need. Please come."

I followed him into the woman's office. An assistant gave me my visas. I signed a form, acknowledging I had been told to check in at the EPD. Bureaucrat took me back out into the lobby. He seemed visibly relieved to know he would have no more dealings with me. He suggested restaurants I should visit and what tourist sights to see in Islamabad.

"The weather will be perfect," he said. Then he became agitated again. "Be careful," he whispered. "All the phones are tapped. Nothing is as it seems."

In my rush to leave Washington, I forgot to make a reservation at an Islamabad hotel. When I arrived, all the hotels were full from an influx of tourists for a cricket tournament between Pakistan and India, the first such competition after years of feuding between the countries.

I picked one of the many taxi drivers mobbing me at the airport and asked him to take me to whatever hotel he thought might have a room. He dropped me off at a real dive. The room was alive with bugs. Standing on the filthy brown carpet, my ankles were ravaged in seconds by invisible monsters leaping off the floor. I could only imagine what the bed would be like.

I unrolled my sleeping bag and was about to drop it in the tub as a makeshift bed when it occurred to me to turn on the water. Cockroaches scrambled out of the drain. Nothing I can do about it, I thought. I mounted a warped chest of drawers where the bugs couldn't get me. I tried to sleep, curled up like an infant until morning.

When I awoke, I needed to send an e-mail to my editor. I walked outside, neck and back painfully stiff, and waved for a taxi. A small yellow car did a U-turn and pulled up beside me.

"Good morning, sir."

The driver stepped out of the car and opened the door for me. He was a slim, dark-haired man with a ruddy complexion. I asked him to take me to an Internet cafe.

"Yes, sir. Where are you staying, sir?"

"A dump."

"I know a good hotel. Grace Guest House."

I shook my head. The taxi driver from the airport had told me he knew a good place, too. Look where I ended up. These guys have friends, family working in hotels. They drum up business for their relatives. Probably get a cut for every guest they bring in.

The taxi driver passed an Internet cafe and turned down a residential street.

"Where're we going?" I asked and glanced at my watch. I really needed to send the e-mail. My editor was a twitchy guy, who got twitchier if he didn't hear from you as he watched every minute pass and considered the money being outlaid for overseas travel.

The driver pulled into the driveway of a large, bungalow-style house. Palm trees rose above it and a water sprinkler sprayed the dark green lawn, over which a second-floor deck jutted, casting long cool shadows.

"Grace Guest House, sir," the driver said.

We went inside and the receptionist showed us a large room. A ceiling fan hummed. The bed was made up and the sheets turned back. I walked across the spotless tile floor to the bathroom and turned on the bathtub faucet, ran my fingers through the warm soothing water.

"You are the man," I told the taxi driver. "Check me in. I'm going to be working here awhile. You need a job?"

"I'll drive for you, sir, no problem."

I stuck out my hand.

"What's your name?"

■ ■ ■

Yeltsin and I drive into Peshawar by midmorning. Mud and burlap vendor stalls and restaurants glut the narrow streets, a dusty hovel. Pickup trucks and dented automobiles swerve around one another, jockeying for position. Sandaled pedestrians ignore the traffic and walk against it in unceasing waves that give no quarter and reduce movement to a crawl.

Trapped in this congestion, Yeltsin and I listen to the latest news of the South Waziristan offensive cackling from his makeshift car radio, a black square of spare electronic parts that amazingly produces sound.

South Waziristan comprises the area west and southwest of Peshawar, forming the most volatile part of Pakistan. Not under the direct administration of the Pakistani government, South Waziristan is virtually autonomous.

In their search for Mr. Big, about six thousand Pakistani soldiers have descended on the tribal lands, scouring for al-Qaida fighters, bombing, burning, and bulldozing the homes and belongings of those who are deemed collaborators—or who are merely uncooperative.

The army has met stiff resistance. Hundreds of soldiers and tribal fighters have been killed. Many of the tribesmen battling the army are former mujahideen, who, in the 1980s, were actively recruited by Pakistan and the United States to resist the Soviet occupation of Afghanistan. They came from all over Central Asia and settled in the tribal regions. They married, had children, and wove their way into the local culture. To many Pakistanis, it is not the soldiers who are martyrs but the Waziris fighting them.

Tribal tradition forbids a host to turn over a guest to an enemy without a fight. So if a "high-value" target is indeed hiding in South Waziristan, he can count on serious backup from tribal leaders.

In the chaos of the bazaar, I ask Yeltsin to take me to a restaurant. I have not eaten since last night. He suggests we find a hotel first and eat there.

"Peshawar," he explains, "is very sympathetic to the tribal leaders."

"I'm hungry," I insist.

"They don't like the West," he says.

"Too bad. I'm hungry. They don't like Musharraf because he does America's bidding. I understand, but I'm still hungry."

Yeltsin shrugs. "As you wish, sir," he says.

He takes my hand and pulls me along the congested sidewalk. We enter a kabob shop. A man stands behind a grill and cuts strips of beef. We sit at a round table and shoo away dogs, skulking for scraps. A waiter stops at our table.

"Why are you with this man?" he asks Yeltsin.

Yeltsin says nothing but his face reddens. The waiter looks at me, clears his throat, and covers his mouth. Without expression, he turns away.

"He won't serve us," Yeltsin whispers, his face clouded with anger and embarrassment. "I told you we should go to the hotel. You are not welcome here."

I watch the waiter studiously ignore us from where he stands behind the kabob grill. My stomach growls.

"Fine, you win. Let's get a room," I say.

"Yes, sir."

Yeltsin and I stand up to leave. A large man blocks our way and motions for us to sit back down.

"Please. You are our guest," he says.

He snaps his fingers and the waiter walks over. His blank expression does not change as the man orders us green tea.

"Why are you here?" the man asks.

"Journalist."

"American?"

"Yes."

"Ahh."

He sips his tea, then introduces himself as Malik Nadir, an elder in the Afrirdi tribe. He left South Waziristan the day before because of the fighting.

"The whole area is boiling," he says.

Nadir digs into his pocket for a mobile phone and jabs in a number. Speaking quickly to the person on the other end, he hands it to me.

"My cousin. I told him to speak English," Nadir says. "There is fighting. Drink your tea and listen."

I hear static, indistinct voices, and the sounds of explosions. A frantic-sounding voice shouts, "Eight, nine helicopters are firing over houses. Helicopters firing inside the compound. Also using RPGs. Heavy artillery."

The line goes dead. I hand the phone back to Nadir, the sound of gunfire fresh in my ear.

"We never had a problem with Osama bin Laden," Nadir says. "We're a target."

He adds sugar to his tea. Men at other tables watch us. A ceiling fan turns from a breeze blowing through an open window and then stops.

"Osama bin Laden was a rich man who devoted his life to jihad. He was not against the Americans but the Soviets. Yet America targeted him and he became anti-American."

The men seated around us nod. The waiter washes dishes listening to Nadir.

"When the Soviets left Afghanistan, the Americans left too, and Osama bin Laden took over. Now the U.S. calls him terrorist. Why is this?"

"Well," I say with some hesitation, "the attacks of September 11th—"

Nadir cuts me off. "You don't have proof. If he is responsible for those attacks, he is not a good person. If he is not responsible, he is a good person. We don't know this."

The other men approach our table and stand behind Nadir. I feel not threatened but confused. I don't know where to begin. If they question the September 11th attacks, what can I say? What can anyone say?

They start talking at once. I turn from one to the other and get dizzy from the bombardment of words.

"You say Osama bin Laden is al-Qaida. That is not a name we know. We say he is with jihad."

"Israel was responsible for your September 11th to give Americans an excuse to attack Muslims."

"What is a terrorist? Who is Osama bin Laden? He is not here."

"Osama bin Laden is no longer the issue. If he is killed, the jihad will not end until Americans stop killing Muslims."

I raise my hands. The men cease talking as abruptly as they began. They watch me. I lower my hands. Yeltsin follows my hands as I drop them to my lap. He watches me, as do the other men. I still can't think of anything to say. I know that, with the blessings of the United States, the Pakistani army has been bombing, burning, and bulldozing the homes and belongings of those deemed collaborators or merely uncooperative.

I can't read Yeltsin's face. He pushes his chair back and stands with the men. For a moment, his gaze toward me is indistinguishable from the other intense yet blank stares I fend off. I am not the West, I insist to myself. I am a reporter, one man, and all I want is to eat.

Yeltsin steps back and turns toward the door.

"Yeltsin, where are you go—"

He turns to me in a rage. "My name is not Yeltsin! Yasin. Yasin. I am named for Abdullah ibn Yasin, an ancient teacher of Islam!"

He lets out a long breath and collects himself.

"You don't understand. Osama bin Laden is not a person," he says, "but a symbol of resistance."

"I'm sorry."

I had not realized how I had offended him. Neither had I appreciated how furious Pakistanis are toward the United States. The men around me are all too aware that it is at America's bidding that the Pakistani army carries out this campaign. The resentment inevitably flows back up the chain to the president of Pakistan and beyond to Washington. For these men, and Yasin too, I am the United States.

"You do not need to apologize," Yasin says in a taut voice. "You are our guest, sir. We should find you a hotel and something to eat."

At night we listen to the radio. Yasin and I will return to Islamabad in the morning, where, according to the radio, a massive protest against the government's military operations has been planned.

The South Waziristan offensive has begun to lose its luster. The high-value target has been downgraded to a Chechen commander or a local criminal who may have escaped from the tribal lands through a series of tunnels. One senior government official concedes there never had been proof that a key terrorist was in the area.

The hotel loses power and the radio shuts off. Yasin and I sit in the dark. He lights a cigarette, and I watch the end flare and fade. Dust sifts through cracks in the window. The fan turns from a hidden breeze. I lean back against the wall and close my eyes. No Mr. Big, I think. No glory. No end to scraping by as a freelancer.

"They will never catch Osama," Yasin says as if he reads my thoughts. "The man maybe, but not his spirit."

He inhales and the cigarette crackles and for a moment lights his face before he fades back into the darkness of the room. Yasin had been right earlier. I didn't understand. Now I do. Osama has assumed a proportion much bigger than himself. I was chasing a phantom in the hopes of achieving my own moment of immortality, while he had long before reached his. No wonder he eluded me.

A girl closes the kitchen door. I hear pots against a table and a woman's voice mingling with the sound of birds.

"Do you want tea or a cold drink?" Mullah Abdul Rashid Ghazi asks me.

"I'm okay."

"Please. You are my guest."

"Okay."

He shouts toward the kitchen. I shift my position on the red-carpeted living room floor and lean against a fat pillow.

"You asked me if I knew the meaning of *jihad*," I say.

"We have different chapters in the Quran," Ghazi says, wiping his glasses on the sleeve of his kameez. "Some of these chapters deal with marriage, prayer, all walks of life of Muslim society. Also there is the chapter on jihad. What do you think it means?"

"A call to arms."

"With no reason?"

"I don't know the reasons."

He nods, looking at me. I sense a question coming but keep quiet. I met him by chance at the Markazi Jamia Mosque in Islamabad where he teaches Islam. He was sitting on the floor in a bare room. A sign on the wall read, BE ALWAYS JUST: THIS IS THE CLOSEST TO BEING GOD FEARING.

Ghazi showed me dozens of classrooms where small, thin boys studied the Quran on wooden tables that came no higher than their ankles. The boys rocked back and forth on their knees, chanting long verses until their voices squeaked and they ran out of breath. The rhythm of the words rose and fell, drifting outside the classroom into stone corridors strewn with sandals.

We saw students studying English, geography, computers, and science. On the balcony of the second floor, I looked over a courtyard filled with leafy trees and bright flowers, where other students completed assignment in the sunlight.

When we had finished walking the school grounds, Ghazi invited us to his home. We drove through narrow streets to the end of a dirt road where his small concrete-block house stood in shadow. As we got out of the car, he asked me if I understood the meaning of jihad. Before I could answer, his mobile phone rang. We walked to the house while he answered, his hand gripping my elbow.

"Jihad starts with yourself. There is something in me that tempts me to do bad things. When I want to control that, it is called jihad, because I am defending the good in me against the bad. It is in support of something the bad wants to oppress. From that place in yourself, jihad moves to a level of killing."

A boy brings us a tray with three glasses of 7-Up. He sets the tray on the floor, and Ghazi reaches over and puts a glass by my feet.

"In Islam, the killing of innocent people is forbidden. You're only allowed to fight someone who has come to fight you. You are allowed an offensive defense. Do you understand?"

"I think so."

"Sometimes I don't think my English is very good."

"It's very good."

"Thank you. If you are worried about yourself, don't be. You are our guest. You have done nothing to justify an offensive defense."

We sip our 7-Up. Yesterday I attended a demonstration against the government. All of the protesters accused Musharraf of killing Muslim women and children at the behest of the United States in South Waziristan.

Their anger fed upon itself, and as the crowd grew, their rage was passed from one person to the next like a virus until it exploded around me. One minute the relatively empty streets spread benignly toward downtown, the next I was enclosed in a mob.

"Murderer!" someone shouted.

Yasin tried to push them away. I was struck from behind and fell, fending off kicks. Yasin picked me up and pushed me through a cluster of outraged faces. We ran into the first place that offered shelter, the Markazi Jamia Mosque. I expected the protesters to follow us inside, but they did not. Silence instead descended around us.

Thinking of that moment, I turn to Ghazi.

"If someone sees me as representative of the United States and they think the United States is a threat to them, couldn't they justify killing me?"

"People ask me, 'What should we do? Can we kill the Americans?

Can we kill the British?' No, it is forbidden in Islam. You have come as our guest. How can I harm you?"

Ghazi's brother walks in carrying a baby. He smiles at me, pressing a hand over his heart, and enters the kitchen.

"That was my son he carried," Ghazi said. "He's one-year-old."

"How many children do you have?"

"Three boys, one girl."

I take another sip of 7-Up. Ghazi finishes his.

"You don't like your cold drink?" he asks.

"No, it's good."

"Why are you not done?"

"I'm not that thirsty."

"What is your purpose here?"

"To get different perspectives of what people see happening in Pakistan. As a journalist, that's what I do."

"Is that your honest answer?"

"Yes."

"I don't think so." He folds his hands and looks at his lap. "You know," he says, "when hatred increases, people are not terrorists, they are depressed. While in depression people do these things you are talking about. But when they are put in a place of justice, they would be convicted. They would be asked, 'The man you have killed, did you do so for your defense?' It is not allowed in Islam."

I finish my 7-Up.

"If the Americans kill my family and then call me a terrorist, am I a terrorist? No, I am an oppressed person," he continues. "I'd want justice. I'd want to have an offensive defense to protect my family. But I can't kill you, an innocent man."

"But if I am the American who is around, I become a target, right? For the perceived behavior of my government? Yes?"

"Not unless you have done something that requires an offensive defense. Let me say there are many depressed people. They are not terrorists. But they are depressed. Hatred in the Muslim world has increased manyfold because of American moves against Islam. So you should be careful. Depressed people do not think so clearly as we do."

I pick up my empty glass to put it on the tray, but Ghazi shakes his head.

"Leave it. You are our guest."

■ ■ ■

The operation in South Waziristan is all but over. Two weeks after it started, the conflict has become a liability for Musharraf. He can't show what, if anything, has been accomplished, other than forging closer ties with the United States, which doesn't give him a lot of street credibility among Pakistanis, who see the American-led war on terrorism as an assault on Islam. An audiotape purportedly from al-Qaida is calling for Musharraf's overthrow. He has begun hinting at a cease-fire.

My twitchy editor, calmer since the story turned out to be a false alarm, gives me permission to return to the States. In October, I will go back to Afghanistan to cover the presidential election.

Before I go, Yasin drives me to a small village outside Islamabad where I want to buy a pair of sandals to replace the worn pair I have now. On the way he picks up his brother-in-law Ahmad, who also needs shoes. We stop at a stall where a vendor sits cross-legged. Yasin points out a pair of leather sandals to me, but the vendor ignores us. Instead he stares off at a bulldozer with the Pakistani flag flying from it. He turns back to me and tells me that in time my beard will be as white as his.

"It all depends on how you live your life and how your life allows you to live. You are young. You have time. I don't."

He faces an unexpected upheaval that will age him further. He and the two thousand villagers he lives with here must move. The government has decided to tear down the village.

"This is not personal property," he explains, wiping his hands on his salwar. "This is government property. They can do with it as they please."

Ahmad shakes his head. He has on a suit and tie and, although he is only twenty-two, wears a serious expression that rarely shows emotion. An unemployed university graduate, he spends much of his time in parks, talking on a cell phone, trying to hustle work.

"This is what the government does," Ahmad says bitterly. "It fights for the United States in South Waziristan while it throws people out of their homes here. They have no jobs and now they will have no homes. Look how old he is. Is he terrorist? No, I don't think so."

The vendor doesn't know what the government will do with the land once the village is demolished. It doesn't matter. It is not his land. Therefore he is not owed an explanation.

"For years I was a peon in the British embassy," he says. "I cut the grass, carried the garbage. I am older now. I can't do heavy work. I hope where they move us to is not far."

Ahmad scowls, kicks at the ground. A few feet away, people line up outside a public call office to use the phone and look at CDs.

CDs are a new phenomenon here. I don't hear music, but the people are quite proud of the advancement. They show me CDs from India and Iran and try to give them to me. Ahmad offers five rupees, the equivalent of a few American cents, for a CD that has a cover illustration of masked men holding military rifles.

"No one in Pakistan can make a living selling CDs," he says.

"The government says leave this place, so we leave," the vendor says. "They might let us rent property elsewhere or they might not. There is great consistency in my life. My life has always been in the hands of others. I am still a peon. Buy some sandals. Please."

Yasin, Ahmad, and I follow a rocky dirt trail toward a small school. We stop outside a cramped compound near the school where a man squats on the ground, stirring coals with a stick. Thin wisps of smoke rise around him. He sets a teapot in the coals, presses his hands to his knees, and stands up.

"I am a jobless person," the man says. "I was a driver, gardener for the Jordanian embassy. My father worked there before me. I was appointed to the job when he died."

Tattered blankets seal off living quarters. Men and women slowly emerge, shuffling toward the fire. Coal dust and dirt fill the lines in their faces. A mangy dog walks around me, sits near the fire, and scratches its ears.

"I have an open mind about the government," the man says. "If they give us jobs, it is a good government. But if not, well, then it is not in our favor."

"It won't be in his favor," Ahmad says. "Count on it."

We leave and stop at the gate of the school. The teachers won't allow us in because the administrator is out. I walk around the school to another group of mud huts. A crude painting of a huge black handgun decorates the metal door of one of the huts. Bullets enter through a window above the gun. Ahmad rubs his hand over the painting.

"Who did this?" he asks a gathering of barefoot children standing behind us.

The children giggle, push and tug one another until they thrust a small, thin boy toward us. He looks about six years old, maybe eight. His hands cover his mouth and he looks away.

"You painted this?"

The boy nods. The other children squirm, watching.

"He is shy," Ahmad says.

"Osama," the boys says.

"Osama? The gun is for Osama bin Laden?" Ahmad says.

The boy blushes. Ahmad and the other children laugh.

"You can see our life here is very poor," a teacher tells me, pushing the children away. "People don't have money. If they shift us to another village and give us a plot of land, what use is that to us? We don't have money to build."

The teacher offers to organize a village meeting so I can hear more about the plight of the village. I tell her I'll attend only if my schedule permits. She gives me a look that shows she knows she has seen the last of me.

"This is not your function," Ahmad says, walking back with me to our car.

"Come," Yasin says. "There are no good sandals here."

Behind us I hear the children chanting, "Osama, Osama, Osama." They smile and wave at us. I hear Ahmad singing softly to himself, "Osama, Osama." Yasin glances at him but says nothing. Then he joins him.

"Osama, Osama."

"There is no future in Pakistan," Ahmad says. "No jobs. I am like these people. I can't afford a house. We have nothing. Only our heroes."

He looks at me, and I wonder if he is goading me for a reaction. To say something that will provide an excuse to unleash on me all his rage. I keep quiet, return his stare long enough to assert myself, and then I glance away to avoid a confrontation. Osama bin Laden. Ahmad's hero. His anger released in images of collapsing towers in New York. I am nothing but a rich Westerner. It's better I say nothing. I should go. Now.

Yasin picks up on my concern and motions me to the car and opens the door for me. I step aside so Ahmad can get in, but Yasin shakes his head.

"Please, sir," he says, pausing to listen to the children still chanting behind us, "you first."

CHAPTER TWELVE

The Mark of History

MAY–SEPTEMBER 2004

At home my mind remains in Afghanistan, but my friends and colleagues take scant interest in the war. I lapse into a lethargic grind of nine to five. Often I think of the boys. What are they doing? I wonder. How are they?

I lose my appetite, do little on weekends but take my dogs out. Like animals in a trance, we walk back and forth on our regular twenty-minute route, two, three, four times a day. When Monday comes I prepare for work again. I make coffee, shower, brush my teeth, feeling as if I am wading through water. I am exhausted by the time I get in my car.

I overhear talk about staff changes at the *Star*, what movies are playing, and whether or not the Kansas City Royals might finish the baseball season better than last year. It is the time of year for vacations, and people around me look forward to days on sunny beaches. I have no interest in seeing any movies, couldn't care less about baseball, and can't imagine I would last more than a day sitting around a beach.

People brush past immersed in the present, the task at hand, what's happening now. I am a bystander. No one expects my participation. They see me but understand, as I do, that I am not here.

Every now and then Afghanistan makes the news. In August seven people, including at least two Americans, are killed when a bomb explodes outside the compound of an American contractor helping to train the Afghan police. A spokesman for the International Security and

Assistance Force in Kabul, says a second bomb was found next to the explosion site, and French explosives experts defused it.

The bombing comes after warnings that the Taliban and other militant groups are planning major attacks in Kabul before the presidential elections. It is the deadliest attack in Kabul since September 2002, when twenty-six civilians died in a car bombing. I imagine the increased security that likely followed the explosion, sealing Kabul off from the rest of the country more than it already was and further isolating Karzai.

Then in September American air strikes against insurgents in Konar Province kill five civilians, including two children, and injure eight others. Twelve insurgents are killed. The U.S.-led coalition asserts that it knows of no civilian deaths.

I put down the newspaper. Outside my window a man hoses down the sidewalk, stepping aside for a couple holding hands to pass. They have no idea.

I type an e-mail to Bro:

I hear things are going to shit in Kabul. You okay? How is your father and family? Here things are fine. It rained like crazy over the weekend flooding some streets. Not as bad as Kabul. No mud slides. I've got to get new tires for my car. I've had two flats this week. The rain that knocked us all for a loop this weekend seems to have stopped. It's sunny today. How are the boys? Do you see them every day? Tell them I said hello and that a package of school supplies is coming for them. That's really about all, Bro. Get back to me and let me know what's going on as soon as you can so I don't worry. Yeah, yeah, yeah, don't let it go to your head. See you.

Bro must be on the Internet because he responds almost immediately. He writes that he is pleased U.S. newspapers covered the bombing, as it has always puzzled him how so few American journalists remain in Kabul, despite ongoing problems. He is working for the United Nations as a data entry supervisor for one division of the voter registration drive. He thanks me for a reference letter I had e-mailed to him and offers to buy me a beer the next time we meet.

"I am a big shot," he writes, and I imagine him laughing.

He says that he continues to work with the boys. Mr. Meat was hired as a janitor at the Mustafa but still attends school. Bro bought bicycles for Mr. Nike and Mr. Gigolo because they did well on some exams.

"Okay, Malcolm. In Kabul everything is going well except for stupid bombings. We're fine. No hurt in my family. Very silly all of this. And dangerous too. My father says hello to you and my wife too says hello. Okay, Malcolm, all the best. Your friend, Bro."

I reread his letter, relieved he still teaches the boys—and envious too. Has he replaced me in their estimation? Why should that matter as long as they have someone mentoring them? It should not, of course. Ego, I imagine Bro saying, silly ego.

I e-mail my editor and remind him of my interest in covering the October presidential elections.

"You're on the rotation," he writes back.

I e-mail Bro. "See you in October. Tell the boys."

OCTOBER 2004

I return to Kabul on a drizzly morning. Bro picks me up at the airport. He has a driver and sits in the backseat of a van in a black suit and tie, tan slacks, and shined shoes.

In my T-shirt and jeans I look like I work for him.

Bro tells his driver to take us to the Mustafa, where he has arranged a room for me. Billboards promote the eighteen candidates running for president. After I check in, we go into the restaurant on the second floor and order our usual—Nescafé for me, tea for Bro. The beer will wait.

I look out the window and watch children beg and offer themselves as "bodyguards" to Westerners. Horses and mules stomp furiously, straining at their bits, and drivers blare their horns as desperate waifs, competing with one another, roll into the roads, biting and punching, while stunned Westerners stand on the sidewalks staring.

"How are the boys?"

"For a long time I have not seen them," Bro says. "I don't know where they are. I am picked up from my home and dropped off every day. I have a driver as you see. What I am trying to say is I am very busy. But I will make time for you."

"But not for the boys?"

He looks at me, suddenly angry.

"I tried, Malcolm. I have a large family to support. Where were *you*?"

We sip from our cups. I consider offering him money to find them, but I realize this is not about money. It's about a moment lost, about disparate lives moving away from one another. What would I think about me if I were the boys? That the Westerner who dropped into their lives was an illusion, a mirage that never really existed. The food they ate at the Herat, the classes they attended at Aschiana, all of it, a dream.

"I'm sorry, Bro. I was just looking forward to seeing them. You did a lot when I wasn't here. I was the one who left. Thank you."

He takes out a cigarette. "Inshallah, they are safe. But, Malcolm, Afghanistan is not the same. For the first time Afghans will be able to choose their own president," Bro says, picking at a fingernail.

I can see he isn't really thinking about the historical importance of the election. Something distracts him. I soon find out what. Today is Bro's four-year wedding anniversary. He should be with his wife, I tell him.

"She is pregnant and grumpy."

I laugh and he offers a rueful smile. We sip bottles of a cold orange drink and watch the traffic build outside.

"The Taliban was in power when I was married so my wedding was very quiet," Bro says. "No music. If the Taliban hears music, they will take the husband to jail for ten days. After ten days in jail, then the husband can make honeymoon."

I notice his lapse into the present tense. After years of such a harsh totalitarian regime, it must be difficult to realize they're gone. I try to imagine an American cop arresting me for playing music.

"It was a very quiet time under the Taliban," he says. "You forgot how to talk to people, because you never went out. If the mullahs see people on the street, they beat them for not being in the mosque."

I wish I had visited here when the Taliban ruled so I could put in perspective the stories I hear about their regime.

"It was a very bad time," Bro says. "We were always afraid of the knock on the door. Now times are better, but we still have problems. Not all the people will participate in the election. They don't want this government because they say the Americans control Karzai. The south is very bad. The east is very bad. No one in my office wants to go there. There is no security."

"What about the Afghan National Army? The U.S. is training them."

"The ANA is garbage. The warlords will kill them. Karzai has no base. Just in Kabul people accept Karzai. Outside Kabul, the people say fuck Karzai. He has so many bodyguards when he leaves the palace he stops traffic all through Kabul. Fuck. He has no money. He spends all his money flying to U.S., India, Japan asking for money."

Bro reaches into his pocket and shows me a Thuraya phone from the regionally based company of the same name that provides satellite phone services to Europe, the Middle East, most of Africa, and Australia.

"In my office, the UN ordered six thousand of these at twenty-five hundred rupees apiece, but we couldn't use them because too many people were afraid to go out in the field and register voters. Twenty-five hundred rupees or this."

He puts the phone on the counter and curses.

"This election is about the future of Afghanistan," he goes on. "Karzai will serve for four years, but in Kandahar I don't think the men will let the women vote. Women there are prisoners. I take my two little girls to the zoo. I get them out of the house, see the city, not locked inside like in Kandahar. When they are older, I will let them choose their life. I will let them choose a love marriage, not an arranged marriage."

"You still think times are better?"

"Yes, they are better. I can choose these things now. Before, I cannot. But I cannot choose if I have no money. After the election I am thinking of going to Iraq. The UN people say they will need staff there. It will be good money, I think. Maybe one, two thousand dollars a month. What do you think?"

"I think you're silly."

He smiles, and I see he remembers moments we had together before. I want to laugh over old times and remove for at least a moment the weight of today.

"Seriously, Malcolm, I have to support my family. There is no job, no future here."

"That's why I worry about the boys."

"I know. It is very sad." He glances at his watch. "Boro. I should go."

"Yeah. Go to your wife," I tell him.

"I will ask my father to drive for you today. You will work with him?"

"Why not?"

"What is it you want to do?"

"Make the rounds, ask about the election. Ministries, you know, the usual."

Bro calls his father, Aziz, talks quickly, and snaps his mobile phone shut.

"He is coming for you, inshallah. You know *National Geographic*? I was watching it on satellite television. A man lived with a lion for twelve months. Twelve months. Imagine. By the time he left, he had tamed the lion. Afghanistan is like the lion, my friend. It needs more time, but when you have a family to support, time is limited."

Aziz and I zip along Charahe Searad Street downtown in his battered station wagon. The sight of a flashing red stoplight ahead of us stuns me. Desperate for roads, schools, hospitals, and housing, local authorities have somehow found power for one stoplight.

"This is reconstruction," Aziz mutters. "Stupid donkeys."

He has no regard for the presidential candidates and won't vote. "They promise more than they can possibly deliver," he says. "The donkey Karzai will win. Every province wants their man to be president. This is one hundred percent the problem. It's all bullshit."

"You sound like an American," I tell him.

A cop frantically waves his stop sign at us. Aziz dismisses him with an obscene gesture. "Stupid!" he shouts.

We dart into the intersection where we tangle in a knot of beeping cars whose drivers, like Aziz, had ignored the light.

"What are you doing?" the traffic cop yells, poking his head through my open window. Aziz reaches over and snatches the cop's tiny stop sign and slaps his face with it. The cop spins away, and Aziz backs up, squeezing us out of the jam by playing bumper pool with the other cars until he maneuvers onto a side street. Stopping, he gets out and examines the dents in his van.

"Stupid donkeys," he says of the other drivers.

We proceed to the U.S. embassy, a huge compound hidden behind high walls and rolls of barbed wire.

"Many donkeys work here," Aziz says. "Donkeys with guns. Donkeys with metal detectors. Donkeys with badges."

On the sidewalk, four-legged donkeys stand in the shade offered by spare trees, stacks of wood piled high on their backs. Impatient men strike them with whips. The donkeys bellow and then move on.

I want to meet with the American ambassador. I saw him in 2002 when the embassy was still in ruins and meetings were arranged in a matter of minutes.

Aziz insists the ambassador is too big an official for me.

"Watch," I say. "He knows me."

A soldier inspects my identification and pats me down rather too vigorously I think. He motions me through the gate, asks the reason for my visit, jots my answer down, talks into a radio, and tells me to wait.

The embassy has a fresh coat of white paint. New windows sparkle in the sun. Barefoot gardeners water red, pink, and yellow roses in lawns of dark green grass. Stern-looking men wearing neckties and carrying briefcases hurry past them.

After thirty minutes a woman in a black suit approaches me. She walks in a stiff, upright manner that must have taken months of practice with a plate on her head.

"The ambassador can't make an appointment with you."

"Why?"

"He's busy."

"So am I."

"I'm sorry."

She turns away, a smart pirouette that sends a few pebbles spinning off her high-heeled shoes.

"Losers," I tell Aziz as I get back in the car.

"Yes," he agrees, with an I-told-you-so look on his face.

Aziz was once a bureaucrat himself. As a teenager in the 1960s, during King Zahir Shah's reign, he was drafted into the army and forced to stand guard in empty lots across from the palace. He survived the ten-year occupation of the Soviet Union and the civil wars that followed its withdrawal in 1989. He hid in the basements of friends when factional fighting reduced Kabul to ruins and the commanders of local militias loyal to feuding warlords forced young men to serve in their armies.

"One day, the Taliban entered Kabul," he says. "I was working at a carpet shop. My boss says, 'We must turn over everything to them.' He leaves and then comes back and sees me sitting at my desk. 'What are you doing?' he asked. I said, 'I am waiting to hand over the office to the Taliban as you said.' He said, 'You stupid donkey, get out. Are you mad? They will beat you.' "

I half listen, distracted. If the boys no longer work in front of the Mustafa, perhaps I might find them at the house of Mr. Gigolo's uncle. I describe that part of Kabul to Aziz. He frowns trying to picture it.

Aziz drives through narrow alleys sluiced with narrow trenches cut by streams of sewage. Children run along the side of the car gleeful for this moment that has broken the monotony of their day. We stop by one house, but I don't recognize the family. We try another house, but again the wrong family. I struggle to remember where Gig's uncle lived but we get lost in dead-end alleys sunk in darkness. I sit in meditation while the car idles. The boys' faces swarm my mind. Finally, I shake my head. I just don't remember.

"Let's go," I tell Aziz.

Driving back downtown we turn onto Jalalabad Road in east Kabul and head for the United Nations office. Aziz wants to show me Bro's office, a father's pride splayed across his tan, smiling face. But the two men at the reception desk insist Bro doesn't work for the United Nations.

"Wrong," I say.

"Not wrong," the first snaps back.

The second asks us to sit and pours some tea.

"These stupid people say my son doesn't work here and they want me to drink their tea," Aziz says, grabbing my arm. "I don't think so, my friend."

He storms back to the van with me in tow. He starts the engine, rests his arms on the steering wheel, and stares out the windshield, a worried look to his face.

"Do you think Khalid could become a donkey?" he says after a moment.

"It's possible."

"I'd beat him," Aziz says, backing up.

We return downtown so I can make the round of ministries, but the offices are closed in preparation for the election.

Aziz drives past the airport back to the Mustafa. Nothing more I can accomplish today. Piles of shattered Soviet military aircraft, tanks, jeeps, and rocket-propelled grenades rise higher than the airport itself. Pieces of an airplane's wing or a jeep's door serve as walls on some nearby huts still scarred from past battles. A billboard announces the construction of Kabul's first Marriott Hotel. Beneath it war widows hold out their hands to passing traffic.

"All this metal was used to destroy Kabul," Aziz says. "You would think we could have done something more with all this metal."

"Donkeys," I say.

"Yes," Aziz agrees. "Stupid donkeys."

On election day, October 9th, I wake up to an overcast morning and wonder, Is this what a history-making presidential election feels like? Cold and damp? Below my hotel window children search for discarded water bottles in heaps of steaming garbage, and dogs lie curled asleep nearby, exhausted from a night of scavenging and fighting.

Power is out, and I make tea with a vendor selling sandals. Beggars squat on the sidewalk, burn scraps of paper to warm their hands. The vendor and I give them our cups to heat. Horse-drawn carts and an occasional truck move past us. Most shops are closed behind gray metal gates that emphasize the bleakness of the weather.

Military checkpoints have sealed off the roads into Kabul for several days. No one can drive in until the balloting closes this evening. The vendor had wanted to vote with his son's family in Wardock, forty minutes south of Kabul, but he did not want to spend the night there.

"It is not our problem if you cannot get back into Kabul," a commander told him. "We can close the road any time. Do your duty and vote. We want to show all the world we can do this thing. Don't trouble me."

U.S. Army helicopters hover overhead, and it is difficult to talk to the vendor, who knows only a little English. The empty streets remind him of Talib time when he stayed inside, fearful of the knock on his door from mullahs with the Ministry of Vice who inspected the length of his beard.

Bro drives me to the polling center at Aisha-E-Durani High School, and we huddle against the cold, waiting for it to open. Women stand near us as the minutes tick slowly toward seven o'clock, when the voting starts. We rub our hands together, shrug off news reports of threats from Taliban fighters denouncing the election.

I am wearing a bullet-resistant vest because of warnings from the

United Nations that suicide bombers might stop outside some of the polling centers. I wonder how many Americans would risk our lives to vote for a president.

"Stay here," I tell Bro. "I'll go in and see if I can crib off someone else's translator. If something happens, I'd rather not be responsible for your children losing their father."

"Right," Bro says. "You shouldn't have that burden. You go. I'll stay."

No one inside speaks English. I wave Bro in. He looks up and mutters either a prayer or a curse, I can't tell.

"I lost my mother and father and my seven brothers in twenty-three years of war," Khalid Razayee, a sad-looking thin man with stubble on his face, tells me. "I lost my wife and my daughter. What is left to take? My vote? But for my house, it is all I have left. It is mine to keep."

Abdul Latif listens to his friend Razayee and nods his head. "For us, we have faced these threats a thousand times before," Latif says. "If shooting starts, if a rocket falls, we laugh. Before, in this place, I have seen fifty, sixty rockets fall. We have seen this so many times before. Maybe today there will be some small problem, but not so big."

Bro compares the photographs in his registration card with other Afghans, and they laugh at the sour expressions on their faces. One young father complains that he had not been allowed to include his son in his picture. A woman shows us two registration cards. She had not liked her photograph in the first card and walked to another registration center to have her picture taken again.

A poll worker shouts, and the men enter one building and the women another. We stand in line outside empty classrooms and wait some more.

UN staff scurry around the dusty halls looking for the ballot boxes, large plastic containers with slits in the top, that earlier had been stacked outside. Sign-in sheets fill small desks, and spare metal frames draped with thin blue cloth serve as polling booths.

"Our first job is to take charge of our future," a man says. "It is not just my opinion that counts today, but all of our opinions."

The poll worker shouts again, and we shuffle single-file into a classroom, scraping the floor with our sandals. I stand aside as the men sign their names and have their registration cards punched. They rub the hole in their cards and appear sad that they had been damaged in this way. Then they dunk their thumbs in a vial of ink to show that they had voted.

Ballots with the names and photographs of eighteen candidates, including Karzai, are handed out at another table.

"If Karzai does not win, that means the Americans have left and our security is bad and there will be war," a poll worker says.

Men slip one at a time without a word behind the curtain of a booth, the fresh smell of the silky curtains wrapping itself around them. Seconds later they emerge with looks that tell me they think there should be something more than marking a card. Something weightier for a first election. But they are left with the simplicity of it and nothing more. They fold their ballots and drop them in the plastic tub. They examine their thumbs and test the durability of the ink by trying to rub it off.

"We are choosing our president," one man tells Bro. "This was a very open process. No problems. Very easy. I knew all the information. I can't read, but I recognized the picture of my candidate. I looked at him very closely to impress upon him his responsibilities."

The lines grow longer with the day and soon stretch outside the schools. Men and women eventually stand side by side as one line enters through one door and another exits out the back.

"We were just waiting for this day to come," a woman says. "Before, three years ago, we women were not happy. We could not leave the house. Now look at us. Please God, one day we will have a woman president."

The mullahs, however, are not pleased.

"From the religious side, because Karzai is supported by the Americans and America puts our religion down, we don't want him as president," Mullah Abdul Ghane of a nearby mosque complains. "He no longer supports our religion, our prophet, our Quran. Democracy may go up, but our religion will go down."

In the evening when the polls close, men and women with purple thumbs stare into space as if to find some spot that embodies this moment of history. But everything appears as it had in the morning except it is night.

"It is finished. What do we do?" Bro asks me.

I hear in his question doubt. Was this the mark of history? Is there nothing more? When will lives change?

He touches his registration card, feels again the hole where it had been punched.

I look at him but have no answers.

CHAPTER THIRTEEN

All the Country Will Be Shaking

MAY 2007

Karzai won as expected, with more than fifty percent of the vote. Millions of people turned out to the polls, and after weeks of threats, the Taliban did not mount any attacks to disrupt the election.

But nearly four years later, the election seems to have mattered little to history or the lives of Afghans. The promised reconstruction touted to thrust Afghanistan into the twenty-first century materializes in haphazard fashion across the country, unveiled in isolated ceremonies by Karzai's lieutenants. Nationwide, roads, schools, and farms still lie in ruins, as does the enthusiasm that first greeted the U.S.-led military coalition.

Karzai conceded that much of the thirteen billion dollars in foreign aid pledged since 2002 was "wasted on high salaries, large overheads, luxury cars, luxury houses that Afghanistan cannot afford at all." He would have been better off saying nothing. His complaints only showed his increasing ineffectualness and isolation. In Kabul money from drug-smuggling warlords fuels the boom, ably assisted by salaried foreign aid workers, wealthy expatriate entrepreneurs, and corrupt government officials.

The U.S. strategy in Afghanistan allowed some Afghan warlords, recruited by the Bush administration, to help fight al-Qaida and the Taliban for control of Afghanistan's flourishing opium trade. They use profits from drug trafficking to fund their armies and amass power under the umbrella of the U.S. war against terrorism, further weakening the already impotent Karzai government.

About fifty thousand foreign troops led by U.S. and NATO military forces have been unable to quash a resurgent Taliban. Outside Kabul suicide bombings, kidnappings, roadside bombs, and violent crime are part of everyday life. The International Committee of the Red Cross found that, in 2006 and 2007, the Taliban insurgency had spread out of the south into the north and west, far from its traditional strongholds.

Afghanistan's renewed explosion of war has quadrupled the rate of violent attacks and frightened many foreign investors. Civilian casualties, including children, from retaliatory strikes by NATO forces against insurgents have only increased resentment toward foreigners.

I follow events in Afghanistan on the Internet and in e-mails from Bro. I had no time to search for the boys while I covered the election. Bro has still not seen them, he writes me. I fret about this. They have just disappeared. Are they still in Kabul or in a village controlled by the Taliban? Where would they be today had I made better arrangements to keep them in school? I can't do anything for them from Kansas City.

Then on a spring evening, as I watch a CNN report on the inroads the Taliban have made around Kabul, I make up my mind. I will return to Afghanistan on my own if necessary and find them. My editors are not interested in another Afghanistan story, so I pitch the idea as a freelance piece to the *Virginia Quarterly Review*. Its editors agree to cover my expenses. I e-mail Bro that I'm returning to find the boys, not to cover news. He is working for a hospital but tells me that Aziz will drive and translate for me as he had during the election.

"You don't have to do this," he writes. "I don't know where the boys are or how to find them. Remember, you left. They expect nothing from you."

"Yes, they do," I write back.

JUNE 2007
Kabul

Watch the suit run, the boys chasing him. War orphans some of them, others carrying their younger siblings, polio afflicted, across their shoulders, hands outstretched, *Money, mister!* Clutching his jacket, shirt, a locust swarm driving this foreigner (diplomat, aid worker, contractor, who knows) to madness.

Aiee!

Shirttail flapping, he tosses money from his pocket, flees past the stylish storefront mannequins of Crystal Light Fashions and Jauque Fashion, past the trays of cream puffs in the windows of Shake Nabal Bakery, and dodges around the red-striped concrete security barriers at Safi Landmark Hotel & Suites before bursting through its gilt-framed doors. The lobby yawns before the boys, and they tilt their heads back and follow the diamond-shaped glass elevator rising eight floors above the marble lobby. When the doors close again, their reflection hangs trapped in glass.

"Tomorrow, you give us five dollar," one of the boys shouts.

Armed guards, scowling and agitated, shoo the boys back with the duct-taped butts of their battered Kalashnikovs, *Boro! Boro! Go! Go!* The boys scatter, the suit's money choked in their hands. They proceed down the road, across the street from the new, hot, blue-tinted Kam Air building. They squint, eye one another, ready to steal from their weaker members if the opportunity presents itself.

Then they see me and stop.

"Nay, not this outsider," my Afghan colleague Aziz tells them in Dari. "Bugger off."

"Boro," says our companion Ahmad Shah Marofi.

Ahead of us we see the boy we have been looking for, twelve-year-old Hamid. I watch him buy a roll of plastic bags from a vendor. Ahmad, his teacher at Aschiana, calls to him. He tells me Hamid knows everyone. I dig into my pocket and show Hamid a photograph of six thirteen-year-old war orphans I helped when I was in Kabul in 2003 and 2004. Hamid shrugs. Maybe he knows them. He can't say for sure. He crooks a finger for me to follow him.

"Who are these boys again?" Ahmad asks me.

I remind him he was their teacher.

"I'm sorry. I don't know them. We see so many."

I put the photo back. The boys would be about seventeen, eighteen now.

Aziz lights a cigarette, offers one to me and Ahmad. His mobile phone rings and he answers a call from his youngest son, Nabil, who asks if we're okay. Everybody buzzing because three Pakistanis were arrested this morning strapped to the gills with bombs for a suicide mission, fifty-two seconds left on the timer. I was with the manager of my hotel when I heard the news. We were standing in the garden by pink rosebushes and a broken stone fountain listening to the radio while I waited for Aziz and Ahmad.

The hotel manager shook his head, told me it was very difficult to combat this "procedure." If someone wants to kill himself, what can you do? He cautioned me not to drive outside Kabul. Taliban everywhere. Always he hears this. Someone says, I saw Talib on the Jalalabad Road. You tell your friends. They tell their friends. Information passes from one person to the next. It could be old but sounds fresh. He doesn't know how to separate truth from rumor. Another way the Taliban mess with your head.

Kabul offers the illusion of bustling normality that makes these threats feel like an aberration, a trick of the mind. Did I really hear that? No, not possible. Kabul is rebounding. No longer is it the vacant capital of my first trip.

Look around.

A Rubik's Cube of dust-clogged, rutted, potholed streets weave through crowded markets, open-fronted mud huts housing butchers, carpenters, auto repair shops, photography studios, and satellite TV stores in the same block. Garishly decorated taxis and buses, donkey carts carrying fresh vegetables, and nomadic shepherds leading caravans of camels and herds of sheep and goats vie for space on roads so congested it can take an hour to drive two miles. Sandal-clad men rush about, carrying wads of fifty-to-the-dollar Afghanis, buying everything that wasn't available under Taliban and Russian rule: satellite dishes, TVs, laptops, sat phones, cell phones, used Toyotas with Pakistani plates and mix-and-match tires. No credit cards, cash only. Electricity runs intermittently, generators hum 24-7. Suited up in flak jackets, sunglasses, and black boots, security contractors walk the streets with the strut of gunslingers.

Plunging into this jostling intensity, Aziz, Ahmad, and I follow Hamid toward the bazaar. We look for my boys in the harsh glare of midmorning where summer temperatures have already reached ninety degrees and hot winds speckle our faces with grit. Hamid seems unfazed by the heat or his daily schedule of school and street hustle. He has attended Aschiana for three months. All of its students survive, as my boys had, shining shoes, washing cars, begging, or, in Hamid's case, selling plastic bags to shoppers at five cents apiece.

Since my last visit, a Dubai businessman had bought the land the school had been renting since 1997 and told them they must leave to make room for a new InterContinental Hotel. Karzai signed an executive order giving Aschiana an acre of downtown land. But a U.S. company, Red Sea Engineering & Constructors, had taken over the land and built a wall around it, saying it was part of twenty-nine acres the company had leased to build a gated community of upscale homes for Western aid workers. Under pressure from Aschiana's backers in Washington, U.S. Ambassador Ronald Neumann pushed Red Sea to cede the acre to Aschiana.

Now the school has land but no money to build upon it. A small compound of four pink brick buildings in downtown Kabul provides inadequate quarters for the more than five hundred children bursting through its doors six days a week.

"Everyone talks about the children," Ahmad says. "They talk of them as the future of the country, but it is talk."

Nearly six years after the Taliban toppled, a manic drive to construct five-star hotels, mansions, and shopping centers for the money men descending on Kabul leaves little room for the needs of its nine thousand street children and countless slum dwellers.

Prior to Aschiana's eviction, hundreds of refugee families on government-owned land in the posh Wazir Mohammad Akbar Khan neighborhood were given the boot when the need for more villas became of paramount concern to Kabul's wealthiest residents. Teetering hovels were bulldozed, and top officials and their lackeys vied for palatial lots.

Behind concrete barriers, villas and malls tower over mud and burlap vendor stalls in a clash of priorities between a tribal Islamic culture, on the one hand, and secular, gotta-have-it, drug-infused venture capitalism, on the other. That hand influences everything including international aid organizations.

Afghans thread their way through a traffic jam of abbreviations emblazoned across land rovers: UN, UNESCO, UNDP, ACF, MACA. No reliable figures exist on the overhead of the 350 Kabul-based aid agencies, but indirect signs, such as air-conditioned Land Rovers, Nissan Pathfinders, Toyota Land Cruisers, and luxurious residences, suggest a high one. The average cost of maintaining a foreign UN employee hovers around $250,000. Security teams cost as much as $20,000 each time an aid convoy leaves Kabul. Add to that, soaring monthly rentals of as much as $15,000 and you have a tidy sum devoted to their upkeep.

Growing public discontent laces tea shop conversations with venomous comments that rise from the gut until spat out in bilious disgust. They call Karzai "America's dishwasher," a demotion from his previously dismissive title "Mayor of Kabul," a ruler with little authority outside the capital. Now Kabul's citizenry won't give him even that much credit.

"Kabul is the heart. If the heart is diseased, all of the country will be shaking," Aziz says. "Afghanistan will be fucked basically."

Hamid stops from time to time so I can show my photograph of the boys to children who clutch at me for money. Then we move on. He takes us down a dusty sidewalk past the Iranian embassy and UNHCR (the organization's refugee agency). Overcrowded buses sag heavily and jobless men sit on a grassy median strip, lethargic and entranced, staring through the gritty air into nothing. Above us an orange billboard promoting a six-hundred-thousand-dollar lottery through a local mobile phone company catches the sunlight.

"Will you invite us to work?" a man shouts to me.

"I have already invited someone," I say pointing to Aziz.

"Today, yesterday, no job," he tells me. "I have no money. My son is in school and needs books."

I offer him ten Afghanis, about fifteen cents. Aziz puts a few more coins in my hands. I give the man the money. I show him the picture.

Swiss chalets, beauty salons, amusement parks, and boutiques for the newly affluent don't provide what the majority of Afghans need: jobs. Most of the foreign companies descending on Kabul bring their own site supervisors and other salaried workers with them. Afghans fill the grunt positions: ditchdiggers, cement mixers, cleanup crews. Few companies train them to fill less expendable positions. When the work ends, so does the job.

"Five days ago, I got a job and cleaned a house for a farmer," the man tells me. He closes his fist around the coins. "I worked eleven hours. I was paid three dollars. It was not enough."

He watches us go, hand outstretched. Hamid cuts through the downtown bazaar. Used blue jeans and denim shirts donated to aid organizations have somehow found their way to the street and hang along steel railings above the drought-parched Kabul River. Pools of stagnant water fill the air with gaseous vapors, and Aziz exhales cigarette smoke in my face to rid my nostrils of the rotted odor, while war widows sit on muddy ground and clutch at my ankles pleading for money. Their children, mouths cracked with dust, stare wide-eyed at the slew of sandals, boots, and shoes passing inches from their faces.

"You promised to take me to Fahim," a man yells at me outside the warped doors of his pharmacy.

"What the hell is he talking about?" I ask Aziz. "Why would I have promised to take him to the former defense minister?"

"He mistakes you for someone else. Every foreigner looks like an American. Russian, Indian, they are all American in the minds of Afghan people, because we are so disappointed."

"We don't want you, go back," the pharmacist shouts. "You made a promise. What has happened to your promise? You remind us we are all in the background. Afghanistan is like a jail. Our guard is NATO. Our warden is Karzai."

Aziz hurries me along.

"We all have limits of how much humiliation we can take," the pharmacist warns me in a final toss of vitriol. "If I eat too much of it, I will vomit."

The sun burns the back of my neck, and we stop for water. Boys gather around me, curious that I am on foot with two Afghans and no vehicle. I look at them closely, but they are not my boys. I pass around the photo. Nothing. They don't know them. More angry men I don't recognize demand I fulfill promises I never made.

"When there was civil war here, all the world was quiet," Aziz says, gripping my elbow. "Now the world is getting quiet again, but it is worse. The people are angrier, hungrier than before."

We wend our way through the crowd of distorted faces snarling for my attention. Hamid climbs a steep, narrow path leading up a mountain toward adobe houses. After an hour we reach the top and enter a square mud hut. Hamid kicks off his sandals, crosses a thickly carpeted floor, and withdraws from behind a curtain a plate of nan, long snowshoe-shaped loaves of bread. He greets his mother. She watches him eat. She has severe rheumatism and cannot work. Her husband,

Hamid's father, died three years ago. Natural causes. Of what, she does not know. Hamid dropped out of regular school to help provide for his family. He sells plastic bags to shoppers. I tell her about the boys, but she remains focused on Hamid. She expects him to earn one dollar a day, enough to buy seven loaves of bread.

"Is bread enough?" I ask.

"No, it is not enough. But with tea it is enough."

When he finishes eating, Hamid removes a fistful of plastic bags from behind a curtain. We follow him out but fall behind as he works his way back down the mountain again, leaping from one boulder to the next. We slide on our asses after him until we reach the street. He pauses at vendor stalls offering his bags to Westerners bargaining over small piles of tea, soap, and nuts. I try to show the boys' photo, but merchants wave Hamid and me away. I am discouraged, but Hamid walks on undeterred.

The wind picks up and knee-high tornado spools of dust spin around us. We turn our heads, feeling the first hints of rain. Soon the heavy drops of water gather speed into a downpour. Aziz, Ahmad, and I duck under the umbrella of a fruit wagon. Shoppers run, and Hamid chases after them, his pink polo shirt clinging to his drenched body. A woman buys a bag from him, covers her head, and hurries away. Then I lose sight of him in the wet torrential blackness that consumes the market.

I awaken early the next morning. The sun has barely risen, and a thin gray light strains through the dust-laden air. Buses from Kandahar have stopped in Kabul, and street children listen to the chatter of the passengers.

"Two months I was in Orbat Village and every night some Taliban came and searched the people, and I saw in Kalot District heavy fighting."

"They fired at a car delivering water to the American base, and then one night the Talib took one hundred dollars from me. They are all thief."

A group of boys listens to their tales. The men shake their heads at what they have seen, and the boys too shake their heads and then hold out their hands for spare change. Rejected, they keep walking. They remind me of my boys when I first met them. Skinny, dirty, easy smiles. I follow them, lost in my memories.

The boys pass men waiting for day labor jobs. A Western suit pulls up in an SUV, and his Afghan driver hops out, picks six men, and barks instructions.

"During work you can't go to sleep, can't go anywhere, because from now until five o'clock you will work, and I will pay you two dollars, and you will have one hour for prayer and lunch and in all this time you will belong to him."

Wandering without purpose, the boys stop to beg outside the office of a Western building contractor. An office manager brings him news of a bomb threat. Very routine, the contractor says. He'll get shut in for hours while they check it out. He'll lose hours, maybe days of production.

The contractor shoos the boys away, and they move on. Ahead of us I see Ahmad roaming the streets to recruit kids for Aschiana. He stops the boys.

"We'll give you food and an education, and you can go to school in the morning or in the afternoon, your choice," he tells them.

He waits as they compete with one another to wipe a driver's windshield for pennies. Then they follow him to his office. Ahmad fills out some forms, as he had once done for my boys. As he concentrates on the forms, the boys, silent and without pause, leave the mildewed office, amid the scratching of Ahmad's pen. I watch them go. Ahmad looks up at the vacant chairs.

"This time, most of our children are sad, they have nothing," he says with a resigned sigh. "You know we have boys and girls whose parents don't have jobs. The students, they want to study, but their families say, 'Don't go to school. Make money for food.'" Without a hint of surprise Ahmad mutters, "That is why these boys have disappeared."

I leave to meet Aziz at the hotel. I see the boys minutes later, leaning over the hoods of parked cars to clean windshields. The Western contractor gives them change. He tells the expat gag: "If you want to be safe in Kabul, move into the U.S. embassy. It's a routine target for insurgent rockets but they always miss." He laughs.

I look at my watch. Not yet six o'clock and already loss and cynicism dominate the day.

■ ■ ■

After another morning following Hamid, Aziz and I sit in Red Hot Sizzlin' Restaurant, part of Red Sea's gated community. I have an idea about our next move to find the boys, but the prices distract Aziz from our conversation.

"A Pepsi is one dollar," he whispers. "In the bazaar you could get four for that." He compares other prices to those of the bazaar, seeing only the amount of food he could buy with another man's disposable income.

"I'll buy the Pepsi," I assure him.

Across from Aziz and me, expats crowd a long rectangular table and order beer and cocktails. The green walls and red brick archways resound with their laughter. Black polo shirts with the Red Hot Sizzlin' logo hang tacked to the wall, and one of the expats asks to try one on. Another man pulls at the corners of his eyes to imitate the Asian features of their Afghan waiter. I glance at a menu of chicken-fried steak and Texas T-bone.

"What are chicken wings?" Aziz asks.

The door opens with more customers. Behind them in the parking lot, smoking cigarettes beside Land Cruisers, stand Afghan drivers. They will wait while their employers finish their dinners and drinks.

Suspected as potential terrorists, Afghans can't enter some restaurants, stores, and sections of the city frequented by foreigners, even when their Western bosses accompany them. Aziz, in slacks and a blue dress shirt, believes he was allowed in with me because he was mistaken for a foreigner, perhaps Indian or Pakistani, presumably associated with an NGO.

"What does that say to the people?" he asks. "It says this is an occupation."

Aziz continues examining the menu. "What are nachos?" he asks. I ignore the question and raise the issue of a road trip. Mr. Bakhsish had family in Bhali Kot, a village outside Jalalabad known for growing poppies. Maybe he moved back. Maybe the other boys followed him. I don't know, but I want to drive there and show his picture around. Aziz would prefer to stay put. The Kabul-Jalalabad Road was recently paved and the five-hour, boulder-strewn drive has been reduced to two hours. But because traffic moves, drivers can find themselves alone in areas still active with Taliban fighters, far from any checkpoints and mobile phone towers.

"If the stupid Talib stop us," Aziz says, pausing to sip his one-dollar Pepsi with the restraint of a champagne drinker, "we will be in deep shit. Do you feel lucky?"

This evening as I pack a bag for Jalalabad, I hear a knock on my door. I open it to Bro. He wears a dark suit, white shirt and tie and dress shoes but otherwise looks the same. Hair a little thinner. Face heavy with long days. But his eyes hold the mischievous spark they've always had.

"Where do we go now?" he asks and then lifts me in his big arms and spins me in a circle like a child.

We walk into the courtyard and sit at a white plastic table beneath a tall palm tree. A fountain gurgles behind a wire cage filled with chirping parakeets. A profound darkness descends, broken by candlelight in the restaurant. I order a beer and green tea from a harried waiter.

"You go to Jalalabad?"

"Tomorrow. Mr. Bakhsish might be there. I don't know."

"At night the Jalalabad Road is not safe."

"We'll leave early."

"Be sure the sun is up. The Taliban go through villages. In the city you will be fine, but outside in the villages they have control. There was a time when the government could have brought in the Taliban, given them a ministry, and fixed the situation. Not now. Now I think it is too late for diplomacy."

He lights a cigarette and offers it to me. I shake my head, and he sticks it in a corner of his mouth. The waiter brings our drinks.

"Your hair is all gray, Malcolm."

"You got some white there too, buddy."

"I make one hundred dollars a month. It is not enough. What I am afraid of is Taliban will come to me and say, I have ten thousand dollars in poppy money for you if you support me. I say yes, because I have no money. I will take it and support you. He does the same with other men, and soon Afghanistan will be like the mafia." Bro pulls hard on his cigarette and sighs.

"It's good to see you."

He looks at me and smiles. "My English is not so good. I don't work with English-speaking people anymore."

"Sounds fine."

"You are married?"

"Not yet. When will you meet me in Miami?"

"When I am no longer married," Bro says and laughs, and I laugh with him. He glances at his watch but doesn't move. He leans his head back and sighs. "Find your boys, Malcolm," he says after a moment. "You should have a family."

In the morning Aziz races along the top of the Kabul-Jalalabad Road as if nothing else matters but the sheer joy of driving without even one bump to jostle us. The novelty of this repaired road, as well as the newly asphalted Kabul-Kandahar Road, has caused nearly as many deaths as insurgent attacks. Afghans drive without caution, any smooth surface beneath their wheels an autobahn intended for unrestrained speed. Pass on a curve into oncoming traffic, why not? Squeeze a car off the road to get around them? Inshallah, we will try. Race into a line of sheep and play bumper pool with their asses? Yes, it's possible. The wrecks of lost gambles lie crumpled in rocky gorges five hundred feet below the road, scraps of snagged clothing and bleached bones tokens of surrender.

Boys on inflated trash bags ride the bucking waves of a white-capped river, swollen from melting snows. It would be easy to think war no longer exists here.

After an hour we pass through Srubee Village and the last military checkpoint before Jalalabad. We stop and buy water. Aziz accuses the vendor of overcharging us by one dollar.

"Stupid donkey," Aziz says as we walk back to the car. "He goes home at night and tells his wife about all the people he's cheated. She is so proud of him. Srubee people are not to be trusted."

We approach Laghman Province, still a Taliban stronghold. I see no one. Aziz drums the steering wheel with his fingers and mutters a quick prayer.

Soon we enter the ghost town of Surhakan Village where, until recently, the Taliban had staged attacks against government forces. To stop the attacks the Afghan army evicted everyone from the village.

We pause to look at the vacant houses, the cold fire pits. I notice a crooked line of rocks in the middle of the road and look up at the mountains to see from where they might have fallen. Aziz looks too and then back at the road.

Without warning, amid an ear-wrenching grinding of gears, Aziz rips the stick shift into reverse. My head snaps forward and back. He swerves around a bus looming large in the rearview mirror, and a truck beeps wildly as we nearly crash into it. Then he stops. The car idles hotly. I hold the back of my neck.

"Jesus! Aziz!"

"I am back driving. The Taliban blocked the road!"

The truck we nearly hit drives around the rocks, as does the bus. We wait. Soon I see them round a curve, passing a horse-drawn cart loaded with firewood. No gunfire. No explosions. No snipers.

"It's okay. Just some rocks off the mountain."

"Yes, I think so too. But if we smell a problem, we go?"

"Yeah man, but chill on the back driving."

The obese, blind, seventy-year-old landowner Qaree Mohammad Shah sits on a cot that sags heavily beneath his burden in the bleak shadows cast by emaciated trees. Two naked infants sleep on a flattened cardboard box at his feet. He spits without moving. He rents land to three farmers, and they and their numerous children sit with him on the hard ground while passing a plate of watermelon. They examine the picture of Mr. Bakhsish and shake their heads. The blind man wipes sweat from his balding pate, and two boys stand behind him and wave scarves to cool his neck. He sighs and tosses nuts in his mouth, rolling them off long, yellow finger nails. The farmers describe the picture of Mr. Bakhsish to him. He too knows nothing about him and spits again with decorous precision.

"I have enough boys to worry about," he says and sweeps his hand before him at the noise of the children. His toothless mouth collapses into each word he speaks, and the stubble on his chin moves with his mouth like an ancient mule chewing. He tips his head back for another mouthful of nuts.

"Who is this boy?"

"Someone I helped."

"Help these boys here. How will they eat now that the destroying people have killed the poppy?"

I pocket the picture of Mr. Bakhsish and look at the vast shorn fields around me, rustled by a hot breeze. A farmer can earn six hundred to a thousand dollars for every two pounds of opium, compared with one dollar for the same amount of rice or wheat.

Soldiers guarding the governor's office in Jalalabad admitted to me that they rarely interfere with poppy farmers. "Narcotics officers," they said, "only destroyed a few acres to pacify the government and the demands of the West."

This year it was Qaree Mohammad Shah's unwitting turn to participate in the crackdown charade. In May, government agents destroyed ten acres of his poppy crop. He now owes two thousand dollars to the drug trafficker who advanced his farmers poppy seeds. He will sell some of his land to pay his debt.

"The destroyers escaped back to their offices, but we will look for them. The next time when a group of destroying people comes, we will fight back. The Taliban tells us the Americans want to deny us our livelihood. I believe them."

"We want to grow poppies," sixty-year-old farmer Abdul Wahed says.

"Because this is my land I am blamed if you grow it."

"What else can I do? I am jobless. I know one man who threw himself in a river and drowned, he was so sad they destroyed his poppy crop."

Wahed points at a field of watermelons and dismisses it as a waste of time. Shah faces the same direction, unseeing, and pats his knees. No money, they both agree. Watermelon is something sweet to eat in the overbearing heat of the day. Shah sighs and pats his stomach, and a boy brings him another plate of nuts.

"If you find your boy, you tell him he can only fight," Wahed says. "We don't have power. Our government is under pressure from the West. It doesn't have power. We are both weak. When we fight, the stronger of the weak will prevail."

On the return trip to Kabul, Aziz drives visibly relaxed, eager to leave Jalalabad and Laghman Province behind. I am disappointed that no one recognized Mr. Bakhshish but not surprised. It was a long shot. Aziz ignores my mood, comments enthusiastically about the novelty of white dividing lines that separate north- and southbound traffic. Much better than the mortar shell casings used to separate lanes in Kabul.

We get stuck behind an American military convoy. A soldier sits behind a .50-caliber machine gun. He raises his hands, won't allow any drivers to pass his armored vehicle. We creep along at ten miles an hour. Aziz and I chafe in the sweltering heat. "One hundred five," Aziz tells me, reading the car thermometer. He speeds up, but the soldier swivels the gun toward us and waves us back. Aziz slows. A UN Land Cruiser passes us and proceeds toward the convoy. The soldier waves it through.

"NGO," Aziz says. "Why don't you tell them you are journalist and maybe we can go too?"

He speeds up to get closer to the soldier so he can hear me. I lean out the window, open my mouth, but the soldier cuts me off.

"Tell your fuckin' hajji driver to back the fuck up!"

I slip back into the car.

"I heard," Aziz says.

In the evening I sit in the garden of my hotel. A suicide bomber killed ten people near Kandahar, including six children, and mandatory curfews have been imposed on the staffs of aid organizations staying here. They drink beers and fill the round tables, scattered across the green watered lawn, with loud conversation. Other guests sit beneath straw overhangs or loiter on the stone walk. A cook grills kabob. Near him two engineers from Pakistan complain about the dearth of equipment the Afghan government is providing them for rebuilding roads. They discuss writing a grant.

"We must include salary for a spokesman," one of the men insists.

"I love proposal writing," his colleague says.

The man renting the room next to me sits outside, sweating from an evening jog. He complains that his new running shoes cut into his heels. He needs to break them in "slow slowly," as the Afghans say. He laughs. He introduces himself. Hans. A German, he advises the government on agricultural projects. I offer him a towel, and he wipes his face. He complains of inadequate coordination between agencies. The Europeans hold back, afraid to get too involved, while the Americans barge ahead without consulting anyone, and the Afghans ignore them both.

"What are you doing here?" he asks.

I tell him about the six boys. He does not hold out much hope that I will find them. "The chances aren't bad," he says, "that at least one of them is dead by now and another is a jihadist. You never know. It will be interesting to see how things look ten years from now, eh?"

I think of the boys as jihadists. It makes a sad kind of sense. What would look better to them? A jobless future or a Kalashnikov and the power and prestige that comes with it? I hope they made a different choice than the one I conclude I would make. However, I won't judge them. If indeed they have taken up the gun, so be it. They have as much right to choose militancy as I had the right in 2004 to leave Afghanistan —and them—behind.

Day after day Aziz and I follow Hamid on his rounds. This morning he pauses at a burlap shack across the street from the Landmark to offer a plastic bag to a woman buying tea. She ignores him and he moves on. Aziz crosses the street to buy cigarettes. The young man selling tea glances at me, turns away, and then looks back. I wait for Aziz and make my way around the cracked sidewalk, anticipating an appeal for money from the tea man.

"Malcolm?" he begins hesitantly.

I stop and we stare at each other. He's about my height, wearing a filthy T-shirt and dusty jeans, hands stained from charcoal used to heat water. Rail thin. He slips on a pair of sunglasses.

"Gig? Mr. Gigolo?"

An embarrassed smile creases his face. He grips my hand and shakes me by the shoulder.

"I saw you!" he says in English. "I saw you! You now come back? Long time."

I say nothing. Mr. Gigolo shows me a photograph a colleague of mine had taken in the Herat Restaurant of the other boys, Bro, and me eating lunch. Mr. Gigolo looks so slight, his hands folded on his lap. Bro and I look tired, hunched over our plates. We all grin at the camera with no hint in our faces that the moment would end. It had ended of course, but by keeping this photo Mr. Gigolo had hung on to that moment, the hope of another time.

"I should have returned much sooner," I tell him.

He shrugs, pockets the photo, and offers me a cup of tea. I try to pay him, but he waves my hand away.

"Your English is very good."

"I learn from Westerners when they buy tea."

"Good," I say and feel relieved no one else assumed my old role, and then shame. It would have been better had someone else picked up where I had left off.

Mr. Gigolo smiles, looks at me, and in his gaze asks for an explanation.

"I had to leave," I tell him after a long pause. "I thought you understood that."

"Yes," he says without conviction.

"I'm a journalist, not a teacher. I should have explained that better."

He stares at the ground.

"You don't understand, do you?" Aziz says.

"No," Mr. Gigolo says.

I sip my tea, avoid looking at him. Shortly after I returned to the States in 2004, a foreigner had offered each of the boys one hundred dollars a month to support their families while they attended school, he says. Like me, the man left, and they never heard from him again. Mr. Gigolo then dropped out of Aschiana to make money that did not rely on the false generosity of strangers.

"I was happy in Aschiana," Mr. Gigolo says. "I can't compare that time to now. I hope to have a good time in the future. I don't know the future. I know just the day and the night one after the other. I never think of what will be beyond. Malcolm, you said you'd come back."

"He has," Aziz says.

"No," Mr. Gigolo says. "He is like the other guy. This is not coming back. What if I had not seen you?"

I stare at the ground without blinking until the sidewalk blurs, and I can no longer avoid saying what I should have said when I first saw him. "It's not your fault," Aziz says.

Mr. Gigolo frowns and then shrugs, stumbling on his limited English. Finally he stares past me and says, "You was nice man."

We shake hands. I did not expect to run into him like this. I had thought that, if I found the boys at all, it would have been more orderly. I thought I'd be in charge. He has grown so much! And his English! He has really learned to speak it. Who has been teaching him? He moved on without me. They all had undoubtedly. What did I expect? That they would be waiting for me? Of course not. I knew better. Still, with his hand in mine I know what I had long suspected. I've lost them.

I make plans to meet Mr. Gigolo later for dinner at our old stomping ground, the Herat Restaurant. He will bring Mr. Nike and Mr. Meat. He has not seen Mr. Ten Dollar, Mr. Chocolate, and Mr. Bakhsish for more than a year. Perhaps they moved to Pakistan? He can't say. I ask Aziz to bring Bro.

I return to my hotel room, sit on my bed, and thumb through a book. My fan won't start. No breeze comes through the open windows. I stand up. I don't hear a sound. The canaries, chirping when I walked in seconds ago, have fallen silent. Then I feel it, a wave followed by an explosion that throws me to the floor. I reach out with my hands until I can get back on my feet. Feeling dizzy, I half run, half stagger outside to the sidewalk and see men fleeing across the street. My ears feel wedged with cotton. Women begging minutes before now scream piercing wails, rocking back and forth. Then they too flee. The street empties in minutes. Not a car or person in sight. Only the solitary clop of a donkey drawing a riderless cart of firewood disturbs the sudden silence.

I run in the direction of the blast, past vendors peering out of their stalls at a black smudge rising in the distance. Other people start off in the same direction, until soon a small crowd of us jogs down the street. We stop at a dirt road cordoned off by police. Before us, twisted and charred, stand the smoking remains of a police academy bus. Blood spatters the ground. Fist-size pieces of flesh lie among the rocks. I hold my stomach and look away. The police, near panic themselves, shout, push, and shove us, raising the butts of their Kalashnikovs until we back away.

Aziz, Bro, and I park outside the Herat and see through its steamed windows Mr. Gigolo, Mr. Nike, and Mr. Meat already seated inside. I embrace them all, but the bombing has replaced any thoughts we had for a celebratory reunion.

"It is sad," the boys say with worried looks. "Sad, sad."

"It shows we are in deep shit," Aziz says.

"Very deep," Bro adds.

We order beef kabob and rice and a round of orange sodas. Our usual. The boys get up and wash their hands, reminding me of the first time we ate here and they lined up at the sink. I ask the boys what they do for money. Mr. Nike repairs bicycles, and Mr. Gigolo reminds me of the night he asked me to buy him one.

"Yes," I say, "I remember."

Mr. Meat sells CDs. They have grown as tall as Mr. Gigolo and

Mr. Meat has lost his potbelly. They earn six dollars a week, as does Mr. Gigolo.

"It is not enough," Mr. Nike tells me.

"Of course not," I say.

Mr. Nike still wears his old windbreaker, although it is far too small for him. He must be desperate if he can't afford another one. Mr. Meat has lost some teeth, and his words slur in the gaps in his mouth.

"Enough about money," I say. "What about girls. Are you married?"

The boys blush and shake their heads and laugh.

"Soon you'll be like every Afghan man and have too many children," Aziz jokes.

The boys laugh harder, and Mr. Meat jerks his hand over his crotch to show what he would do if he had a wife, eyes popping when he realizes Aziz, Bro, and I saw him, and Mr. Gigolo and Mr. Nike erupt into further hysterics.

"It's good to see you," Mr. Nike says to me. "Maybe next time you'll bring us an American girl."

The thought of returning reminds us all I will be leaving. Again. Slowly their laughter fades amid the clatter of dirty dishes being stacked on trays by rushing waiters. A ceiling fan stirs the warm air. I reach for a Kleenex to wipe sweat from my forehead. The boys watch me, all humor gone from their eyes. I avoid their gaze.

"You're late," Mr. Meat says. "It took you a long time to come back."

"It did, I know."

"Why?"

"Things. My job did not want to send me."

"We had stopped expecting you," Mr. Nike says.

Their faces sag with regret. Until this moment, I had been relegated to memory. I have returned, but their lives and expectations are very different than before. The need to help feed their families has taken precedence over school and a future. Economic difficulties force one out of every three school-age children to work in order to help their families survive. The prevalence of child labor is creating a generation of illiterate Afghans who will likely remain trapped in poverty. Even if they wanted to attend school, their options would be limited. More than half of the government schools in Kabul have no buildings and use rented space or tents instead.

"I'd hoped to come back earlier," I say.

"He is here now," Bro tells the boys.

It is too late, I think. We had a moment filled with possibilities in 2003, but we lost it.

The sight of the boys reciting their lessons helped ease the despair I felt lurking beside me among all those I could not help. I can feed, clothe, and help educate these boys I see every day begging outside the Mustafa, I had thought. Amid all the loss here, I can do that much.

Now what can I do?

A waiter stops at our table and distributes plates heaped with brown rice. I watch the boys scoop the food with their fingers as they had at our first lunch when anything seemed possible. I do not want to feel hopeless about them. I do not want them to give up on me.

The man who offered them money to stay in school had the right idea. I weigh whether I can afford wiring three hundred dollars a month to their families. I tell them I will try. It would be a small gesture not to be mistaken for a massive aid package, but it would give three young Afghan men a chance and fulfill an unspoken pledge I had made to them.

I tell them what I'm thinking. Aziz offers to handle the money, disbursing it weekly so the boys don't spend it all at once. I know he expects to take a little off the top for himself. I understand. Without me here, he will be as poor as the boys.

"I will make no promises," I tell them.

Bro nods approvingly. The boys look at him and then me without expression. They understand. They have been through my promises before.

The next morning, I pack my duffel bag for my return trip to the States. Boots, shirts, pants, socks, sandals. Aziz rummages through my wastebasket for plastic bottles, packets of aspirin, and other items I tossed to make room for souvenirs. The Ministry of Public Health has offered him a data entry position for seven dollars a day. He starts in a few weeks.

"It is more than the boys," he says, "but it is not enough."

I make my bed, fold the bathroom towels. I leave no sign I slept here. I have some time before I head for the airport. Aziz will wait for me in the car. "Inshallah," he says, "nothing will happen today to delay your flight."

"Do you feel lucky?" he asks on his way out.

I do, yes. Each visit here continues a journey that began as an extraordinary intersection of two paths, Bro's and mine, that by all rights never should have crossed. But I will leave Afghanistan behind as certain as Aziz will stay. There's nothing either of us can do about that. Home calls us all.

I'd heard a similar sentiment during my embed from a village elder. "You try to help us and we thank you," he told our patrol's American commander. "But many people have tried to help us and have not come back. You'll be gone in two or three years. Maybe we see you again, maybe not. But we'll still be here. And you will not."

War hardens people, especially the young. They roam the streets with feral dogs. They skulk in shadows, sleep in ruins. They assault strangers for money and are not dissuaded by slaps to the face. They steal. They join militias, longing to fight the kind of fight that destroyed their families. War withers the part of their soul that survives.

"Let me tell you about Afghan people," Hajji Din Mohammed, the governor of Nangarhar Province told me in his Jalalabad home in 2003. Photographs of his two dead brothers hung on a wall. The Taliban killed one. The other was assassinated. "We are like a butcher. A butcher kills sheep that have done him no harm. He has to. He must not feel, because he does this to survive. He holds their heads in his hands. He cuts their throats, looking into their frightened eyes. He kills all day without feeling, one lamb after the other.

"My two brothers are dead. Yet I continue to work for all of Afghanistan. I must. For Afghan people, sorrow does not stop us. After years of war we can look at death many times and not feel. For myself and all Afghan people, our hearts are like a butcher's."

Western diplomats often say that Afghans must eventually take responsibility for Afghanistan. None of them has explained the time frame for "eventually" in a country that, as a doctor in the 82nd Airborne Division said to me, "remains back in the year 1260."

Those of us who have covered the Afghan war think these diplomats are articulating the escape clause in U.S. foreign policy: We did our best. It's time you help yourselves. We're out of here.

Years ago, as a social worker, I had my own escape clause. I used to tell homeless people to quit drinking. Find work. Be accountable. All of life's bounty awaits you if you just shape up, blah, blah, blah.

Eventually I realized that poverty and despair were more complicated than I had wanted to believe. Moral platitudes had helped me avoid responsibility for the disappointments and failures that awaited the poor, Americans and Afghans alike.

I finish packing and look out my window. No boys or Bro. I'm not expecting them, just thought they might drop by one last time. But they have their lives as much as I have mine. Maybe more so.

I leave my room. In the hotel lobby, the receptionist studies an English-language textbook. He attends Kabul University. He points to a word and asks me to pronounce it.

"City," I say. "City."

"City?"

"Yes."

He points to another word. *Bridge.* Aziz beeps. I glance at my watch.

"I have to go. I'm leaving."

"Yes, I know this. But you will be back?"

"Inshallah," I say and reach across the desk to shake his hand. "Why not?"

Epilogue

Dear Bro:

Try as I might, I have been unable to wire money to the boys. For some reason my bank can't complete the transaction despite months of trying. The wire is not received in Kabul, I'm told, every time I attempt to send it. No one seems to know why.

Mr. Nike called me and said he believes I am sending money but that you and your father are holding out on them. I told him that was not the case, but he is young, angry, and disappointed. Let's arrange a phone call so I can talk to them all. Mr. Gigolo knows enough English to understand me better than Mr. Nike. We have been here before. Commitments made, I leave. Obstacles arise, delays. Frustration, suspicion, and disappointment follow. Four steps forward, three steps back. Afghanistan, man, Afghanistan.

I will return to Kabul soon and bring money for the boys, but I do not think it should be doled out in monthly installments as we had discussed. Instead we should set up a bank account and put it away for the day when the boys—and, frankly, you and your family—might need to get out. From your e-mails and the news it's clear the situation is much worse now than at my last trip in 2007, and it sucked then.

Recently I read that the Taliban attacked the Ministry of Justice and occupied the building for more than an hour. That's right downtown, isn't it? Then I saw that other Taliban attackers assaulted the Ministry of Education and the Ministry of Justice Correction Department. A lot of people had to die to get Afghanistan back on the front page of daily newspapers. The Taliban managed a well-coordinated attack, designed to persuade the power center that government cannot protect them. If the response is anything less than overwhelming, the clock is running out on the current government.

It seems to me Kabul is under siege with the Taliban operating a shadow government that has spread north from Kandahar and has now penetrated the capital. I remember in 2007 you told me not to travel to Wardak Province, just a forty-minute drive from Kabul. The Taliban had taken over district centers there, set up checkpoints, and would kidnap foreigners.

Against your advice, Aziz and I drove to Lowgar Province to interview Mohammad, a man he knew who had been released from Guantanamo Bay. On the way into Lowgar, I noticed some women who turned away from me when I looked at them. A group of men sat under a distant tree. They wore long beards and black turbans, and I wondered if they were Taliban. Less than three years earlier the government had controlled all the provinces near Kabul.

Not anymore.

Mohammad told me his year in Guantanamo was a mistake. He said he had done nothing wrong except to live in a former Taliban stronghold and own a gun. When he was released, he said he was required to take an oath of loyalty to the Karzai government. Now, all this time later, he stays close to his farm. U.S. troops have searched homes in Lowgar since his release—but not his. Afghan police stop by his house and ask about his family but nothing more. Mohammad no longer owned a weapon. The Taliban watched the roads at night, the Americans by day, he said. But he reserved his anger for the Americans. The Taliban never took him from his family, he said.

When we finished the interview, Aziz and I followed Mohammad out the door. I looked over his shoulder at the flat desert, the mud huts and the men, women, and children. The United States has lost them too—loyalty oath or no.

You know, the more I think about it, Bro, the more convinced I am that we should get you and your family American visas. It may be time for you to visit Miami Beach. You would have to fly to Pakistan, as I understand the American embassy in Kabul does not issue visas. Of course that would mean I should get the boys visas too. This doesn't get any easier.

Did I tell you about the time I met a Taliban in Pakistan? I was there reporting on the 2005 earthquake that killed thousands in Pakistani Kashmir. One morning in my hotel a young man who said he was a Taliban fighter told my translator he wanted to speak to me. He said his name was Hamza. He had been fighting in Indian-controlled Kashmir and had never seen an American before. He showed me his battered Kalashnikov. Smiling, he said he would not kill me because he knew I was there to help.

It seems this insight has been lost in Afghanistan. Mismanagement and mounting civilian casualties have led many Afghans to conclude that the West is not there to help.

Do you ever drive by the Mustafa? I don't know if I told you, but I visited the hotel shortly before I left Kabul in 2007. It felt abandoned. No more contractors, journalists, hangers-on. The lights were out, the bar closed. The few guests I saw roamed the empty halls cloaked in prayer shawls as if they were in a temple. I drank tea in the dark with the one staff member on duty, who told me he was no longer paid. He had stayed on because it was a job, and even if he earned nothing it was better to work than not. So we sat together in silence and waited for whatever it was that would come that night or any other night. And I think in a larger way, Afghanistan too waits without expectation. We don't know what it awaits, but suspect it won't be for the better.

If you visit Miami Beach, you will be surprised how little notice Americans pay to news coming out of Afghanistan. Actually, that probably won't be your first thought, with crowds of bikini-clad babes wandering around. But I'm aware that the deteriorating situation has not created general concern. I don't know why that is. I guess your war doesn't have much entertainment value. Fighting in mountains and spare villages lacks the video game appeal of Iraq's urban combat.

Perhaps Afghanistan is so different from the United States that Americans can't find enough commonality to care. When the Iraq War started I remember watching TV in the Mustafa. U.S. tanks drove on Baghdad freeways. Damn, they have roads, I remember thinking. How nice would that be?

There was this American soldier in Orgun-e who stood out because he didn't complain about all the media attention on Iraq like the other grunts. He said Iraq kept his family distracted from what was happening in Afghanistan and therefore they didn't worry about him.

They must be worried now.

I have met American soldiers in Kansas City who fought in Afghanistan. On occasion I hang out with them. We compare experiences, joke about me embedding with them again, but what we seek in one another are places we can't re-create outside Afghanistan, memories shared and shelved.

Outside of one tent on the Kandahar base stood a pole with arrows pointing in all directions. So many thousand miles to Australia, so many to Britain, so many to the United States. So many soldiers from all over the globe seeking a way home. Anywhere but this desolate base, this hostile ground, this forgotten war.

"What was it like?" I'm asked, just as I might be asked, "What's up? How's your day?" Not really interested in the answer unless it conforms to the one they already have, the one they are comfortable with, that corresponds to the yellow wristband they wear to show support for the troops. I have learned not to listen and to offer vague answers if I must. Standoffish, aloof, low social skills—think what they will, I have forgotten the language.

I met an Afghan in Kansas City who worked as an interpreter for the U.S. Army. He told me he never stopped thinking about his house in Kabul. Seven rooms. Dozens of carpets on the floor. The people here are very nice, he said, but he feels strange, alone. Not many Afghans in Missouri. The mosques are too far for him to walk. The air is wet and sticks to him. Everything is so clean. Fragile. What can he touch without making it dirty? Afghanistan was a paradise despite the dry heat and dust and dirt and fighting. "I love my tired country," he said. I showed him your picture, but he shook his head and shrugged. He did not know you. I seek connections stored in my brain, lost in the world.

I look forward to seeing you and the boys again and getting this money thing straightened out. I never wanted kids and now I've got five counting on me, and I've let them down once more. It's the integrity of the effort, Dr. Mark told me, the integrity of the effort, even if the results are minimal. But how much is necessary to call it progress? How many false starts are acceptable before I lose all credibility with the boys? If I have learned anything from Afghanistan, results—or the lack of them —matter.

You should know I have been studying Dari without much success. When I speak it, I sound like I'm clearing my throat and have a bad cold. I continue trying to practice the few Dari words I know on any Afghan who will listen to me. Hotel clerk, vendor, soldier. I try my best to speak clearly the short, quick greetings you have taught me with what I hope is the proper accent.

Sobh ba khayr. Good morning.

I then pause and consider whether or not I should say something more and risk uttering incomprehensible nonsense, afraid I might tumble into the mush of "uh . . ." The silence lengthens. But the patient, encouraging smile of my listener urges me on.

Nam-e shoma chist? What is your name?

My listeners respond with the unadorned simplicity that any foreigner could understand. They say their name, offer another smile, followed by a gentle nod that urges me to continue, implying with silent assurance that together we will find our way to understanding, although we venture on uncertain ground.

Man zhornalist astom. I am a journalist.

Like a mountain climber seeking a foothold, my face pressed against the hard granite, I feel alive and part of something.

Acknowledgments

I owe a debt of gratitude to my editors at the *Kansas City Star* and the Washington Bureau of Knight Ridder Newspapers, now McClatchy, for giving me the opportunity to work in Afghanistan and Pakistan.

I also cannot thank enough the editors at the *Virginia Quarterly Review*, *Missouri Review*, *West Branch*, and *Ascent*, among other small "literary" magazines, for publishing some of these chapters as separate stories and urging me to write this book.

I want to thank all those who helped me along the way in the early drafts of this memoir, especially Scott Canon, Susan Hartman, Bill Luening, Chuck Murphy, and Heather World.

Elizabeth Stein edited a rough draft and helped me shape it into a book. Without you, it would still be in my computer.

Peter Bosch, Steve Connors, Steve Komarow, Jonathan Landay, Darren McCollester, Sudarsan Raghavan, David Swanson, and Lucian Truscott had years of experience reporting overseas and in war zones, and were kind and patient enough to show me the ropes.

Jesse Barker, Stella Ferrer, Grace Hobson, Sharon Hoffman, Lee Hill Kavanaugh, Dale Maharidge, Joe Ruklick, and Matt Stearns have always encouraged me as a writer and have kept me going when I thought of throwing my computer through a window.

San Francisco State University professor Molly Giles treated my first fumbling efforts at writing with respect and never stopped encouraging me.

David Littlejohn, you have been my mentor, professor, and, most important, friend. This book would not have happened without you.

I must extend my appreciation to Dale M. Titler and my late aunts Elvira Villafane and Jo Perry. The three of you taught me to follow my dreams and not compromise them.

Everyone at Beacon Press has made this a wonderful writing experience, especially my editor Gayatri Patnaik and editorial assistant Joanna Green.

To my agent Will Lippincott, who had the unenviable task of reading draft after draft of this memoir, refusing to let go of it or me.

To my mother and father, for putting up with the travels of their wayward son, and to my brother Michael, who bore the brunt of their worries. And to my late brother, Charles A. Garcia Jr., and to *mi padrino,* Oscar A. Villafane: you both told stories better than most people I know and encouraged me to write mine down.

Finally, many thanks to my former coworkers at Hospitality House and at St. Vincent de Paul Society's Ozanam Center for your support as I took my first awkward steps away from social work and toward a journalism career.